KARL POPPER

One of the most original thinkers of the twentieth century, Karl Popper inspired his own and subsequent generations of philosophers, historians and politicians.

The essays presented here, specially written for this volume, offer a fresh philosophical examination of key themes in Popper's philosophy, including the philosophies of knowledge and science, and political philosophy. Drawing from some of Popper's most important works, the contributors address Popper's solution to the problem of induction and his views on conventionalism and criticism in an open society, while exploring his unique position in twentieth-century philosophy. The contributors also examine the current relevance of Popper to understanding liberal democracy along with his critique of tribalism. Additionally, they offer new evaluations on Popper's relationship with analytic philosophy in general, and with Wittgenstein in particular, and draw on the studies of Isaac Newton and Albert Einstein to assess Popper's conception of science.

This volume offers new insights on key topics from some of Popper's most important work and is essential reading for students of Popper and anyone interested in political philosophy and the philosophy of science.

Contributors: Alan Musgrave, Semiha Akıncı, Philip Catton, Wenceslao Gonzalez, Jeremy Sheamur, Peter Munz, Christian List, Philip Pettit, Graham Macdonald, Alan Ryan, Anthony O'Hear, Jeremy Waldron

Philip Catton is Senior Lecturer in Philosophy at the University of Canterbury, New Zealand. **Graham Macdonald** is Professor of Philosophy at the University of Canterbury.

KARL POPPER

Critical appraisals

Edited by
Philip Catton and Graham Macdonald

Routledge
Taylor & Francis Group

LONDON AND NEW YORK

First published 2004
by Routledge
2 Park Square, Milton Park, Abingdon, Oxon, OX14 4RN

Simultaneously published in the USA and Canada
by Routledge
270 Madison Avenue, New York, NY 10016

Routledge is an imprint of the Taylor & Francis Group

Alan Musgrave 'How Popper (might have) solved the problem of induction',
reproduced with kind permission from Cambridge University Press. First
published in *Philosophy* (date forthcoming), Cambridge University Press

Typeset in Goudy by The Running Head Limited, Cambridge
Printed and bound in Great Britain by MPG Books Ltd, Bodmin

British Library Cataloguing in Publication Data
A catalogue record for this book is available from the British Library

Library of Congress Cataloging in Publication Data
Karl Popper: critical appraisals / edited by Philip Catton and Graham
Macdonald. – 1st ed.
p. cm.
1. Popper, Karl Raimund, Sir, 1902–94
I. Catton, Philip, 1956– II. Macdonald, Graham.
B 1 649.P64K34 2004
192–dc22
2004002913

ISBN 0–415–31970–6 (hbk)
ISBN 0–415–31971–4 (pbk)

CONTENTS

CONTENTS

CONTRIBUTORS

Semiha Akıncı is Associate Professor of Philosophy in the Faculty of Communication Sciences at Anadolu University, Turkey. She took her degrees from the Middle East Technical University in Ankara, and these included a Master's on Popper as well as a Ph.D. on the metaphysics of possible worlds. Her publications are diverse, as she writes on philosophy of science, ontic commitment, possible worlds, human rights, the environment, theodicy and education.

Philip Catton is Senior Lecturer in Philosophy at the University of Canterbury, New Zealand, where he heads up the programmes in history and philosophy of science and also mathematics and philosophy. His early degrees are from New Zealand, and his Ph.D. is from the University of Western Ontario. He has published on the philosophy of space and time, ecology, and problems with the deductivist image of scientific reasoning.

Wenceslao J. Gonzalez is Professor of Logic and Philosophy of Science at the University of La Coruña in Spain. He has been a visiting researcher at the University of St Andrews, the University of Münster and the London School of Economics, as well as Visiting Fellow at the Center for Philosophy of Science, University of Pittsburgh. He is the editor of *Philosophy and Methodology of Economics* (1998) and *Lakatos's Philosophy Today* (2001). He has published numerous articles on scientific methodology, economics and individual rationality.

Christian List is a Lecturer in Political Science in the Department of Government at the London School of Economics. He took his degrees from the University of Oxford, modulating from mathematics and philosophy into political science, and subsequently held several visiting and postdoctoral positions at Oxford, ANU, MIT and Harvard. His publications range over topics in political philosophy, rational choice theory, philosophy of economics and philosophy of science.

Graham Macdonald is Professor of Philosophy at the University of Canterbury, New Zealand. His research areas are philosophy of social science, philosophy of mind, and teleosemantics, on which he has published in journals such as

Mind and Language, Philosophical Quarterly, Analysis and *Proceedings of the Aristotelian Society*. He is co-author of *What Philosophy Does* and *Semantics and Social Science*, and editor or co-editor of numerous volumes, including *Fact, Science, and Morality* (with Crispin Wright) and *Philosophy of Psychology* (with Cynthia Macdonald).

Peter Munz is Emeritus Professor of History at the Victoria University of Wellington, New Zealand. He is the only person to have been a student of both Popper and Wittgenstein. He is the author of several books on early medieval history as well as of several books on philosophy, including *The Shapes of Time, Our Knowledge of the Growth of Knowledge: Popper or Wittgenstein?*, *Philosophical Darwinism: On the Origin of Knowledge by Means of Natural Selection* and *Critique of Impure Reason*. His new book, *Beyond Wittgenstein's Poker: New Light on Popper and Wittgenstein*, is in press.

Alan Musgrave is Professor of Philosophy at the University of Otago, New Zealand. He took his degrees at the London School of Economics, where with Imre Lakatos he edited *Criticism and the Growth of Knowledge*, an outstandingly influential collection of essays assessing the competing views about science of Popper and Thomas Kuhn. His chief interests are the theory of knowledge and the history and philosophy of science, in which areas he has published widely including his books *Common Sense, Science, and Scepticism* and *Essays on Realism and Rationalism*.

Anthony O'Hear is the Weston Professor of Philosophy at the University of Buckingham, UK and is Editor of the journal *Philosophy*. Among his many interests in philosophy are philosophy of science; philosophy of religion, aesthetics and culture; political philosophy; and ethics. His books include *Karl Popper, Beyond Evolution: Human Nature and the Limits of Evolutionary Explanation, After Progress*, and *Philosophy in the New Century*.

Philip Pettit teaches political theory and philosophy at Princeton, where he is William Nelson Cromwell Professor of Politics and at the University Center for Human Values. He works on the foundations of cognitive and social science, and moral and political theory. Among his recent books are: *A Theory of Freedom: From the Psychology to the Politics of Agency* and, with Geoffrey Brennan, *The Economy of Esteem: An Essay on Civil and Political Life*.

Alan Ryan is Head of New College, University of Oxford, and Tutor there in political philosophy. His main interests are political philosophy, philosophy of the social sciences, and the history of ideas. He has written and edited several books on John Stuart Mill, theories of property and the philosophy of social sciences. His most recent books are *John Dewey and the High Tide of American Liberalism* and *Liberal Anxieties and Liberal Education*.

Jeremy Shearmur is Reader in Philosophy at the Australian National University. He obtained his degrees from the London School of Economics, where he worked for eight years as Popper's assistant. His research areas include political philosophy, philosophy of science and social science, moral philosophy, and mid-twentieth-century social and political theory, in all of which he has published widely, including the recent books *Hayek and After* and *The Political Thought of Karl Popper*.

Jeremy Waldron is the Maurice and Hilda Friedman Professor of Law and Director of the Center for Law and Philosophy, Columbia University. He has written on a wide range of topics in social, legal and political philosophy. His books include *The Right to Private Property*, *Nonsense Upon Stilts* (ed.), *Liberal Rights*, *The Dignity of Legislation*, *Law and Disagreement* and *God, Locke and Equality*. He is also the author of numerous articles in law journals and is a member of the American Academy of Arts and Sciences.

PREFACE

The majority of papers appearing in this volume were given at a conference held in Christchurch, New Zealand, 12–14 July 2002, celebrating the centenary of the birth of Sir Karl Popper (28 July 1902). There are many people to thank for their assistance in making the conference such an agreeable and successful occasion. We would not have been able to effect the participation of so many distinguished speakers without very generous sponsorship from Jade Software Corporation Ltd. We would like to thank Sir Gil Simpson for this sponsorship, and Professor Martin Holland for being instrumental in obtaining it. The University of Canterbury provided assistance through the Erskine Fellowship fund; in this regard we appreciate the support of Professor Daryl Le Grew and Professor Robert Kirk. Financial assistance was also provided by the Goethe Foundation (Wellington).

The pre-conference administration was accomplished with remarkable efficiency and exceptional good humour by Carol Hiller, to whom we are indebted for keeping us sane. The registration desk at the Conference was staffed by postgraduate students from the Department of Philosophy and Religious Studies.

The participants also merit considerable admiration for the way in which they rapidly overcame fatigue due to jet-lag, contributing vigorously to the discussion of all the papers. Karl and Hennie Popper's thought that New Zealand was 'half-way to the moon' was no doubt caused in part by the means of transport at their disposal (ship), but even with modern jet planes the journey to Christchurch can be energy-sapping. Some of the contributors flew directly from the Viennese Centennial Popper Conference. To all of them, and to those who have contributed papers to this volume who did not make the conference, a very big thank you.

Graham Macdonald would like to express gratitude to the University of Canterbury for an Erskine Fellowship that funded leave in 2001 which enabled him to do some of the organising for the Popper Centennial conference, and to the Philosophy Department in King's College, University of London, for hosting him during this leave. He would also like to thank the Philosophy Department at the University of Connecticut, USA, for its hospitality during his study leave from the University of Canterbury in 2003–4, during which time this volume was prepared for publication. Philip Catton likewise thanks the University of Canterbury for an Erskine Fellowship that funded leave in 2002–3 during which he reshaped and improved his contribution to the present volume, and to the Center for Philosophy of Science at the University of Pittsburgh for hosting him during that leave.

INTRODUCTION

Philip Catton and Graham Macdonald

Sir Karl Popper's work has been among the most controversial, and influential, in twentieth-century philosophy. Born 28 July 1902 in Vienna to parents Simon and Jenny, Jews who converted to Lutheranism in 1900,[1] Popper made his impact on the German-speaking philosophical world with the publication of *Logik der Forschung* in 1934. It was received by his peers with both acclaim and criticism.[2] *Erkenntnis* had it reviewed by two philosophers whose views could hardly have been more different. Hans Reichenbach wrote:

> The results of this book appear to me completely untenable . . . I cannot understand how Popper could possibly believe that with respect to the problem of induction his investigations mean even the slightest advance.

while Rudolf Carnap wrote that Popper's book was 'one of the most important contemporary works in the field of the logic of science'.

The English translation (by Popper, with the assistance of Julius and Ian Freed) produced a somewhat similar reaction. Karl Mendelssohn thought *The Logic of Scientific Discovery* was

> laborious and complicated reading. In fact, I did not immediately notice that in my review copy 16 pages were missing . . . Long and detailed discussion culminates in the well-known truism that you can never prove an effect to be non-existent.
>
> (*New Scientist*)

Yet at the same time Richard Wollheim enthused that Popper had produced 'one of the most important philosophical works of our century. . . . a masterpiece of lucidity. . . . [B]oldness of design and . . . of execution place this work amongst the best and greatest of its age' (*The Observer*).

These contrasting comments are typical of the divergent reactions to Popper's philosophy throughout his life. Some have hailed him as the most important philosopher of the twentieth century; others think of his contribution as constituting merely a footnote to the developments in positivist and neo-positivist philosophy of science. Over against this latter estimation, probably held more in the United States than in Europe, stand the following facts. The idea that for a discipline to be scientific its hypotheses and theories have to be falsifiable has been immensely influential, particularly among scientists themselves. One has only to read the account Sir John Eccles gives of his path-breaking experimental work on inhibitory and excitatory synaptic action to find something very rare, a philosopher's methodological advice influencing empirical research (Eccles 1982). The effect that the accusation 'Unfalsifiable!' has had on whole disciplines has been immense – and for the most part salutary. It is arguable that psychoanalysis has never recovered. The related idea that the informational content of a hypothesis is one of its central virtues has also been influential, at the very least as an essential corrective to the positivist emphasis on confirmation, this emphasis tending to lower the informational content of hypotheses. And Popper's work on the propensity interpretation of probability has been widely discussed and debated, with its proper place within the field of interpretations of probability still undecided.

Again, Popper's political philosophy has been valued less among political philosophers than politicians. The appeal to freedom in an open society, and what was taken to be an associated individualism, resonated with some conservative politicians, who perhaps mistook Popper's vehement anti-collectivism for support for their own 'privatising' preferences. Whether or not this is the correct way to read his political thought is highly debatable – his plea for 'small-scale' social engineering by no means rules out a fairly significant role for the state to play. (There has also been a tendency to conflate, and confuse, Popper's views with those of his more anti-statist friend Hayek, a tendency only recently being countered by more discerning analyses – see especially Simkin 1993, Appendix 2.) Popper's political philosophy developed against the background of two major political and social catastrophes, fascist Germany and the communist Soviet Union, and it is perhaps no accident that its influence has been most felt in Eastern Europe. Here once more we find Popper's thought having a surprising impact, given that philosophers overall have been remarkably uninfluential in shaping political events.

Most of the chapters in this volume were delivered at a conference celebrating the centenary of Karl Popper's birth. The idea behind the conference was to use the centenary as an occasion to critically assess some of the central features of Popper's philosophy. The conference was held in Christchurch, New Zealand, where Popper had been a lecturer in philosophy from 1937 to 1945, and where he completed two of his major works, *The Poverty of Historicism* and the two volumes of *The Open Society and Its Enemies*. In the first part of this introduction we would like to briefly re-appraise the significance of this time in Popper's life. Then in the second part we will briefly discuss this volume's contents.

Popper in New Zealand

In many ways this period may well have been the most productive, as well as the happiest, of Popper's life. It may seem strange to say this given the widespread view that Popper's time in New Zealand was one in which he was out of touch with what was going on in the philosophical world. In *Karl Popper: The Formative Years*, Malachi Hacohen's magisterial biography of Popper (which finishes when Popper leaves New Zealand), Chapter 8 is titled 'Social Science in Exile 1938–9' (Hacohen 2000). Stefano Gattei, reviewing this book, talks of 'Popper's exile to New Zealand': 'Then Popper went to his New Zealand exile, and virtually disappeared, out of touch and influence' (Gattei 2001).

In their acclaimed book *Wittgenstein's Poker* Edmonds and Eidenow sarcastically comment that in 1937 Popper 'took up his first full-time lectureship – in New Zealand, hardly the beating heart of philosophy' (Edmonds and Eidenow 2001, p. 211).[3]

One gets the impression that the time spent in New Zealand was both miserable and an unfortunate break in Popper's philosophical career. Edmonds and Eidenow suggest (2000, p. 218):

> if he had gone to England in 1937, he would not have spent some of his most productive years outside the mainstream of philosophy. He would have had the chance to establish himself academically – and to work and debate alongside Wittgenstein.

Popper himself gives some credence to this treatment of that time. 'Had he gone to Cambridge, he remarked to Michael Nedo, Wittgenstein and his school would have been eclipsed' (ibid.).

There is, of course, some truth in this view. Hacohen (2000, p. 342) reports a letter from Popper to Kaufmann reading: 'We live here a life without a trace of external events. You have no idea how physical distance, something rather abstract, becomes profoundly and terribly concrete here in New Zealand . . .' and that Hennie suggested New Zealand was 'half way to the moon' (Hacohen 2000, p. 343). And any feeling of exile may well have been exacerbated by Popper's poor working conditions. He was given a remarkably heavy lecturing load, being the only full-time philosopher in Canterbury University College. By the time he left, Popper had, single-handed, delivered the following lecture courses: Logic, Ethics, History of Philosophy, Introduction to Philosophy, and Moral Philosophy. Moreover he had supervised research work on: Bacon's Theory of Science, Kant's Criticism of Theism, Spinoza's Political Philosophy, and Bergson's Theory of Intuition and Change. In addition, a friend, Colin Simkin, reports that Popper's 'office' was unsuitable for much philosophical thought, it being 'a small room in a ramshackle wooden building above a carpenter's shop where a buzzsaw was often in operation' (Simkin 1993, p. 184, fn. 3).

Popper also complained to the University authorities that, despite the number of philosophy students doubling since his appointment in 1937, requests for increased assistance had been turned down, that he had been forbidden to ask the departmental student assistants for help (permission was granted *after* he had accepted the position at LSE), and that he had a lower salary than any other of the Senior Lecturers given this status in 1941. And if all this wasn't enough of a disincentive to do research, there was also some friction between Popper and his Head of Department, Professor Sutherland, a psychologist. Both had applied for the Professorship, Popper accepting the lecturing position when his application was turned down.[4] The Chair Committee in London, consisting of Professors F. Clarke, A. Harrop, J. MacMurray and G. E. Moore, although reporting that Popper was 'a philosopher in every sense of the term', recommended Sutherland on the grounds that he was already well known in New Zealand.[5] (At least Popper was considered for the Chair. When he had, earlier, applied for a Chair at the University of Queensland he did not even make the short list, despite having Professors Stebbing, Carnap, Russell, Moore and Bohr as referees.[6]) It is reported that Sutherland made Popper pay for any paper he used for non-teaching purposes (Simkin 1993, p. 183, Hacohen 2000, p. 339), though this may have been a general University requirement. At the time the University was, if anything, opposed to its lecturers doing research, regarding 'time spent on research as time filched from the primary job of teaching' (Simkin 1993, p. 183). This attitude Popper, with the help of many friends, did his best to change, but even up to the time he left he had to answer for time spent on non-teaching activities. Responding to a question (in a questionnaire) from the Chancellor of the University of New Zealand as to whether he had used University time for his research, Popper replied, 'Certainly not. All the research work carried out by me was done during the vacation, during the weekends, and at night, to the complete sacrifice of any leisure for myself and my wife (who worked as my typist).' (Popper Archives, University of Canterbury.)

It has been suggested (cf. Sandall 2001) that Popper's relationship with Sutherland deteriorated partly as a consequence of their very different opinions about 'tribalism'. Sutherland's psychological research was connected to Maori culture, his view being that prior to European colonisation Maori had lived in equilibrium with their environment, this producing a state of 'mental and moral stability' (Sutherland quoted by Sandall 2001, p. 119).[7] Popper's advocacy of the open, critical society could be seen as being in direct opposition to anyone supporting a 'closed', tribal community, and so might have been interpreted as being in direct opposition to Sutherland himself. Whatever the cause, it is claimed that the relationship between the two men became so bad that Sutherland 'instigated a campaign of harassment against Popper, eventually alleging to the police that the visiting European was probably an agent of influence for the Axis powers – if not an actual spy' (Sandall 2001, p. 125).[8] Whether there is any truth in this claim is unclear,[9] but there is no doubt that the war made life more difficult for foreigners. Findlay claims that 'war-fever' hit New Zealand, and those with German accents became 'pariahs overnight, and even our friend Lady Wood . . . was, on account of her undecipherable accent, suspected of being a spy' (Findlay 1985, p. 33).

So how can we suggest that this was a happy time in the lives of Karl and Hennie Popper? There are many indications that they found New Zealand an agreeable place in which to live. In his autobiography Popper talks of New

Zealand as being the 'best governed country in the world, and the most easily governed', with the inhabitants being 'like the British . . . decent, friendly, and well-disposed' (Schilpp 1974, p. 89). Although the University as an institution did not do much to encourage research, Popper found many friends with whom to talk and exchange ideas. Colin Simkin has already been mentioned: it was Simkin who introduced Popper to the work of the Austrian economists. Others were Hugh Parton (chemist), Frederick White (physicist), Robin Allan (geologist), George Roth (radiation physicist), Alan Reed (a lawyer), and Margaret Dalziel (English) – who took over Simkin's role as 'English editor' of *The Open Society* when Simkin was engaged in war duties.

Popper must have been much flattered by the reception given to his philosophical views; it was clear that a number of academics in Christchurch and beyond were influenced by both the philosophy of science and Popper's political philosophy. When John Eccles arrived in Dunedin to take up the position of Professor of Physiology at the University of Otago, he writes that he heard 'marvellous stories . . . about the academic stir that was being made by a philosopher, Karl Popper, in Canterbury University College at Christchurch' (Eccles 1982, p. 221). Eccles invited Popper to give a week-long course of five lectures at the University of Otago:

> The train was very late, so the lecture perforce had to start about 30 minutes late to a crowded audience of at least 500 in the largest lecture theatre of the University. It was a unique occasion for the University, so remote and in war-time.
>
> (Eccles 1982, p. 221)

Eccles also writes of trips he made via Christchurch to Wellington, relating how on one occasion

> we were deep in discussion until the ship departed beyond shouting distance. Two days later, when the ship arrived at 6.30 a.m. at Lyttelton, I was amazed to find Karl on the wharf for a renewal of the conversation that continued on the drive to his lovely home in the Cashmere Hills for breakfast, and so to the train departing from Christchurch to Dunedin.[10]
>
> (Eccles 1982, p. 223)

J. N. Findlay's experience of Popper was similar; he recounts that his stay in New Zealand (which he describes as 'perhaps the most beautiful country in the whole world' – Findlay 1985, p. 24)

> was made more interesting by a philosophical and personal friendship with Karl Popper . . . with whom I regularly exchanged visits over the two hundred or so miles that separated us. Discussions with Karl Popper were for me immensely profitable, but they were also exhausting, as he

5

never knew when to stop and would go on explaining intricate formulae while we were driving among the scenic beauties of the Cashmere Hills.
(Findlay 1985, p. 26)

The contrast between this and Findlay's experience of Popper in London is enormous. He recounts that though they were now separated only by the width of the Strand and Aldwych, their relations were more distant than they had been in New Zealand: 'His views of people, always violently moralistic, became more and more prejudiced, and he attributed defects of character to most of those who differed from him philosophically' (Findlay 1985, p. 40).

It is also clear that the Poppers had many friends in New Zealand, and seemed to live more gregariously than they did after moving to England. Simkin reports that Popper used to drop in to his home between lectures for a chocolate or ice cream to satisfy his sweet tooth, and it is clear from the voluminous correspondence with George and Edith Roth that the Roths spent a lot of time with the Poppers attending plays and concerts.[11] Popper was also involved in the Workers' Educational Association (WEA) partly organised by George Roth, and clearly had a rapport with the non-university students from varying backgrounds. In the early 1970s George Roth writes to the Poppers about a WEA course on 'Freedom and Determinism' attracting 69 students in the 40- to 85-year-old age group:

> The lecturer is an amazingly competent delightful young University Faculty member (David Novitz (MA (Rhodes), D.Phil. (Oxon)) who reminds us (not just in looks but in many of his mannerisms and in his presentation of the subject to this type of audience) of the young Karl Popper when we knew him when we first met him. Can you understand that we take great delight in the course?
> (Popper Archives, University of Canterbury)

The picture one gets 'from the outside' is one of a very active and enthusiastic philosopher revelling in his contacts with other academics and enjoying relaxing with friends – when not working. That he appreciated these friends is clear from this response to the Chancellor's questionnaire when he left New Zealand:

> I wish to make especially one point clear: owing to the interest and understanding of these friends, I never felt isolated in New Zealand. I never felt for a minute that I was lacking mental stimulus. In this respect I have not only to thank the active research workers among my colleagues, but also a great number of students in the University, as well as in the WEA and the Royal Society.
> (Popper Archives, University of Canterbury)

That his friends appreciated him is also clear, and Popper could hardly have failed to have been pleased by the favourable reception and attention given to his ideas.

Compare this with what happens when he gets to England, where he always felt an outsider and unappreciated. ('Popper's relationship with the philosophical establishment in his adopted country was always chilly; from early in his career he may have despaired of British audiences for their inability to appreciate his originality' – Edmonds and Eidenow 2001, p. 215.) The thought that, had he not gone to New Zealand, he would have vanquished Wittgenstein, is hugely improbable. English philosophy at that time was dominated by Oxford and Cambridge, and Popper's relationship to those institutions was always problematic. (He is reported to have said that Oxford had 150 philosophers and no philosophy. See Edmonds and Eidenow 2001, p. 216.) And the ease of life in Christchurch was missed. Hennie writes to the Roths in May 1946:

> The School [LSE] has started again and Karl is rather exhausted. Life is very rushed, he is always in a hurry, and buses and underground are crowded, noisy and take up the best part of the day; time required from our place to the School when one is lucky – just over an hour (but one isn't lucky often).
>
> (Popper Archives, University of Canterbury)

And it is reported that soon after arriving in England Popper 'began to withdraw from conferences and professional gatherings, choosing increasingly to work in isolation at home. . . . [T]he heroic period, tackling the fundamental questions, was over' (Edmonds and Eidenow 2001, p. 214).

All of this would suggest that Popper's time in New Zealand was not the unfortunate interlude it has been made out to be. There may even be a case for saying that without this 'exile' some of Popper's most valuable work might never have been completed. The truth probably lies somewhere between the two extremes; in some ways this time was (as both Karl and Hennie were wont to complain) 'poor and miserable' (Hacohen 2000, p. 460), in other ways it was productive and fulfilled. It was, at any rate, a sufficiently happy time for Karl to write to the Roths on 29 July 1970, 'I would like to retire to New Zealand, but Hennie is against it' (Popper Archives, University of Canterbury).

The chapters in this volume

The chapters in this volume review Popper's work, and develop themes from that work, in a critical vein consistently with Popper's methodological advice. The topics discussed cover many of the major issues explored by Popper in his most important works. We begin the volume with discussions of Popper's philosophy of knowledge and of science, and we end it with discussions of Popper's political philosophy. Several chapters in the middle link these two broad spheres of Popper's philosophical interest.

The opening chapter by Alan Musgrave addresses the problem of induction – 'Hume's argument for the shocking conclusion that any evidence-transcending belief is unreasonable' – and carefully examines the solution to this problem that Popper claims to have achieved. Musgrave contends that Popper generated confusion about the nature of his solution, and may not himself have been entirely or always clear about what it is. Consequently many followers of Popper have evaded Hume's challenge rather than answering it. Instead of proposing a way that evidence-transcending belief can after all be reasonable, they have pretended that preoccupation with belief is itself somehow misguided. Musgrave insists that 'this is not answering Hume, it is changing the subject'.

According to Musgrave, Hume rests his argument on two premises, the first his inductive scepticism and the second 'the justificationist principle that it is only reasonable to believe what you can justify'. Musgrave proposes that the best way to understand Popper's critical rationalism is as upholding the first of these premises but rejecting the second. He argues that we are all already committed to rejecting the justificationist principle, and he discusses how in the face of its rejection we may still claim the right to possess a contentful notion of conjectural knowledge: 'to know is to reasonably believe what is true' (rather than to believe what is reasonable and true).

Semiha Akıncı confronts the notorious fact that while Popper attacked conventionalism, specifically of the types espoused by Henri Poincaré and Pierre Duhem, he has himself been labelled a conventionalist by many philosophers, including Robert Ackermann, Joseph Agassi, A. J. Ayer, Imre Lakatos and Anthony Quinton. Despite this Popper continued to insist 'I am not a conventionalist (whether modified or not)'. In an historically sensitive analysis, Akıncı distinguishes between various quite distinct expressions of conventionalism in the philosophy of science. Crucially, Akıncı distinguishes between 'epistemic' conventionalism according to which conventional decisions have to be taken concerning the very content of our knowledge, and 'epistemological' or 'methodological' conventionalism according to which conventional decisions have to be taken during the process by which knowledge is generated. While Popper eschews the former kind of conventionalism in relation to all science, it is by a conventional decision of the second kind that he does so. Using her distinction, Akıncı makes evident that while Popper consistently pitted himself against 'epistemic' conventionalism his approach to doing so thoroughly committed him to 'epistemological' or 'methodological' conventionalism.

Philip Catton, drawing on studies of some accomplishments of some groundbreaking historical scientists including Isaac Newton and Albert Einstein, opposes Popper's general conception of science as a process of conjectures and refutations. Endorsing Newton's contention that there is a more cogent method for science than guess-and-test, Catton details the ways in which this more cogent method remains none the less in its own right fallible. He argues that Newton himself explicitly recognised the fallibility of the method he preferred, so that, *pace* Popper, Duhem, Lakatos and Einstein, it is neither the case that Newton exaggerated the cogency of his method, nor that hypothetico-deductivists have a monopoly on the fallibilist stance in philosophy of science.

Catton discusses reasons (first pointed out by Jon Dorling) for saying that Einstein very much followed this method of Newton's, despite officially endorsing something like conjectures-and-refutations as the method of science (thus helping to inspire Popper's philosophy of science).

Newton's method involves non-hypothetico-deductive deductions-from-phenomena, a form of inference that Catton discusses in relation to the more general conception of *measurement*. He argues that measurement performs, in addition to the negative function, recognised by Popper, of confronting a theory with a potential counter-instance, a positive function, not recognised by Popper, of *deductively warranting* a theoretical conclusion modulo the acceptance of an empirical claim and a background of theoretical assumptions. This is illustrated by historical examples, showing how impressive such warrants can be when they compound with others for one and the same conclusion (in the circumstance of 'consilience', or thus of the theoretical harmonisation of facts). According to Popper, insofar as a theory is scientific and true, it accurately predicts what we observe. Catton proposes the quite different view, that insofar as a theory is scientific and true, it concertedly harmonises phenomena. He concludes by discussing the freedom underlying scientific creativity. He urges that Popper, the positivists and Thomas Kuhn (in his very different way) held in view only a negative kind of freedom in theoretical creativity, namely scientists' freedom to conjecture anew. Over against this view, Catton insists that the freedom of the greatest scientists is positive: it reforms theory in a maximally *responsible* way, that is to say, in the most measured and thus most harmonising way possible.

Wenceslao Gonzalez reminds us that Popper's emphasis on prediction is nuanced. Popper famously emphasised prediction in his general methodology of science, but he is no less famous for the scepticism he propounded about the supposed ability to predict the course of human history. Popper opposed the thesis of determinism in all connections and was to that extent committed very deeply to the unpredictability of events. About human affairs, he thought that there are reasons in principle to expect that the scope of what can be predicted is very limited. So this invites careful consideration of the role he thought prediction could and should play in scientific investigations.

On the one hand, Popper insists that the theories of the natural sciences should be capable of yielding predictions against which they can be tested. On the other hand, Popper defends a method for social science that he calls the *logic of situation*, the understanding of human behaviour in terms of rational decision-making in a situation. Popper thinks that in social science, unlike in natural science, predicting particular events is bound to be difficult, yet predicting event-types comes easily. Gonzalez considers the implication of these ideas to the field of economics, where he offers a diagnosis different from Popper's as to why prediction is difficult. It is not that (as Popper held) only economic event types are predictable, not singular economic events; rather it is that both singular economic events *and* economic event types are inordinately complex. Where well reasoned prediction in economics is possible at all it is, *pace* Popper, not less liable to be of a singular event than it is of an event type.

Jeremy Shearmur explores the anomalous position of Popper in twentieth-century philosophy, Popper being neither a 'continental philosopher' nor a conventional analytic philosopher. Three facets of this divergence from analytic philosophy are explored: Popper's attitude to logic, his coherentist epistemology, and his anti-naturalism. Regarding the first, Shearmur urges that Popper's instrumentalist attitude to logic differs from that of important proponents of analytic philosophy. For Carnap and Quine logical analysis was viewed as revealing the underlying structure of the claims we are making, and so enabling us to discern the truth. For Popper truth is apt rather 'to emerge from the contention of substantive, competing viewpoints', and there is no sure way to generalise about the form that it might take. Shearmur also advocates revisiting, and improving on, Popper's anti-psychologistic epistemology, seeing this view as resulting in 'a layered coherence theory of knowledge (but not of truth)'.

Finally, Shearmur notes that despite his high regard for science Popper eschewed naturalism – the predominant '-ism' in current analytic philosophy. Shearmur explores this anti-naturalism in the context of moral philosophy, proposing that Popper could be seen as recommending an anti-naturalistic ethical realism. This view is discussed using Michael Smith's argument against the plausibility of such a position as a foil. Shearmur makes a case that philosophical inquiry would be richer if it better engaged with distinctive alternatives such as Popper's.

Peter Munz studied first under Popper and then under Wittgenstein. This unique association surely raises the interest for scholars of Munz's historical reminiscences in his contribution to this volume. His chapter here, however, is not only about history, it is also about philosophy, for it criticises both Popper and Wittgenstein for what they failed to learn from one another. Munz urges that Popper and the later Wittgenstein complement one another, the commonalities between them having the potential for each to correct and strengthen the other's philosophical viewpoint in some ways.

Among the commonalities between Popper and the later Wittgenstein was their shared opposition to any account of linguistic meaning given in only ostensive terms. Unlike Popper, however, Wittgenstein provided a positive account of how linguistic meaning could transcend mere ostensive meaning, an account in which types of linguistic expressions are said to have their meaning via the mutual consent and habits of the users of those expressions. But then again, Popper, unlike Wittgenstein, was enormously concerned to detail the qualities of practical endeavour and social organisation that leave a community open to the detection of error and thus place them upon the path towards truth. Popper armed us, appropriately in Munz's view, against the relativism which so clearly crept into the philosophy of the later Wittgenstein, by 'showing that propositions which are true as well as meaningful can only be generated in socio-political orders which are free and open enough to allow unlimited criticism'. In short, had it only been possible for these two men to interact at the level of productive dialogue, the philosophies of both of them would have benefited. Munz concludes, pessimistically but fairly, that neither Popper nor Wittgenstein had the temperament to make such collaboration likely.

Popper often emphasised that since social scientists are members of the society they study, whatever they conclude in their researches can then affect that society and thereby alter that which they mean to be theorising about. The chapter by Gonzalez, introduced above, discusses this point, but the chapter by Christian List and Philip Pettit moves it to centre stage. As mentioned above, Popper made much of the fact that social science was in the awkward position of being unable to predict the future, and this for a reason unrelated to problems of induction. Here the problem is that future social events depend on the action of individuals, and those actions depend on the knowledge available to the actors. Any present predictor has to know what knowledge those future actors have in order to be able to predict the actions, and that was precisely knowledge unavailable to any present predictor, given the likelihood that future knowledge would incorporate new discoveries. Such knowledge may also incorporate knowledge of the predictions made, hence permitting actions contrary to those predicted. List and Pettit call this a reflexivity problem: knowledge of the theory underwriting the prediction may lead actors to produce actions contrary to the theory's prediction. They explore such reflexivity in the context of Condorcet's jury theorem, which is expressed as follows:

> Suppose that each individual member of some decision-making body has an equal chance greater than 0.5 of making a correct judgment, and suppose further that all individuals' judgments are independent from each other. Then the jury theorem states that the majority will make a correct judgment with a probability approaching 1 as the number of individuals increases.

List and Pettit note that a voter who knows Condorcet's theorem may make their judgment depend on the way others vote, hence undermining support for the correctness of that judgment delivered by the majority of votes. Such a voter will be taking an epistemic 'free-ride' on others' judgments, but in so doing will devalue the epistemic support provided by a majority vote. List and Pettit discuss reasons why this problem is liable to be significant in many spheres where the jury theorem ideally would be applicable, spheres, that is, where the theorem indicates why a particular social mode of knowledge production would have integrity provided that free-riding doesn't occur. They also show that some practical ways in which one might have hoped that the problem could be averted and the jury theorem restored to significance do not work. The conclusion (surely both political philosophical and important, yet based on an insight in the philosophy of science) is that epistemic free-riding is a serious problem. Popper therefore had his finger on the pulse of something significant.

Graham Macdonald's chapter likewise interlinks philosophy of science and political philosophy, in his case by examining the role of experience in both scientific knowledge and ethical reasoning. In his philosophy of science Popper limited the role of experience to that of causing beliefs, denying it any epistemological role on the grounds that experience as such is merely psychological and thus is without logical traction – '*statements can be logically justified only by statements*' (i.e. experience is not the right sort of thing to be inference-worthy). Yet in his political and ethical philosophy Popper implied otherwise. There, a person's experience of pain (for example) seems to Popper to give us immediate reason to help the person if we can. Is this difference in Popper's viewpoint across the two domains defensible? Macdonald argues that it is not, and that we can improve Popper's epistemology by accommodating it better on this point to Popper's ways of thinking about ethics. He shows how Popper could have accepted a moderate amount of psychologism, in a way that would not only underwrite an epistemological role for experience, but also strengthen Popper's own endorsement of evolutionary epistemology. Knowledge need not be sentences all the way down.

The connections between open societies – democracies – and science is taken up by Alan Ryan, who asks three questions. Is science good for democracy? Is democracy good for science? And are

the ways in which scientists come (or should come) to a consensus about the way the world works a model for the ways in which the citizenry comes (or should come) to a consensus on what government ought to do about those things that governments exist to do?

Ryan argues that the answer to the second question is a guarded 'yes'; recent history suggests that intellectual freedom is necessary for good science, and such intellectual freedom is one of the features of an open society. The third question is addressed more fully. Ryan notes that the authority provided by (scientific) knowledge tells against Popper's view that there is a natural affiliation between science and liberal democracy, and the views of Thomas Hobbes, a supporter of both science and authoritarian government, also suggest otherwise. Hobbes and Popper share an analytical framework composed of an austere theory of rationality applied to agents in a situation, but differ hugely in their approach to political accountability. For Hobbes the Sovereign is not accountable, while for Popper political accountability is an essential feature of an open society. It is here that one finds the connection he forges between science and politics, the 'great virtue of science' being

the notion that we are accountable for our beliefs. What this means is that Popper's philosophy of science does not so much support a liberal and democratic politics; it just is that politics in cognitive action.

However, in Ryan's view 'the actual practice of science and political democracy work against Popper's picture'. Concerning the actual practice of science, Ryan touches on some of Kuhn's contentions and discusses their negative impact on Popper's point of view. Concerning the actual practice of political democracy, he examines factors causing the popular participation in governmental decision-making to have largely faded away. Ryan proposes that John Dewey's picture of science and politics provide a better basis for giving a partial affirmative answer to his second question. He then turns to the third question – is science good for democracy? – and suggests that there are grounds for some doubt, given both the necessity for much of scientific education to be authoritarian and the increasing emphasis placed on such an education by funding authorities.

The issue of the role of criticism in an open society is taken up by Anthony O'Hear, who critically appraises the book of Popper's that he thinks in retrospect may be judged Popper's most important – *The Open Society and Its Enemies* (OS). O'Hear would like to see the perspective of this book refined, clarified and developed further for the twenty-first century. To this end he questions the conception of an open society in Popper's OS, pointing to respects in which this conception is utopian or otherwise over-simple. Thus when Popper insists that social institutions must be maintained in ways that leave them forever under critical scrutiny and liable to be changed in light of changing knowledge or requirements, he proffers this demand under the conception that institutions are all about problem-solving. O'Hear insists that this is not the case; institutions rather are the vessels through which particular traditions are transmitted, and they have intrinsic value for the people who support them. For this reason,

> an institution forced by Popperian social engineers to declare its aims and objectives, and then held accountable against a diet of targets met and problems solved, is more than likely to lose morale and to wither and decline

rather than contributing as best it might to producing what people find worthwhile. This fact points to there being a need for humans to value their traditions even somewhat prejudicially. They cannot view them only or always with a merely critical disposition.

O'Hear suggests that by the time Popper wrote 'Towards a Rational Theory of Tradition' in 1949 (just four years after he published OS), he came to distance himself not only from the rationalists he explicitly criticises, but also from his own earlier rationalistic stance. Popper retracted 'the implicit contrast of *The Open Society*' between (in O'Hear's words) 'irrational communities, with no commitment to reason, and rational open societies with no basis in tradition. The open society, where and in so far as it exists, exists as part of a given tradition'.

According to O'Hear the challenge is to work out better than Popper did not only what such a tradition may look like, but also what it is about human nature and human flourishing that makes it good.

13

Jeremy Waldron explores Popper's critique of tribalism in *The Open Society and Its Enemies*, assessing its significance for the critique of contemporary cultural identity politics. In the tribal society, according to Popper's characterisation, the norms of that society are regarded as natural rather than conventional, and so are not reflected upon with a view to criticism and change. Such a society is vulnerable to change whenever there is interaction with other societies in which the norms may differ, and this provides for a different kind of tribalism, one in which the nostalgic desire for the old ways produces deliberate attempts to reinstate them. Waldron argues that these attempts are doomed to failure, as once reflection on normative differences has become part of the culture, the practice of unreflective observance of the norms is impossible to recapture.

Similarly, Waldron suggests, present-day partisans of cultural identity must acknowledge that the customs and mores of cultural minorities cannot be uncritically maintained. It would be far better for 'the members of minority cultures in modern societies . . . to engage their norms as political proposals for solving the problems of wider society, rather than as fiercely defended aspects of individual identity'.

Waldron finds support in Popper's 'The Myth of the Framework' for his own argument against the relativistic claim that customs and norms from different cultures are incommensurable. He follows Popper in urging the promulgation of very high expectations concerning the ability of different peoples to engage one another in fruitful debate.

Notes

1 For a comprehensive intellectual biography of Popper from 1902 to 1945, see Hacohen 2000.

2 The third impression of *The Logic of Scientific Discovery*, which was published by Hutchinson, is unusual in that it includes on the dust-jacket both praise and criticism of the work. All of the appraisals reported in the present paragraph appeared there (see Popper 1959).

3 See also Adam Gopnik, who writes (Gopnik 2002, p. 90): 'In exile in New Zealand in the forties, Popper gave this insight [science wasn't the name for knowledge that had been proved true; it was the name for guesses that could be proved false] a surprising twist in the greatest of his books, *The Open Society and Its Enemies*.'

4 Other applicants for the Chair included the Hegelian scholar Errol Harris and 'Professor A. Garnett' from the University of Transylvania.

5 This information is contained in the Popper archives at the Macmillan Brown library, University of Canterbury.

6 The person appointed, William Kyle, had an MA from the University of Queensland, and long service in the Queensland Department of Public Instruction. (Information provided by Professor Alan Rix, Dean of Arts, University of Queensland.)

7 We are grateful to Michael Grimshaw for drawing our attention to Sandall's article.

8 Sandall is here reporting a conversation with Colin Simkin, a lecturer in economics at the University, who helped Popper correct his English for the early parts of *The Open Society*.

9 Hacohen reports that the police inquiry may have been a matter of routine (Hacohen 2000, p. 391).

10 Lyttelton is a port a few miles to the south of Christchurch. Cashmere Hills, a suburb of Christchurch, is on part of a small range separating Lyttelton harbour from Christchurch.
11 Roth was an Austrian Jew rescued from Europe by a New Zealand committee set up to save those threatened by Hitler's onslaught. It appears that Popper had some role in this committee.

References

Eccles, J. C. 1982. 'My Living Dialogue with Popper', in P. Levinson (ed.), *In Pursuit of Truth*, Atlantic Highlands, NJ: Humanities Press.

Edmonds, D. and J. Eidenow. 2001. *Wittgenstein's Poker*, New York: HarperCollins Publishers.

Findlay, J. N. 1985. 'My Life', in R. S. Cohen, R. M. Martin, and M. Westphal (eds), *Studies in the Philosophy of J. N. Findlay*, Albany: SUNY Press, pp. 1–69.

Gattei, S. 2001. 'Review of M. Hacohen's *Karl Popper: The Formative Years 1902–1945*', in *British Journal for the Philosophy of Science*, vol. 52, pp. 815–25.

Gopnik, Adam. 2002. 'A pilgrimage to Popper', *New Yorker*, 1 April, pp. 88–93.

Hacohen, M. H. 2000. *Karl Popper, the Formative Years, 1902–1945: Politics and Philosophy in Interwar Vienna*, Cambridge: Cambridge University Press.

Popper, Karl. 1959. *The Logic of Scientific Discovery*, London: Hutchinson.

Sandall, R. 2001. 'Popper in New Zealand', in his *The Culture Cult*, Boulder, CO: Westview Press, pp. 111–95.

Schilpp, P. (ed.). 1974. *The Philosophy of Karl Popper*, La Salle, IL: Open Court.

Simkin, C. 1993. *Popper's Views on Natural and Social Science*, Leiden: E. J. Brill.

1

HOW POPPER (MIGHT HAVE) SOLVED THE PROBLEM OF INDUCTION

Alan Musgrave

The problem of induction is posed by Hume's argument for the shocking conclusion that any evidence-transcending belief is unreasonable. That argument rests upon two premises: (1) Hume's inductive scepticism and (2) the justificationist principle that it is reasonable to believe only what you can justify. Popper's answer to Hume was (or might have been) critical rationalism, which accepts (1) but rejects (2).

Most Popperians are not critical rationalists in this sense. Their so-called 'critical rationalism' has nothing to say about beliefs or their rationality, and confines itself instead to 'third world considerations'. But this is not answering Hume, it is changing the subject. Other ways of changing the subject are jettisoning truth as the aim of inquiry, or going in for some peculiar epistemic theory of truth.

The most common philosophical objection to critical rationalism is that it must smuggle in inductive reasoning somewhere. However, this objection itself smuggles in precisely the justificationist assumption (2) that critical rationalism rejects. Demanding a justification for critical rationalism smuggles in the same assumption.

Critical rationalism means that we may reasonably believe what is false – though if we find out that what we believe is false, it is no longer reasonable to believe it. Similarly, according to critical rationalism reasonable beliefs need not be reliable beliefs, beliefs produced by a reliable belief-producing process – though if we find out that a belief-producing process is unreliable, it is no longer reasonable generally to adopt beliefs of that kind.

Critical rationalism can contain a notion of 'conjectural knowledge': to know is reasonably to believe what is true.

1 Introduction

The situation with Popper's philosophy is most peculiar. There are twelve or twenty folk, the self-styled 'Popperians', who think it is the bee's knees. Most philosophers ignore them. Popper's philosophy of science is popular among scientists. Most philosophers of science think it fatally flawed. Popper talks about 'The Growth of Scientific Knowledge'. Most philosophers regard him as a sceptic who

16

thinks scientists know nothing. Popper says he is a 'critical rationalist' and extols the virtues of reason. He is one of the *Four Irrationalists* discussed in a recent book of that name.

The problem of induction is the key to all this. Popper said, famously and immodestly, 'I think I have solved a major philosophical problem: the problem of induction'. He admitted that 'few philosophers' agree with him. He said this was because 'few philosophers have taken the trouble to study . . . my views' (1972, p. 1). Popper's explanation of his neglect is as insulting as it is mistaken. Many philosophers have studied his views *and found them wanting*. The most important reason for the peculiar state of affairs regarding Popper's philosophy is that his solution to the problem of induction is rejected. That is why Popper is dismissed as a sceptic and an irrationalist. That is why the Popperian edifice is viewed as a house of cards, which collapses as soon as its foundation is scrutinised.

What exactly *is* Popper's solution to the problem of induction? I think I know, and have tried several times to explain it, and to say why the key philosophical objections to it miss the mark. But the Popperians object violently to my views, and accuse me of a litany of sins (justificationism, psychologism, messing about with 'second world considerations', belief philosophy, and so forth). As for Popper himself, he never endorsed my account of what his solution is, and in the course of his own voluminous writings on the matter said things difficult to reconcile with that account. However, neither did Popper ever explicitly reject my account. Perhaps he did not fully understand his own ideas. Perhaps I am the only person who understands Popper, including Popper himself! (This paradox is consistent with Popper's own view that any work has a 'life of its own' and may not be fully understood even by its producer.)

So I shall first explain again how I think Popper solved, or might have solved, the problem of induction. Then I shall defend that solution against the most widespread objections to it. I take no credit for what follows – I think I learned it from Popper. But I will take the blame, if I did not learn well and it is all wrong.

2 The problem of induction and Popper's solution

The problem of induction is posed by the following argument of David Hume's:

1   We reason, and must reason, inductively.
2   Inductive reasoning is logically invalid.
3   To reason in a logically invalid way is irrational.
    Therefore, we are, and must be, irrational.

The problem this argument poses is: can Hume's irrationalist conclusion be avoided? This formulation of the problem is Popper's. Other formulations are more common, such as 'Can induction be justified?' or even 'How can induction be justified?' But these beg the question against some possible solutions, notably Popper's.

Popper's formulation of the problem highlights Hume's originality. That inductive reasoning is logically invalid (premise (2) above) had already been pointed out by Aristotle, Sextus Empiricus, Francis Bacon and countless others. Hume's originality was to combine this well known logical triviality with other things to produce an intellectual bombshell. What other things? Inductive reasoning is arguing from experience. It is arguing from the premise that all observed As were Bs to the conclusion that the next A will be B, or that all As are Bs. The invalidity of inductive reasoning means that no argument from experience can establish that its conclusion is true, or probable (more likely to be true than not). But it is only reasonable to believe something if you have shown that it is true, or probable (more likely to be true than not). *Ergo*, any experience-transcending or evidence-transcending belief is unreasonable. The Greeks thought we were rational animals. Hume thought us irrational, no better than dogs and cats, who are also inveterate inductive reasoners.

Hume's intellectual bombshell can be pedantically set out as follows:

Inductive scepticism: since induction is invalid, no evidence-transcending belief can be justified (shown to be true, or probable).
Justificationism: it is only reasonable to believe what has been justified (shown to be true, or probable).
Therefore irrationalism: no evidence-transcending belief is reasonable.

Many philosophers before Popper grappled with Hume. All of them accepted his first premise (1), that we do and must reason inductively. All of them disputed either (2), inductive reasoning is logically invalid or (3), to reason in a logically invalid way is irrational, or both. Popper disputes (1). He says that induction is a 'myth'.

When Popper says that induction is a 'myth', is he making the factual or psychological claim that no one ever argues from experience? If he were, he would be refuted every time someone actually did argue from experience. No, it is Hume's assumption that we *must* reason inductively that is Popper's real target. Most philosophers share Hume's assumption. We must reason inductively if we are to have any justified evidence-transcending beliefs. Only justified beliefs can be reasonable beliefs. Hence, if we are to avoid Hume's irrationalism regarding evidence-transcending beliefs, we must reject his inductive scepticism.

Popper also rejects the irrationalism. But he accepts the inductive scepticism. Hence, he must reject justificationism. He must think that it may be reasonable to believe what has not been justified, established as true or probable. Most philosophers think this is crazy. After all, to believe something is to think it true. So a reason for believing something must show that it is true or probably true.

However, the term 'belief' is ambiguous. It can refer to the thing believed, and it can refer to the act or state of believing that thing. Talk of 'reasons for beliefs' inherits this ambiguity. Do we mean a reason for the thing believed, or a reason for the believing of it? Obviously, we mean the latter. After all, one person might

18

have some reason for believing something, and another person believe the same thing for a quite different reason or for no reason at all. Suppose, as is traditional, that the thing believed is a *proposition*. What might a reason for a *proposition* be? Logic tells us. A conclusive reason for a proposition P is another proposition R that entails that P is true. And an inconclusive reason for a proposition P is another proposition R that entails that P is probably true, more likely true than not, or at least, more probable than it was without R. (Of course, we need a logical theory of probability, a generalisation of deductive logic, to make good the idea of one proposition being an inconclusive reason for another.)

Now the mere existence of a reason for a proposition cannot be a reason for believing that proposition. After all, there are always propositions that entail any proposition. And if a theory of logical probability can be worked out, there are always propositions that 'probabilify' any proposition. If propositions were reasons for believing propositions, there would be (conclusive or inconclusive) reasons for believing any proposition whatever.

No, it must be that *believing* one thing might be a reason for believing another. After all, people do come to believe things by inferring them from other things that they believe. So perhaps we should say that a reason for believing P is that you believe R, and infer P from R. But then everybody might have a conclusive reason for everything they believe, if they believe P and waste mental energy inferring P from itself! Or if they believe some stronger R from which they deduce P. Or if they believe some weaker R which 'probabilifies' P (assuming that a theory of logical probability can be worked out).

When is believing R and inferring P from it, a *good* reason in the epistemic sense for believing P? Well, your belief in R had better be reasonable, and your inference had better be valid. (Here, deductivists like Popper and me part company with inductivists. Deductivists think that the only valid inferences are deductively valid inferences, that there is no inductive logic.) But it cannot be that the *only* good reason for believing P is that you have inferred it from another belief R, for which you have good reason. That is *logomania*, the view that only reason or reasoning provides a good reason for believing anything. Logomania leads to infinite regress, as sceptics long ago pointed out. All inferential beliefs (beliefs obtained by inference from other beliefs) must rest on non-inferential beliefs. But logomania entails that non-inferential beliefs are unreasonable – from which it follows that all beliefs are unreasonable.

So, everybody who is not a total irrationalist must reject logomania. Everybody who is not a total irrationalist must think there are good reasons for believing P that do not involve inferring P from other propositions we believe. Everybody who is not a total irrationalist must think that some non-inferential beliefs are reasonable beliefs.

The prime candidate for non-inferential belief is, of course, perceptual belief. I take it for granted that people acquire perceptual beliefs as a result of their perceptual experience, and that this is not to be analysed as inferring the propositions believed from any other propositions. Perceptual experiences cause us to

19

acquire perceptual beliefs. Having a table-experience or seeming to see a table causes us to come to believe that there is a table in front of us. Coming to believe something is an act or action that we perform. Since reasons for actions are also causes, seeming to see a table is both a cause and a reason for the act of coming to believe that there is a table. But having a table-experience or seeming to see a table is not a reason for the content of the belief, the proposition that there is a table. Only a proposition can be a reason for a proposition. The distinction between belief-acts (believings) and belief-contents (propositions) is crucial here.

Is perceptual experience a good reason, in the epistemic sense, for perceptual believing? I propose that it is. A good reason for believing that there is a table in front of you is that you seem to see one. Perceptual beliefs (acts of believing) are reasonable beliefs (acts of believing). Perceptual beliefs are not necessarily true beliefs. And if you somehow find out that your perceptual belief is false, then it will no longer be reasonable to persist in that belief. But unless and until you find out that a perceptual belief is false, it is reasonable to think it true.

I said that having a table-experience is not a reason for the proposition that there is a table in front of you. But what if we formulate a proposition about the experience? What is the relation between the proposition 'I have a table-experience' (E) and the proposition 'There is a table in front of me' (T)? Obviously, E does not entail T – nor, according to deductivists, is there any fancy non-deductive logic in which the inference from E to T is 'sound' or 'cogent'. But T, combined with other assumptions, does entail or predict or explain E. So E represents the results of a successful test of H. And if in any doubt, there are other tests that we can perform. In plain English, we can see whether we can touch as well as see the table, or ask others if they also see it, and so forth. All this is no more than common sense.

Suppose we accept that unrefuted perceptual beliefs are reasonable non-inferential beliefs, and now consider non-perceptual beliefs. It is tempting to suppose that non-perceptual beliefs are only reasonable if they can be validly inferred from reasonable perceptual beliefs. But this is where Hume's inductive scepticism comes in! If inductive scepticism is correct, then non-perceptual or evidence-transcending beliefs cannot be validly inferred from perceptual beliefs or evidence. It follows, if justificationism is correct as well, that non-perceptual or evidence-transcending beliefs cannot be reasonable beliefs.

If we accept inductive scepticism, but reject this irrationalist conclusion, then we must reject justificationism. Logomania does not apply to our perceptual beliefs (believings). And it does not extend to our evidence-transcending beliefs (believings) either. We now need a positive story about which evidence-transcending believings are reasonable, and why. Popper's critical rationalist story is as follows. Faced with an evidence-transcending hypothesis H, there are two ways we can proceed. We can try to justify H, give reasons for it, show that it is true or probable. Or we can try to criticise H, give reasons against it, show that it is false. Hume's inductive scepticism means that the former will not work. We should forsake the way of justification in favour of the way of criticism. No invalid inductive reasoning is involved in rejecting an evidence-transcending hypothesis H as false because it contradicts some perceptual or evidential belief. But suppose our critical endeavours fail, and H stands up to our efforts to criticise it. Then this fact is a good reason to believe H, tentatively and for the time being, *though it is not a reason for the hypothesis H itself.*

Our critical endeavours may involve us in believing, or coming to believe certain evidential propositions E. But E is not a conclusive reason for H, since induction is invalid. Nor is E an inconclusive reason for H, since probabilistic induction does not work. Never mind. We do not *infer* H from E, and believe it because of having made such an inference. Rather, our reason for believing H is the fact that (putting it in a nutshell) E has not falsified H. What of the evidence, E? We do not *infer* E from anything more basic, and believe it because of having made such an inference. Our reason for believing E is (again putting it in a nutshell) that it gives a natural explanation of our perceptual experience.

3 Popperian scholasticism

By 'Popperian scholasticism' I mean the tendency to squabble about words, in particular, about the word 'belief'. Hume's conclusion was that no evidence-transcending belief is reasonable. Anybody who disagrees with this conclusion must think that some evidence-transcending beliefs are reasonable. But Popperians say we should forget about beliefs and their reasonableness, drop 'belief philosophy', engage instead in 'epistemology without a knowing subject'. We should focus, not on 'second world' or psychological considerations, but on 'third world' considerations about theories, propositions, the contents of beliefs.

Popper says that, like E. M. Forster, he 'does not believe in belief'. What Forster did not believe in was unreasonable beliefs, dogmas, articles of faith, irrational commitments. Forster was giving an eminently sensible piece of (second world) advice, that many philosophers would agree with. The advice assumes that there is a difference between reasonable and unreasonable beliefs. Hume's shocking conclusion was that evidence-transcending beliefs are unreasonable, however tentatively held.

Popper preferred to talk, not of believing a theory or thinking it true, but of *preferring* one theory to another, or *choosing* one theory over another, or *adopting* one theory rather than another. Popper also said that the aim of scientific theorising is truth. But to prefer or choose or adopt a theory, when your aim is truth, is to believe it. David Miller prefers to talk of *classifying things as true* rather than *believing* them (see his 1994, further discussed in my 1999, chapter 15, section 10). But to classify something as true is also to believe it. These terminological fads sit oddly with Popper's repeated declaration that 'words do not matter'. They also sit oddly with the distinction between second and third world considerations. Choosing, preferring, adopting and classifying are all things that epistemic subjects do, are all second world phenomena.

Connected with the terminological fads is the matter of *verisimilitude*. Popper dreamt of working out a theory of verisimilitude or closeness to the truth, which would enable us to say that one false theory is closer to the truth than another false theory. Armed with such a theory, we could still aim at truth, and prefer one theory to another, yet believe neither theory to be true – provided we believe that this false theory is closer to the truth than that one. The verisimilitude project, appealing though it was, fell on hard times, for reasons that need not now concern us. (I have also come to suspect that verisimilitude was unnecessary, anyway. What we need is not verisimilitude, but rather *approximate truth*, to be analysed as simple truth of approximations, or of parts of theories. But this need not now concern us, either.) What does concern me here is that dropping truth in favour of verisimilitude cuts no *epistemic* ice. Judgments of verisimilitude depend upon judgments of truth, and are just as conjectural as judgments of truth. If belief in any evidence-transcending hypothesis is unreasonable, so is belief that one evidence-transcending hypothesis is closer to the truth than another. Popper, who started the verisimilitude industry, made this very clear at the outset (although some of his later formulations muddied the waters).

Many philosophers, browbeaten by Hume, give up on truth as the aim of science and put something weaker in its place. Bas van Fraassen's 'empirical adequacy' is the best-known and most-discussed example (see his 1980, further discussed in my 1999, chapter 5). We are not to believe (think true) any evidence-transcending hypothesis. Instead, we may only believe (think true) a meta-claim to the effect that an evidence-transcending hypothesis is empirically adequate, contains nothing but truths about observables. Meta-claims about empirical adequacy and the like succumb to analogues of Humean scepticism and irrationalism, since empirical adequacy is evidence-transcending just as truth is. For this reason John Watkins waters down the aim of science still further, into empirical adequacy *as far as we have looked into the matter* (see his 1984, further discussed in my 1989).

Other philosophers say we aim at truth, but go in for some peculiar new epistemic conception of what truth is. We might propose an *empirical adequacy theory of truth*, according to which an empirically adequate theory is *by definition* a true theory. (Van Fraassen did not, of course, propose such a theory, despite what Arthur Fine says.) Again, to believe a theory (think it true) turns out, when the meaning of 'true' is cashed out, to be believing a meta-claim of empirical adequacy.

None of this is answering Hume – it is agreeing with him and changing the subject. You do not answer Hume by confining yourself to 'third world considerations', or by striving ineffectually to avoid the term 'belief', or dropping truth as our aim, or by going in for some peculiar epistemic concept of truth. You only answer Hume by making out that his inductive scepticism is false, or that his justificationism is false. Most answers take the former course. Popper, rightly understood, takes the latter.

4 Does Popper smuggle in induction?

The most widespread objection to Popper's answer to Hume is that it must smuggle induction in somewhere. This is the objection urged, in one form or another, by the countless philosophers who have read Popper and found his theory wanting. But, I shall argue, the philosophers who press this objection *themselves smuggle in precisely the assumption that Popper rejects.*

To investigate this, let us confine ourselves, as Popper's critics do, to the case of a severely tested but unrefuted hypothesis, which enjoys a high 'degree of corroboration'. Popper says this gives us good reason to adopt the hypothesis as true (that is, believe it), and to use it to make predictions. Here is the Achilles' heel where induction is smuggled in! Popper must be assuming that predictions from well-corroborated hypotheses will be true, while predictions from refuted hypotheses will be false. Or he must be assuming that predictions from well-corroborated hypotheses are more likely to be true (more probable) than predictions from refuted ones. Either way, induction is smuggled in. His 'degrees of corroboration' were supposed to be backward-looking reports on past successes and failures. Backward-looking reports say nothing about future performance. So Popper must be smuggling in an inductive principle linking past success to future performance, he must be assuming that corroboration is a guide to truth or high probability. Without this assumption, he must endorse Humean irrationalism about all evidence-transcending beliefs.

This criticism assumes that a reason for believing something must be a reason for what is believed. That is why the critic says that Popper must be assuming that corroboration is a guide to truth or high probability. But Popper has rejected the view that a reason for believing something must be a reason for what is believed. Popper agrees with Hume that corroboration does not show that a hypothesis is true or probable, is not a reason for what is believed. But it is a reason for believing the hypothesis. The critic begs the question, by taking for granted precisely what Popper denies.

An epistemic principle lies behind all this. The principle says that the fact that a hypothesis is well corroborated is a good reason to adopt it, tentatively, as true. Call this principle CR (for 'corroboration report', or for 'critical rationalism'). Is CR an inductive principle? Well, traditional inductive principles such as 'Nature is uniform' were metaphysical principles, whereas CR is epistemic. Traditional principles were metaphysical because you need a metaphysical principle to show truth or high probability. And tradition – specifically, justificationism – demanded that a reason for believing something must be a reason for what is believed. This is what Popper denies. Of course, if you assume justificationism, you will also assume that lying behind CR there must be a metaphysical principle linking corroboration with truth or probability. After all, what reason might we give for CR, other than such a metaphysical principle? Induction is smuggled in after all.

But epistemology is one thing, metaphysics another. Call CR an 'epistemic inductive principle', if you like. This principle neither implies nor assumes that well-corroborated theories are true, or more likely to be true than not. It says only that it is reasonable to adopt such theories as true. Can we separate epistemology and metaphysics? Justificationism says not – a reason for believing (epistemology) must be a reason for what is believed (metaphysics). Can it be reasonable to believe falsely? If it can, then the (epistemic) reason for believing falsely cannot be a conclusive (metaphysical) reason for what is believed. Everybody will agree that any reasonable theory of reasonable belief must make room for reasonable yet false belief. Everybody will agree, too, that if the state of the critical discussion changes, and we find a reason to think something false, then it is no longer reasonable to adopt it as true. What we say in such cases is that what we reasonably believed turned out to be wrong, not that it was wrong or unreasonable for us to have believed it. Can it be reasonable to believe unreliably? If it can, then the reason for believing unreliably cannot be an inconclusive reason for what is believed. But surely corroborated hypotheses must be, if not true, at least more likely to be true than not, if it is reasonable for us to believe them? Surely, we must show that the method of corroboration is a reliable method, which produces more true beliefs than false ones, if it is to be a rational method? No. Just as a belief need not be true, or shown true, to be reasonable, so also a method of forming beliefs need not be reliable, or shown reliable, to be reasonable. Of course, if the state of the critical discussion changes, and we find out that the method of corroboration is *unreliable*, then it will no longer be rational to persist with it. No sceptic has shown this, but methods are corrigible, too. CR is an epistemic principle only, about what it is reasonable to think true, not a metaphysical principle about what is true or more likely true than not. If you assume that a reason for believing something must be a reason for what is believed, you will also assume that this epistemic principle must be underpinned by a metaphysical one. But this is justificationism again.

The demand for a reason for CR assumes for epistemology precisely what critical rationalist epistemology denies. It assumes that a reason for adopting CR must be a reason for CR. A consistent critical rationalist should refuse to give a reason for CR. As the critic rightly sees, a reason for CR will be a metaphysical inductive principle, anathema to critical rationalists, and no use anyway because we would immediately be asked for a reason for the reason, and so on, *ad infinitum*.

This does not mean that CR must be adopted arbitrarily or irrationally. A consistent critical rationalist can give a reason for *adopting* CR. The reason for adopting CR is that it has withstood philosophical criticism better than rival epistemic principles. This is what Popper does when he describes our epistemic predicament as he sees it. There are no reasons, conclusive or inconclusive, for evidence-transcending hypotheses. Induction being invalid, there are no conclusive reasons for them. Probabilistic induction having foundered, there are no inconclusive reasons for them either. Combine these Humean sceptical results with justificationism, and the result is Humean irrationalism. But if we reject justificationism, a new possibility opens up. There is nothing more rational than a thorough and searching critical discussion. Such a discussion may give us a good reason for believing an evidence-transcending hypothesis that survives it – though not, of course, a good reason for that hypothesis itself. Such is the reason for *adopting* CR.

Some of this, such as the rejection of probabilistic induction, is still contentious. But even if we set that aside, and accept that CR withstands philosophical criticism better than rival principles, a new objection presents itself. *All this is circular!* We are being told that it is reasonable to adopt CR *by CR's own standard of when it is reasonable to adopt something.* Nobody sceptical of CR is going to find this convincing.

Is this new objection devastating? I submit that it is not. For what are the alternatives to circular reasoning of this kind? You might give no reason for adopting CR, and admit that your belief in your theory of reasonable belief is irrationally adopted. Or you might give some reason for adopting CR that is not of a critical rationalist kind, again admitting that your belief in your theory of reasonable belief is not itself reasonable by its own lights, and inviting the demand for a reason for your reason, *ad infinitum*. Circularity is preferable to either of these alternatives – *just*.

You can count this an objection to CR if you like. But take comfort from this – *any general theory of reasonable belief will be subject to the same objection.* For any general epistemic theory is either reasonably adopted by its own lights (circularity), or not reasonably adopted by any lights (irrationalism), or reasonably adopted by other lights (hence irrational by its own lights once again). So this objection to CR, if it is an objection, cannot tell against CR and in favour of any rival view.

(It was William Warren Bartley III who urged the superiority of a *comprehensive* rationalism, a rationalism that could be rationally adopted by its own lights, a rationalism that could subsume itself. Anything less is subject to the *Tu Quoque Argument* – 'So you too are irrational – about your theory of rationality!'. Robert Nozick has said that circularity or self-subsumption of this kind is not a vice, but a virtue. I disagree. I disagree because self-subsumption is too easily had. 'My granny told me that I ought to believe everything she tells me' subsumes itself – but it is no triumph. Circularity or self-subsumption is no virtue. It is merely, at this level of abstraction, the least of the vices.)

5 Conjectural knowledge

Popper's last major attempt to explain his solution to the problem of induction was called 'Conjectural Knowledge: My Solution of the Problem of Induction'. It is one of Popper's most scholastic productions.[1] Despite all the scholasticisms, Popper nowhere defines what 'conjectural knowledge' is. I suggest the following definition on his behalf: A conjecturally knows that P if and only if (a) A believes that P, (b) P is true, and (c) A reasonably believes (is justified in believing) that P, in the sense of CR. The parallel with the traditional justified true belief (JTB) account is obvious. Like that account, it denies that we can know a falsehood. (I do not agree with those Popperians who flirt with the idea that 'false knowledge' makes sense.) It differs from the traditional JTB account only over the 'justification condition'. It rejects the traditional justificationist principle. Indeed, if you accept that principle, justified true believings must be justified true beliefs.

Let us leave knowledge behind, and get back to belief. I have talked much about belief, about its act/content ambiguity, and about the critical rationalist view that we can justify an act of believing without justifying a belief-content. What about Forster's dictum 'I do not believe in belief', which Popper said he agreed with? Well, critical rationalism means that Forster's dictum contains a deeper truth – deeper than 'I do not believe in dogmatically held irrational commitments'. Beliefs are transitory – beliefs change. *Reasonable* beliefs are transitory, too. It was reasonable for Aristotle to believe things (given the state of the critical discussion in his time) that it is not reasonable for us to believe (given the state of the critical discussion in our time). The epistemic problem of problems is: What ought I to believe? Critical rationalism does solve this problem, rather than dodging it. It says that we ought to believe that which best survives the critical discussion in our time. This simple formula takes us outside the self-defeating and played-out circle of justificationist ideas, and into an exciting arena where the theory of criticism occupies centre-stage. If the foregoing is correct, then Popper does answer Hume, as opposed to changing the subject. But Popper's answer to Hume simultaneously shows that we can get beyond Hume's problem. Induction or inductive logic is a myth, after all, because we do not need it. Conjectures and critical inquiry about them is all we need.

Karl Popper was right to call his paper 'Conjectural Knowledge: My Solution of the Problem of Induction'. And despite his critics, he was right to talk about 'The Growth of Scientific Knowledge'. Science is our best epistemic engine. Its self-corrective critical method has provided us with lots of knowledge – conjectural knowledge. Science contains much that we believe, that is true, and that we reasonably believe to be true.

Notes

1 Consider, for example, the following (Popper 1972, pp. 21–2):

Pr1 Upon what theory should we rely for practical action, from a rational point of view?
Pr2 Which theory should we prefer for practical action, from a rational point of view?
   My answer to *Pr1* is: From a rational point of view, we should not 'rely' on any theory, for no theory has been shown to be true, or can be shown to be true.
   My answer to *Pr2* is: But we should *prefer* as a basis for action the best-tested theory.
   In other words [sic!], there is no 'absolute reliance'; but since we *have* to choose, it will be 'rational' to choose the best-tested theory. . . .
   Of course, in choosing the best-tested theory as a basis for action, we 'rely' on it in some sense of the word. It may even be described as the *most* 'reliable' theory available, in some sense of this term. Yet this does not say that it is 'reliable'.

What are we to make of this passage, with its unexplained distinction between 'rely for practical action' and 'prefer for practical action', its plethora of unexplained scare quotes around the word 'rely', its talk of senses of the word 'reliable' that are nowhere explained, and so on?

References

Miller, David. 1994. *Critical Rationalism: a Restatement and Defence*, Chicago, IL: University of Chicago Press.

Musgrave, Alan. 1989. 'Saving Science from Scepticism', in Fred D'Agostino and I. C. Jarvie (eds), *Freedom and Rationality: Essays in Honor of John Watkins*, Boston Studies in the Philosophy of Science, vol. 117, Dordrecht, Boston, London: Kluwer, pp. 297–323.

Musgrave, Alan. 1999. *Essays on Realism and Rationalism*, Amsterdam and Atlanta, GA: Rodopi.

Popper, Karl. 1972. *Objective Knowledge*, Oxford: Oxford University Press.

Van Fraassen, Bas. 1980. *The Scientific Image*, Oxford: Clarendon Press.

Watkins, John. 1984. *Science and Scepticism*, London: Hutchinson.

2

POPPER'S CONVENTIONALISM

Semiha Akıncı

In this chapter I examine various types of conventionalism and compare Popper's philosophy of science with those conventionalist philosophies of science. I conclude that it is not possible to arrive at one unique definition of conventionalism. In this light I re-examine the claim that Popper, despite his official opposition to conventionalism, is himself a conventionalist. Whether Popper may be called a conventionalist or not depends upon our characterisation of conventionalism. However, I make out clear reasons why Popper is not a conventionalist of either the Poincarean or the Duhemian type.

1 Introduction

When we survey Popper's writings we find a lot of forthright criticism of conventionalism. Yet some philosophers claim that Popper is himself a conventionalist. For instance M. Deutscher claims (1968, p. 273) that if Popper is not a sceptic, or an adherent of a form of coherence theory of truth, then Popper must opt for a form of conventionalism. S. Amsterdamski (1975) and R. J. Ackermann (1976) also claim that he is a conventionalist.

Anthony Quinton (1973), A. J. Ayer (1974), and J. Agassi (1974) all claim that there are strong conventionalist elements in Popper's philosophy. One well-known philosopher of science, Imre Lakatos, also claimed that not only are there some conventionalist elements in Popper's philosophy, but Popper is a true conventionalist. 'Popper's methodological falsificationalism is both conventionalist and falsificationist' (Lakatos 1978, p. 22).

Popper always objected to the above accusations. He said, 'I am not a conventionalist (whether modified or not)' (Popper 1974, p. 1117). In the following pages I will try to clarify this paradoxical situation.

I will first make a short classification of criticisms that claim Popper is a conventionalist. Then I will survey two basic philosophers who are accepted as being conventionalists by almost everybody. Finally, I will compare Popper's approach with these other approaches in order to arrive at a conclusion.

2 Some criticisms to the effect that Popper is a conventionalist

Generally criticisms raised against Popper can be subsumed under two groups. The first group of criticisms deals with the nature of Popper's classical *modus tollens* argument. For instance, Amsterdamski claims (1975, p. 93) that the principle of falsification is based on the well known classical *modus tollens* argument: $(T \rightarrow B)$, $\neg B$ $\therefore$ $\neg T$. However in an experiment we test not only the theory but also 'the theory in conjunction with background knowledge' (ibid.), including auxiliary hypothesis and initial conditions. If we accept that Z is the background knowledge, the *modus tollens* argument becomes:

$$(T \wedge Z) \rightarrow B$$
$$\neg B$$
$$\therefore \neg(T \wedge Z)$$

In the face of the above argument we are at liberty to change Z and thereby preserve our theory. From this we can say that no experiment is crucial and to accept that an experiment is crucial is conventional. To falsify the theory T we must accept the conclusive truth of Z and this acceptance is conventional. Later we will see that this criticism is almost the same criticism that was raised by Duhem's conventionalism. According to Duhem it was not possible to isolate a certain hypothesis from the whole theory and for this reason he claimed that it must be a conventional decision which hypothesis is taken to be falsified.

The second group of criticisms is concerned with the nature of basic statements in Popper. They are singular statements that are used in *modus tollens* arguments. Popper says (1959, p. 104):

> Every test of a theory, whether resulting in its corroboration or falsification, must stop at some basic statement or other which we decide to accept. If we do not come to any decision, and do not accept some basic statement or other, then the test will have led nowhere.

He at the same time claims (1959, p. 106) that 'basic statements are accepted as the result of a decision or agreement; and to that extent they are conventions'. According to Amsterdamski (1975, p. 92):

> [o]n the one hand, we need a convention according to which we accept that the given sentence is a basic one, i.e., empirically testable. On the other hand, we need a convention on the force of which we temporally stop the process of justification at this testable statement.

We know that Popper's basic statements determine the empirical content of a theory. Anthony Quinton claims that if these statements determine the empirical content, and if these statements are conventions, then Popper must be a conventionalist. Deutscher, on the other hand, claims that if Popper is not a sceptic or a defender of coherence theory of truth, he must be a conventionalist because of the nature of basic statements. And more importantly Lakatos asks (1978, pp. 165–6):

> [w]hy not extend Popperian hard-headed conventionalism from the acceptance (without belief) of some spatio-temporally singular statements to granting similar acceptance to some universal statements and even beyond that, to some conjectural weak inductive principle?

We have seen that these two groups of critics openly claim that Popper is a conventionalist. However when we survey the articles, we see that each philosopher uses 'conventionalism' in his own sense, and for this reason the issue cannot be decided without clarifying what 'conventionalism' means. To determine the basic characteristics of conventionalism in the usual sense, I next endeavour to clarify the stand of some of the best known conventionalist philosophers.

3 What is conventionalism?

When we survey the above criticisms we see that they do not contain an explicit expression of what conventionalism is. Mostly their arguments are confined to the following line of reasoning. Since Popper accepts that there is no absolute line of discrimination between background knowledge and the hypothesis under test, he must be a conventionalist; since basic statements are determined by the decisions of the scientists, he must be a conventionalist; since there are some decisional elements in Popper's philosophy, he must be a conventionalist, etc. We see that these are all piecemeal criticisms against Popper's philosophy, which fail to do justice to the sweep and the unity of his doctrine as an integral system. As a whole Popper's system has many philosophical implications and I doubt that a philosopher can be labelled a conventionalist without taking into account his whole theory, that is, his ideas about truth, his ideas about logic, his ideas about the function of reason, etc. To be a conventionalist is to take a serious clear-cut stand in philosophy, and in order to call someone a conventionalist, one must show that at least the basic philosophical implications of conventionalism in the problem concerning the confrontation of our knowledge with reality must be present in that philosopher's doctrine. In other words, to be justified in calling Popper a conventionalist, we must have a clear understanding of what conventionalism is and we must show that Popper's system has these characteristics.

However, to arrive at an explicit understanding of conventionalism is not as easy as it seems to be. When we survey the writings of some philosophers whom everybody agrees are conventionalists, first of all we see that the word 'conventionalism' is mostly used in an evaluative sense to praise or degrade a philosopher who ostensibly subscribes to it. For example Popper uses it in order to degrade a certain philosophical stand, but Lakatos characterises Popper as a conventionalist in order to praise him. However, to clarify conventionalism, I think it would still be best to take the best-known representatives of conventionalism and then derive their common characteristics. While doing this we must be aware of the fact that these well-known representatives do not agree even among themselves upon what conventionalism is. For instance Poincaré accuses Le Roy of being overly conventionalistic (1946, pp. 321–6). Duhem explicitly asserts (1976, p. 30) that the views of Poincaré and of Le Roy are incorrect. Popper, on the other hand, when talking about conventionalism mentions (1959, p. 78n) the names of Poincaré, Duhem, Dingler and Eddington. In order to lessen the above confusion the best thing to do will be to ignore some minor figures and focus on the most prominent players, namely, Poincaré and Duhem.

4 Poincaré's conventionalism

'The "laws of nature" are simple; and, these conventionalists hold, are our own free creations; our inventions; our arbitrary decisions and conventions' (Popper 1959, p. 79). Popper characterises conventionalism in the above words. Although Poincaré is the best-known conventionalist philosopher of science, philosophers find the origin of conventionalism in Kant. Popper also describes a resemblance between Kantianism and conventionalism:

> Kant's idealism sought to explain this simplicity by saying that it is our own intellect which imposes its laws upon nature. Similarly, but even more boldly, the conventionalist treats this simplicity as our own creation. For him, however, it is not the effect of the laws of our intellect imposing themselves upon nature, thus making nature simple; for he does not believe that nature is simple. Only the laws of nature are simple.
>
> (Ibid.)

In the above quotation, Popper points out the differences between Kant's philosophy and conventionalism. In Kant it is our mind that makes nature simple. The mind has its own categories which are imposed upon nature. If these categories or forms are simple, then nature must be simple, because we cannot discuss whether objective nature (thing in itself) is simple or not. However, in conventionalism, according to Popper, nature is not simple but the laws of nature which are our own creations are simple. Although nature itself is not (claimed to be) simple, scientists describe it as if it were simple. The difference that Popper has pointed out between conventionalism and Kantianism is very important for us, because there are some philosophers such as Lakatos who tend to equate conventionalism with the active interference of our minds, of our theories being imposed upon nature (as in the case of Kantianism), and therefore they claim that since Popper accepts this interference he must be a conventionalist. However, Popper

31

will not accept that Kantianism is a form of conventionalism. Conventionalism is the view according to which the simplicity of nature is grounded upon the way we choose to describe nature, since there are alternative ways of describing nature, and we can choose one or another of these at will. In the case of Kantianism our subjective categories and the phenomenal world have to correspond to each other. However, no such correspondence is claimed by conventionalists. The way we choose to describe things is, to an important extent, independent of how things are, but depends on how we prefer to describe them. As a result conventionalism will amount to the view that some facts about nature, like the laws of nature, depend upon our subjective taste, and empirical reality does not uniquely determine this choice; we are left with lots of room for making decisions.

According to Poincaré it is, as Adolph Grünbaum states (1961, p. 142) possible to give 'either an Euclidean or a non-Euclidean description of the same spatio-physical facts' and it is legitimate 'contrary to Newton to speak, of alternative metrisations of the time continuum *which issue in correspondingly* different systems of chronometry and physical law' (ibid.).

Poincaré's argument, in Poincaré's own words (1946, p. x), is as follows:

> The question has also been put in another way. If Lobachevski's geometry is true, the parallax of a very distant star will be finite, if Riemann's is true, it will be negative. These are results which seem within the reach of experiment, and there have been hopes that astronomical observations might help us to decide between the three geometries. But in astronomy 'straight line' means simply 'path of a ray of light'.
>
> If therefore negative parallaxes were found; if it were demonstrated that all parallaxes are superior to a certain limit, two courses would be open to us: we might either renounce Euclidean geometry, or else modify the laws of optics and suppose that light does not travel rigorously in a straight line.
>
> It is needless to add that all the world would regard the latter solution as the more advantageous.

Poincaré goes on to state (1946, p. 235) that 'to ask what geometry it is proper to adopt is to ask, to what line is it proper to give the name straight?'. In fact Poincaré 'advanced the more comprehensive thesis that most if not all the general "principles" of physics (such as the principle of inertia) are conventions' (Nagel 1961, p. 260). The crucial idea in the above arguments is that in the description of reality any geometry can be used by making the necessary revisions in the definition of straight line. According to Poincaré geometrical axioms cannot be true or false:

> [T]he enunciation of a fact can only be true or false. This is not so of any proposition: if this proposition is the enunciation of a convention, it can

not be said that this enunciation is true, in the proper sense of the word, since it could not be true apart from me and is true only because I wish it to be.

(1946, p. 327)

A geometrical system is adopted because a certain geometry is the most convenient one. The conventional element in a physical theory is not only the geometry it uses.

Peter Alexander states the position this way (1967c, p. 362):

For example, the principle of inertia, according to which a body under the action of no force can move only at a constant speed in straight line, is neither a priori nor experimental. It was originally conceived as experimental but has become a definition and so cannot now be falsified by experiment. Scientific conclusions are always conventional to some extent since alternatives to any hypothesis are always possible and, other things being equal, we choose those which are most economical. Because we have no means of knowing that the qualitative features of our hypothesis correspond to the reality, it does not make sense to regard the chosen hypothesis as the one true hypothesis.

What are the basic characteristics of Poincaréan conventionalism? First, there are some elements in a physical theory which cannot be true or false; second, it is always possible to preserve a certain geometry by changing the definitions of some concepts.

What is Popper's stand against the above form of conventionalism? There is one important similarity between Poincaré and Popper. They both agree that the same empirical facts can be explained by different theories. According to Popper, many different conjectures may explain the same facts and the scientist chooses one. According to Poincaré, by contrast, to describe the same facts more than one geometry can possibly be used and scientists choose the simpler one. However, while according to Popper the chosen one should be falsifiable, according to Poincaré no such falsification is possible. What are the sources of this difference? Their epistemic views about the role of scientific theories are totally different. Alexander states (1967c, p. 363) that

Theories do not set out to explain, although they may provide possible explanations. They are devices enabling us to connect and predict phenomena but not to describe reality in all its details. The assertion that, for example, atomic theories explain the behaviour of matter implies that we are able to establish the actual existence of atoms as delineated by the theories. But this is a metaphysical and not a scientific assertion because such existence can never be established by scientific means.

33

According to Popper, however, theories are conjectures that explain reality and for this reason they must be true or false. When a theory asserts that atoms exist, it tries to describe reality. Although the concept of atom is in the third world, that is in the world of concepts, there is a counterpart to it in the first world, the physical world. Just for this reason 'in so far as scientific statements speak about reality, they must be falsifiable: and in so far as it is not falsifiable, it does not speak about reality' (1959, p. 314).[1] For Popper, although there might be some conventional elements or decisional elements in a scientific theory, they are not related with the content of a physical theory. The content of a theory, the assertions about what exists or not, the assertions about the geometrical structure of the physical universe cannot be conventional. Just for this reason there is only one theory that explains reality. There can only be one such theory, because there is only one 'first world'. However, for Poincaré there can be more than one theory, because some assertions of a physical theory are only definitional and for this reason more than one theory can describe reality. This is so, because we cannot give a 'genuine' explanation of the world though we can 'provide' possible explanations. So once a scientific community chooses a scientific theory, they may preserve a theory forever. For this reason Lakatos calls Poincaré a 'conservative conventionalist'. When we examine Popper's views about conventionalism in geometry, we see that they more or less agree with Nagel's criticisms. According to Popper (1959, p. 72) the axioms of any system, e.g. those of Euclidean geometry

> may be regarded either
> (i) as *conventions*,
> or they may be regarded
> (ii) as empirical or scientific *hypotheses*.

When a certain axiom is regarded as convention it becomes an implicit definition.

> An axiomatic system interpreted in this way cannot therefore be regarded as a system of empirical or scientific hypotheses (in our sense) since it cannot be refuted by the falsification of its consequences; for these too must be analytic.
>
> (1959, p. 74)

However in scientific theories geometry is

> correlated with, or interpreted by, the concepts of another system, e.g. physics. The possibility is particularly important when, in the course of the evolution of science, one system of statements is being explained by means of a new – and more general – system of hypotheses which permit the deduction not only of statements belonging to the first system, but also of statements belonging to other systems. In such cases it may be

possible to define the fundamental concepts of the new system with the help of concepts which were originally used in some of the old systems.

(1959, p. 75)

In other words, for Popper, geometry acquires an empirical and falsifiable character by being interpreted. For Kant, by contrast, geometry is the geometry of the empirical world, but since it is a form in our mind, there is only one geometry to which the empirical world must conform. For Poincaré there are many geometries, and the question of which one is more suitable for being applied to the actual world is not settled decisively by empirical data.

We can summarise the relationship between Poincaré and Popper as follows. Popper is a realist and for this reason believes that theories are true or false. There is no part of a physical theory that cannot be falsified. In fact according to Popper not just the geometry of a scientific theory, but every part of a scientific theory can be falsified except logic. Indeed not only universal statements, but also singular statements that express the facts can be falsified, because the conjectural element is present in every part of our knowledge and there is always a possibility that this knowledge might not correspond to reality. Poincaré's conventionalism, on the other hand, is closer to the instrumentalistic approach. Although he accepts that there is a falsifiable part of a theory, there is a non-falsifiable dogmatic part also. In other words there are some ultimate non-changing elements in our knowledge. According to him a theory is rejected not because it is refuted by the objective world, but rejected only when a more convenient theory has been found. 'Moreover,' writes Alexander (1967a, p. 217), 'we may simultaneously hold two contradictory theories that are useful for dealing with different ranges of phenomena. There is no objection to this if the theories are not claimed to be true.'

Thus we may conclude that Popper's and Poincaré's epistemic views are different in a very important sense. If by 'conventionalism' we mean the view according to which theories are not (empirically) true or false, Popper is not a conventionalist.

However, we may ask whether Popper's proposals can prevent the conventionalist argument which claims that a geometry can be preserved by changing the definition of 'straight line'. Popper accepts the idea that we may change the explicit definitions of some of the concepts of an axiom system: 'changes in these definitions are permissible if useful; but they must be regarded as modifications of the system, which thereafter has to be re-examined as if it were new' (1959, p. 83).

Certainly this is a methodological rule and nobody can claim that by proposing methodological rules it is possible to prevent conventionalism. Popper knows the fact that logically it is possible to preserve a theory forever by changing explicit definitions or by changing the background knowledge or initial conditions. Therefore he claims :

Only with reference to the method applied to a theoretical system is it at all possible to ask whether we are dealing with a conventionalist or an empirical theory. The only way to avoid conventionalism is by making a decision: the decision not to apply its methods. We decide that, in the case of a threat to our system, we will not save it by any kind of conventionalist stratagem.

(1959, p. 82)

According to Popper scientists are not conventionalists because they decide not to be conventionalists. What is paradoxical here is that scientists decide conventionally not to be conventionalists.

At this point we must differentiate two types of conventionalism. The first type is related to the content of knowledge claims. For example if we say that a certain part of a theory is conventional, we are asserting that there is a part in our knowledge that is independent of the empirical world. Poincaré's conventionalism is such a conventionalism, i.e. epistemic conventionalism. The second type of conventionalism is related to the methods used in scientific practice. This type of conventionalism can be called methodological conventionalism. It is certain that Popper is not a conventionalist in the first sense. What can we say, however, about the methodology he proposed? In the above passage he claims that science is demarcated from non-science by using a non-conventionalist methodology. The problem is whether Popper can succeed in proposing a non-conventionalist strategy. Is to propose a non-conventionalist strategy not itself a matter of convention?

5 Duhem's conventionalism

M. Hesse claims (1976, p. 188),

[I]f by conventionalism is meant, as Poincaré appearently intended in regard to the geometry of physical space, that any given total theoretical system can be imposed upon any logically possible experience, then surely to class Duhem as a conventionalist is a mistake. For neither Duhem nor Quine say anything to imply that a total system is not refutable by experience.

Certainly according to Poincaré any geometry can be imposed upon experience, and since the geometry that a theory accepts has a definitional status it cannot be refuted by experience. Duhem opposes this kind of irrefutability, because according to him there is no such definitional part in a theory. The geometrical part of a theory can be refuted because it enters

as essential foundation into the construction of certain theories of rational mechanics of chemical theory, of crystallography. The object of these theories is to represent some experimental laws; they are schematisms intended essentially to be compared with facts.

(Duhem 1976, p. 37)

According to Duhem, Poincaré underestimates the role of experiment. There is no a priori conceptual part of a scientific theory that is immune to revision, and many changes in the history of science prove this fact (Durham 1976, pp. 33, 36, 37). If we accept that Duhem opposes the irrefutability of scientific theory then why do we call him a conventionalist?

The classical *modus tollens* argument falsification schema is as follows: $H \rightarrow O$, $\neg O \therefore \neg H$. From the schema it is evident that for falsification to take place we must be able to isolate the hypothesis we will test. According to Duhem this isolation is not possible, for the simple reason that no hypothesis can be isolated. In a scientific test many assumptions, rules of inference and a set of auxiliary hypotheses are involved and 'the physicist can never subject an isolated hypothesis to experimental test, but only a whole group of hypotheses' (1976, p. 8). For example from Newton's theory of light the proposition, *p*, that 'light travels faster in water than in air' (p. 7) is deduced. The problem for an experimental scientist is to devise an experiment to test observationally whether this proposition is true or false. Foucault proposed such an experiment and in the end it was observed that light was propagated less rapidly in water than in air. Certainly this result falsifies the proposition *p* that was deduced from Newton's theory of light. Duhem claims that from this result 'we may conclude, with Foucault, that the system of emission is incompatible with the facts' (p. 8).

> But in condemning this system as a whole by declaring it stained with error, the experiment does not tell us where the error lies. Is it in the fundamental hypothesis that light consists in projectiles thrown out with great speed by luminous bodies? Is it in some other assumption concerning the actions experienced by light corpuscles due to the media through which they move? We know nothing about that. It would be rash to believe, as Arago seems to have thought, that Foucault's experiment condemns once and for all the very hypothesis of emission, i.e., the assimilation of a ray of light to a swarm of projectiles.
>
> (Ibid.)

In other words, for Duhem a scientific test can only be represented as $(H_1 \wedge H_2 \wedge H_3) \rightarrow O$, $\neg O \therefore \neg(H_1 \wedge H_2 \wedge H_3)$. When the observation contradicts a scientific prediction we can say that something is wrong with a system of hypotheses but we cannot determine which hypothesis in particular is false. The experiment does not designate which hypothesis should be changed. A scientist has to act like a doctor in the sense that 'The doctor to whom a patient appears cannot dissect him in order to establish his diagnosis' (p. 9). A scientist cannot dissect a theory into isolated hypotheses and discover the false one. This holistic argument of Duhem gives the first reason for the impossibility of a crucial experiment.

Among modern philosophers, Willard Quine defends almost the same holistic views. Like Duhem, Quine claims that 'it is misleading to speak of an empirical content of an individual statement' (Quine 1976, p. 60). In fact Quine's holism is more thoroughgoing than Duhem's. For Quine, not only a scientific theory but 'the totality of our so-called knowledge or beliefs, from the most casual matters of geography and history to the profoundest laws of atomic physics or even of pure mathematics and logic, is a man-made fabric which impinges on experience only along the edges' (p. 59). According to Sandra Harding:

> Quine's thesis is stronger than Duhem's, for where Duhem claimed that the physicist can never be sure that no saving set of auxiliary assumptions exist which, together with the target hypothesis, would entail the actual observational results, Quine seems to hold that saving hypotheses always exist: 'Any statement can be held true come what may': Quine's thesis is also more general than Duhem's, for Quine extends Duhem's claim for conventionalism in physics to include the truths of logic as well as *all* of the laws of science.
>
> (Harding 1976, p. xii)

Duhem's second argument for the impossibility of crucial experiments is as follows. Let's grant that it is possible to falsify a certain hypothesis. Let's assume that we have isolated two hypotheses and devised an experiment such that if a certain observation occurs, one of the hypotheses will be falsified and if that observation does not occur, the other hypothesis will be falsified: $(H_1 \rightarrow O, \neg O \therefore \neg H_1)$, $(H_2 \rightarrow \neg O, O \therefore \neg H_2)$. Let's assume that O was observed. Now Duhem asks the question: Can we conclude from this that H_2 is false and therefore H_1 is true? According to Duhem this is not possible because although we can derive from the experiment that H_2 is false, there is an infinite number of hypotheses that may imply O. For this reason we cannot determine which hypothesis among this infinity of hypotheses is true. Duhem's example (in his 1976, p. 11) is as follows:

> Light is a body. If the contrary is the case, then light is a wave: But it would be difficult for us to take such a decisive stand; Maxwell, in fact, showed that we might just as well attribute light to a periodical electrical disturbance that is propagated within a dielectric medium.

The above two arguments, that is, the impossibility of isolating a certain hypothesis, and the impossibility of arranging a crucial test are usually cited as the most important characteristic claims of Duhemian conventionalism. The decision to change a certain hypothesis is conventional. In fact the falsification of a certain theory is somewhat conventional. According to Duhem, it results as follows. Conventional repairs in different parts of a theory can eventually mean that the theory loses its simplicity. In that case the theory is changed by the good sense of the scientists, by the 'reason which reason does not know' (p. 38).

When we examine Duhem's cited arguments we notice that a different component was introduced to the discussion of conventionalism in the history of the philosophy of science. In Poincaré we have seen that there is an a priori part in scientific theories. In his case non-falsifiability is the result of a methodological problem, namely, the problem of isolating certain parts of scientific theories. Although Duhem's epistemic views have close connections with Poincaré's approach, Duhem's importance in the history of philosophy of science is in his elaborating the methodological aspects of conventionalism. This is important for us because while philosophers are criticising Popper they mostly do not differentiate between being a methodological conventionalist and being an epistemic conventionalist. Popper in no sense can be claimed to be an epistemic conventionalist because he simply does not believe in any type of a priori knowledge. A priori knowledge means absolute knowledge, and in Popper no absolute knowledge is possible. All knowledge is conjectural, even singular observation statements. We may say that non-falsifiability is the common characteristic of Poincaréan and Duhemian conventionalism. But the sources of non-falsifiability are different and for this reason there are differences in their conventionalisms. Popper does not elaborate this difference either. It is true that he proposes different counter-arguments against Poincaré and Duhem. However, when Popper uses the word conventionalism, he means basically non-falsifiability. Since he does not clarify the distinction between Poincaré's and Duhem's conventionalism, he misses some close similarities between himself and Duhem with respect to methodological problems. We will focus on this later.

We may summarise as follows Popper's criticism of Duhem's claim that crucial tests are not possible: *pace* Duhem, we can sometimes know which part of the theory is false. Duhem is mistaken for two reasons:

(a) A crucial test is conducted to choose between two distinct theories, T_1 and T_2. While we design the crucial test we assume that the background knowledge in each is the same.

$$(Z \wedge T_1) \to O \qquad\qquad (Z \wedge T_2) \to \neg O$$

$$\underline{\neg O} \qquad\qquad\qquad\qquad \underline{O}$$

$$\therefore \neg(Z \wedge T_1) \qquad\qquad \therefore \neg(Z \wedge T_2)$$

In this case, since the background knowledge in each case is the same, it is possible to blame only one of the two theories; and therefore it is possible to design crucial experiments.

(b) Also it is possible to design crucial experiments to test their background assumptions. (Cf. Popper 1965, p. 112.)

The basic difference between Popper and Duhem is on point (b). Since Popper is a fallibilist, he believes in the testability of all our knowledge. It is possible to test our knowledge, even though this may take forever. According to Popper, Duhem and Quine do not realise the piecemeal nature of our tests:

though every one of our assumptions may be challenged, it is quite impracticable to challenge all of them at the same time. Thus all criticism must be piecemeal (as against the holistic view of Duhem and of Quine).

(Popper 1965, p. 238)

However, from the above ideas we must not derive the conclusion that Popper believes in conclusive falsification. Although he opposes Duhem on this issue, Popper also admits that a falsification experiment is a matter of decision: 'Thus it is decisions which settle the fate of theories' (1959, p. 108). However, Popper, as we have said above, does not concentrate on the aspect of Duhem's claim that crucial tests are not possible. He still thinks that the basic characteristic of Duhem's conventionalism is to be found in his epistemic views, and instrumentalistic inclinations.

Like Poincaré, Duhem believes that scientific explanation is impossible. According to him to explain is 'to strip reality of the appearances covering it like a veil, in order to see the bare reality itself' (Alexander 1967b, p. 423). But science depends upon observation and appearances. For this reason it cannot reach reality except through appearances. Reality can be explained only by metaphysical reasoning. This attribution of a non-explanatory function to scientific theories leads Duhem to instrumentalism.

Popper claims that the basic difference between Duhem and himself is that, while Duhem is an instrumentalist, he himself is a critical realist (Popper 1965, p. 99n.). By characterising Duhem as an instrumentalist Popper is also pointing to the close connections between instrumentalism and conventionalism. This is not surprising, because if a theory does not describe reality, in other words, if it is a convention, then simplicity becomes the differentiating characteristic between theories. And simplicity is a pragmatic, instrumentalist criterion. Instrumentalist philosophers 'all assert that explanation is not an aim of physical science, since physical science cannot discover the hidden essence of things' (1965, p. 104). According to Popper (ibid.) 'Duhem seems to think (on lines reminiscent of Kant) that there are essences but they are undiscoverable by human science (though we may, somehow, move towards them)'.

If theories cannot describe essences, they cannot describe anything so they must be mere instruments. If a theory is an instrument, then it cannot be true 'but only convenient, simple, economical, powerful, etc.' (ibid.). We see that Popper still thinks Duhem's conventionalism is due to his instrumentalistic inclinations. It is true that Duhem's approach contains such a component. But his importance in the philosophy of science comes from his noticing the methodological impossibility of conclusive falsification. Duhem is one of the first philosophers who noticed the fact that the decision component in scientific practice is very important. Although Popper differs from him in epistemic matters, Popper has also noticed the importance of decisions and in this sense he resembles Duhem. Popper claims that decisions play a role in the acceptance of background knowledge, in not applying conventionalist stratagems etc. The most important decision, however, is in the acceptance of basic statements, and many of the critics claim that this acceptance makes Popper a conventionalist. Let us now examine the character of decisions concerning basic statements.

6 Basic statements

According to Popper, theories are stated in the form of generalisations which are put forward as conjectures. From these general statements singular statements about observable facts are derived by deduction, and *modus tollens* arguments are based on these statements. Popper describes these 'vital' singular statements as 'basic statements'. 'We need them in order to decide whether a theory is to be called falsifiable, i.e. empirical. And we also need them for the corroboration of falsifying hypotheses, and thus for the falsification of theories' (Popper 1959, p. 100).

According to Popper, the objectivity of science is derived from its being constructed on an 'empirical basis', and this empirical basis consists of basic statements.

In the philosophy of science these basic statements are mostly considered as observation sentences in the sense familiar from logical positivism. It is true that Popper sometimes gives this impression when characterising basic statements. He says these statements tell us that a particular thing or event is in a particular region of space-time. 'This event must be an "observable event", that is to say, basic statements . . . must be testable, inter-subjectively, by "observation"' (1959, p. 102). This quotation gives the impression that we justify basic statements, and that we justify them by observation. But does Popper in fact hold this view? The answer is that he does not. Paradoxically, Popper does *not* believe that a basic statement can be justified by observational experiences: 'Experiences can *motivate a decision*, and hence an acceptance or a rejection of a statement, but a basic statement cannot be *justified* by them – no more than by thumping the table' (p. 105).

So a basic statement will be about an observable event but at the same time it is not capable of being justified by experience. Why does Popper arrive at such a paradoxical view?

Popper argues that three different views can be taken about the status of basic statements: dogmatism, psychologism, infinite regress. These three views can be stated as Fries's trilemma. On the one hand we have language and on the other the world. By the help of language we make statements about the world. The problem is how will we accept or reject these statements. According to Fries only three positions are possible. Either we accept some positions dogmatically or we justify them by some method. Only two methods of justification are possible. The first method says one statement is justified by another statement and this leads us to an infinite regress of justifications. Popper prefers the dogmatist and infinite regressionist positions. The third possibility is the possibility which Popper calls psychologism.

This is more or less the view defended by the empiricist philosophers. According to them it is possible to escape from this prison of statements because there are some sentences which can be directly compared with perceptual experiences. They are atomic sentences which contain only neutral observation terms. In other words, according to Logical Positivism, there are some sentences which can directly be compared with facts.

To clarify the matter we must look more closely at that kind of observation sentences. The nature of the connection between a fact and the sentence which expresses this fact is perhaps the most important problem in the history of philosophy. The empiricist approach to this problem is most evident in David Hume's approach. (Cf. Harold I. Brown 1977, pp. 15–17.) According to Hume every fact corresponds to an impression, so observation statements in a sense contain terms that correspond to impressions. Bertrand Russell defended more or less the same view. (Cf. Brown 1977, pp. 18–21.) Russell claimed that every factual proposition must be reducible to phenomenal terms. Later this stand was transformed to a programme which aimed at showing that not only a singular sentence but the whole physical theory must be reconstructable from a purely neutral observational base. One natural consequence of this naive empiricist position was its inductivism. They thought that neutral observational vocabulary was possible because we human beings learned that vocabulary through repetition.

However, according to Popper, pure observation sentences cannot exist for two basic reasons. First, our observations are theory-impregnated. Popper claims that every observation has a theoretical element in it. Second, every statement necessarily involves universal terms. In the statement 'Here is a glass of water' 'glass' and 'water' are universals and they cannot be reduced to raw sense-data. In the above two respects Popper differs from Logical Positivists.

Eventually it was understood that the relationship between facts and statements is not so simple. A 'Fact' is different from the statements that express it. Neurath is one of the first Logical Positivists who noticed that a theory which is a system of statements cannot be compared with a fact. It can be compared only with a statement that expresses this fact.

> It is always science as a system of statements which is at issue. Statements are compared with statements, not with 'experiences', 'the world', or anything else. All these meaningless duplications belong to a more or less refined metaphysics and are, for that reason, to be rejected. Each new statement is compared with the totality of existing statements previously coordinated. To say that a statement is correct, therefore, means that it can be incorporated in this totality. What cannot be incorporated is rejected as incorrect. The alternative to rejection of the new statement is, in general, accepted only with great reluctance: the whole previous system of statements can be modified up to the point where it becomes possible to incorporate the new statement . . . The definition of 'correct' and 'incorrect' proposed here departs from that customary

among the 'Vienna Circle', which appeals to 'meaning' and 'verification'. In our presentation we confine ourselves always to the sphere of
linguistic thought.

(Neurath, as quoted in Scheffler 1967, pp. 93–4)

Thus in Neurath's view '[e]very law and every physicalistic sentence of unified
science or of one of its sub-sciences is subject to . . . change. And the same holds
for protocol sentences' (Scheffler 1967, p. 94). Neurath, after elaborating the
connections between facts and statements, arrived at a purely conventionalist
position. According to him it was possible to change the protocol sentences and
the scientists were free to change them if they wanted to preserve their theories.
As a result Neurath's approach was transformed into a totally conventionalistic
stand.

Popper also noticed that a statement is different from a fact. Popper criticises
Neurathian conventionalism in this respect (1959, pp. 96–7). Even so, we may say
that the difference between statements and facts is the basis of Popper's epistemology. According to Popper all concepts, statements and statement systems are
placed in the third world. The first world contains objective fact. Our observational activity and other activities of the mind are in the second world. The
peculiarity of the activities in the second world is that it is not possible for
the mind to work without concepts. In other words, any attempt to understand the
first world must be through the third world. So in Popper although the objective
world and the world of concepts exist, they exist separately.

Many of the critics argue implicitly in the following way. Popper opposes the
idea that a statement can be reconstructed in the positivistic sense. Popper
opposes the idea that a statement can be justified by observation. Popper accepts
the idea that 'statements can be logically justified by statements' (p. 106) and
that '[b]asic statements are accepted as the result of a decision' (ibid.). So
Popper's basic statements must depend upon decisions, and therefore upon conventions. This line of argument is not cogent, because it makes the mistake of
confusing logical relevance with empirical relevance. It is a logical fact that a
statement is different from the fact it expresses. Popper has noticed this. The
problem is whether this acceptance necessarily forces a philosopher to a conventionalist stand. The crucial point of the above argument is that the decisional
element in basic statements makes them conventions. Let's examine the decisional element in basic statements. The decision involved in basic statements has
two components: a logical component and an empirical component.

From a purely logical point of view, its decision may be called 'arbitrary'
insofar as the accepted statement (verdict) is in no way logically deriv-
able from any other ('given') statement . . . The verdict plays a role
comparable to the decision to accept or to reject Euclid's axiom of parallels, or the Archimedean axiom. In all these cases, the decision may
be called 'arbitrary' in the logical sense mentioned; but it is far from

being 'totally arbitrary': in all these cases it is motivated by the search for truth.

(Popper 1974, p. 1111)

Since basic statements cannot be derived from other statements and since basic statements are different from the fact itself, there is an element of arbitrary decision from the logical point of view. But a basic statement also has an empirical component. A statement expresses a fact. It has a content and this content of a basic statement is compared by observation, and whether the fact to which the content alludes is actual or not is determined by observation. There is no logical route from observation to the statement itself, but this does not make a basic statement totally arbitrary. Non-existence of a logical connection does not mean non-existence of an empirical connection. All critics who claim that Popper is a conventionalist make the mistake of confusing logical connection with empirical connection. An observation provides the empirical connection. It is the motivating reason for acceptance of a basic statement, but it is not a logical reason.

It would incidentally be a complete misunderstanding to assimilate my view to any form of 'conventionalism': the 'conventional' or 'decisional' element in our acceptance or rejection of a proposition involves in general no element of arbitrariness at all. Our experiences are not only motives for accepting or rejecting an observational statement, but they may even be described as inconclusive reasons. They are reasons because of the generally reliable character of our observations; they are inconclusive because of our fallibility.

(1959, p. 106)

If basic statements had been decided only by logical considerations, they would have been purely arbitrary decisions. According to Popper the most basic characteristic of conventionalism is its endorsing arbitrary decisions, and the most obvious example of arbitrary decision is the subjective criterion of simplicity. The acceptance of basic statements is not purely arbitrary, because they are accepted as a result of observation. Popper's most explicit example, mostly neglected by the philosophers of science, is as follows: Let's take the example of the verdict of a jury. The jury asks some questions and gets some answers from the accused person. Also the jury ask questions of the eyewitnesses. All these answers are singular statements about an event. Then the jury comes to a decision. Now although the decision of the jury is a convention in a sense, because it is a decision, will we call this agreement a pure convention? No, because the empirical events influence the jury. But it is certain that all that the eyewitnesses have said and the guilty person has said might be false and that the verdict might be incorrect. The jury reaches an agreement by using criminal law. This criminal law is a universal statement in a sense. The jury takes the singular statements of eyewitnesses and of the accused person and by combining these singular statements with universal law comes to a decision. In this case the jury decides according to some rules. They are designed to discover the truth. Scientific procedure resembles this example in many respects. For example, the judge, just like a scientist, tries to justify or to deduce his conclusion by combining laws – universal statements – with the accounts of eyewitnesses – basic statements.

Popper's stand, as expressed above, may be summarised as follows: basic statements cannot be justified by observation, because there is no logical connection between a fact and a statement such as the inductivists claim. As far as logical connection is concerned, basic statements are arbitrary and conventional. But this does not mean that they are pure conventions, because empirical considerations play a role in their acceptance as in the case of the verdict of a jury. So from an empirical point of view they are not conventions. From these ideas it is clear that when Popper speaks about conventionalism he mostly means epistemic conventionalism, that is the stand which endorses the non-existence of empirical reasons for the acceptance of a theory or a statement. However, he is not consistent in his usage. Sometimes he equates conventionalism with endorsing decisions (every kind of decisions). 'Basic statements are accepted as the result of a decision or agreement; and to that extent they are conventions' (1959, p. 106). 'We cannot say that a test statement is "justified" by perceptions: it is, I suggested, more nearly like the "verdict" (vere dictum: spoken truly) of a jury, and it can therefore be said to be a decision or convention' (1974, p. 1110).

He even characterises his methodological rules as conventions: 'Methodological rules are here regarded as conventions' (1959, p. 53). It is evident from these quotations that when Popper talks about conventionalism, he means the endorsing not only of arbitrary decisions, but of any kind of decisions.

Summary and conclusion

Conventionalism in the sense of Poincaré

a) The nature of decisions

For Poincaré, decisions have to be taken concerning the very content of our knowledge. This kind of decision characterises epistemic conventionalism. Like Popper, I call this kind of decision arbitrary. For instance the decision to accept a certain geometry is, according to Duhem, governed by an arbitrary criterion, that is, the criterion of simplicity. The decision to accept a particular geometry for the world on these grounds is a priori.

b) Truth and falsity of scientific theories

In this type of conventionalism, parts of a scientific theory that are decided by conventionalistic decisions cannot be true or false. They are definitions (see Poincaré 1946, p. 327).

c) Falsifiability or non-falsifiability of scientific theories

The conventional part of a scientific theory (geometry, law of inertia, all the laws of mechanics) can not be falsified by experiment, because they are definitions. It is always possible to preserve a certain geometry by changing the definitions of some concepts (see Alexander 1967c, p. 362). According to Poincaré, a theory is rejected not because it is refuted by the objective world, but rejected only when a more convenient theory has been found. Poincaré's conventionalism is related to the content of knowledge claims. He asserts that a certain part of a theory is conventional and independent of the empirical world. The conventional laws from which we learn something about the world are conventional and therefore non-falsifiable.

Conventionalism in the sense of Duhem

a) Nature of decisions

For Duhem there are two types of methodological decisions. In the first type we make an experiment and decide to modify a certain hypothesis of a theory and in the second type the community of scientists decide by their 'good sense' to falsify the whole theory. These decisions function after the experiment.

b) Truth and falsity of scientific theories

Duhem is an instrumentalist in holding that explanation is not the aim of physical science. There are essences which cannot be discovered by human science. If theories cannot describe essences, they cannot describe anything so they must be mere instruments. If a theory is an instrument, then it cannot be true or false but only simple, convenient (see Alexander 1967b, p. 423; Popper 1965, p. 104). Duhem in his epistemic views is a conventionalist because he does not believe that theories can be true or false.

c) Falsifiability or non-falsifiability of scientific theories

There is no definitional part of a scientific theory that is irrefutable. According to Duhem we cannot isolate the hypothesis which we will test, and we cannot know at the end of a test which hypothesis is falsified. There is a methodological difficulty in determining which hypothesis to falsify. So the falsification of a certain theory and a certain hypothesis depends upon methodological conventionalistic decisions.

Conventionalism in Popper

a) The nature of decisions

For Popper the decision can be roughly listed as follows: the decision not to employ conventionalistic methods, the decision not to accept auxiliary hypotheses whose introduction diminishes the testability of the system, the decision to classify which statements are basic statements, the decision to accept that an experiment is crucial, the decision not to accept ad-hoc hypotheses, the decision to accept the background knowledge as well corroborated, etc. If endorsing decisions were sufficient to make a philosopher an epistemic conventionalist, certainly we would be obliged to regard Popper as conventionalist. But for Popper the decisions concern scientific practice. Such conventions are not about *how* the world is, but about when we are *justified* in making singular claims concerning the world. Popper's position is not *epistemic* but only *epistemological* conventionalism. The decision element in basic statements does not determine the content of basic statements. It is used to determine which statements are to be called basic and when to stop the infinite derivation. That is, from a universal statement we can derive infinitely many singular statements. We decide to call some of them 'basic' and these are used in test procedures. Furthermore each such statement can be tested further and we decide to stop the process at a point. Also it is used to determine how many of them are to be considered sufficient for corroboration or refutation. As we have seen this decision does not determine the content of singular statements. The decisional element enters at the methodological level and Popper is a *methodological conventionalist*.

b) Truth and falsity of scientific theories

Popper is *not* an *epistemic* conventionalist, because he is a critical realist and believes that theories are true or false. He believes in the correspondence theory of truth, but also acknowledges the important role which decisions play in scientific practice.

c) Falsifiability or non-falsifiability of scientific theories

Methodological conventionalism asserts that while empirical assertions may be discredited, they cannot be conclusively refuted. Popper equates conventionalism with non-falsifiability. 'According to this conventionalist point of view, laws of nature are not falsifiable by observation' (1959, p. 79). According to the epistemic conventionalism, the conventional parts of theories are definitions and therefore no kind of falsification is possible. For Popper we know that the most important problem of philosophy of science is the problem of finding a criterion that demarcates science from non-science. This criterion is the criterion of falsifiability. That is, a statement or a system of statements is scientific if it can be falsified by experience. For Popper not only universal statements but also singular statements can be falsified. As a result Popper is against Poincaré's and Duhem's epistemic conventionalism. However, at the methodological level, he may be called a conventionalist.

Note

1 Popper acknowledges in a footnote (1959, p. 314n) that he is paraphrasing Einstein. 'Einstein said: In so far as the statements of geometry speaks about reality, they are not certain, and in so far as they are certain, they do not speak about reality.'

References

Ackermann, Robert John. 1976. *The Philosophy of Karl Popper*, Amherst, MA: University of Massachusetts Press.

Agassi, Joseph. 1968. 'The Novelty of Popper's Philosophy of Science', in *International Philosophical Quarterly*, vol. 8, pp. 442–63.

Agassi, Joseph. 1974. 'Modified Conventionalism is More Comprehensive than Modified Essentialism', in P. A. Schilpp (ed.), *The Philosophy of Karl Popper*, vol. 2, La Salle, IL: Open Court, pp. 693–97.

Alexander, Peter. 1967a. 'Conventionalism', in Paul Edwards (ed.), *The Encyclopedia of Philosophy*, vol. 2, New York: The Macmillan Company and The Free Press; London: Collier-Macmillan Limited, pp. 216–19.

Alexander, Peter. 1967b. 'Duhem, Pierre Maurice Marie', in Paul Edwards (ed.), *The Encyclopedia of Philosophy*, vol. 2, New York: The Macmillan Company and The Free Press; London: Collier-Macmillan Limited, pp. 423–5.

Alexander, Peter. 1967c. 'Poincaré, Jules Henri', in Paul Edwards (ed.), *The Encyclopedia of Philosophy*, vol. 6, New York: The Macmillan Company and The Free Press; London: Collier-Macmillan, pp. 360–3.

Amsterdamski, S. 1975. 'Fact and Theories: Conventionalism', in R. S. Cohen and Marx W. Wartofsky (eds), *Between Experience and Metaphysics: Boston Studies in the Philosophy of Science*, vol. 25, Dordrecht: Reidel, pp. 88–115.

Ayer, A. J. 1963. 'Professor Popper's Work in Progress', in *New Statesman*, vol. LXV, no. 1664, p. 155.

Ayer, A. J. 1974. 'Truth, Verification and Verisimilitude', in P. A. Schilpp (ed.), *The Philosophy of Karl Popper*, vol. 2, La Salle, IL: Open Court, pp. 684–93.

Bartley, W. W., III. 1976. 'Critical Study: the Philosophy of Karl Popper, Part I: Biology and Evolutionary Epistemology', in *Philosophia*, vol. 6, pp. 463–94.

Bartley, W. W., III. 1982. 'Critical Study: the Philosophy of Karl Popper, Part III: Rationality, Criticism, and Logic', in *Philosophia*, pp. 121–221.

Brown, Harold I. 1977. *Perception, Theory and Commitment: the New Philosophy of Science*, Chicago, IL: University of Chicago Press.

Deutscher, Max. 1968. 'Popper's Problem of an Empirical Basis', in *Australasian Journal of Philosophy*, vol. 46, pp. 277–88.

Duhem, Pierre. 1954. *The Aim and Structure of Physical Theory*, Princeton, NJ: Princeton University Press.

Duhem, Pierre. 1976. 'Physical Theory and Experiment', in Sandra G. Harding (ed.), *Can Theories Be Refuted?* Dordrecht: Reidel, pp. 1–40.

Feigl, Herbert and Grover Maxwell (eds). 1961. *Current Issues In the Philosophy of Science*, New York: Holt, Rinehart and Winston.

Grünbaum, Adolf. 1961. 'Law and Convention in Physical Theory', in Herbert Feigl and Grover Maxwell (eds), *Current Issues in the Philosophy of Science*, New York: Holt, Rinehart and Winston, pp. 140–55.

Harding, Sandra G. 1976. 'Introduction', in her *Can Theories Be Refuted?* Dordrecht: D. Reidel Publishing Company, pp. ix–xxi.

Heil, John. 1981. 'On Saying What There Is', in *Philosophy*, vol. 156, pp. 242–7.

Hesse, Mary. 1976. 'Duhem, Quine and a New Empiricism', in Sandra G. Harding (ed.), *Can Theories Be Refuted?* Dordrecht: Reidel, pp. 184–204.

Jones, Gary and Clifton Perry. 1982. 'Popper, Induction and Falsification', in *Erkenntnis*, vol. 18, pp. 97–104.

Kuhn, Thomas S. 1977. *The Essential Tension*, Chicago, IL: University of Chicago Press.

Lakatos, Imre. 1978. *Philosophical Papers*, vols 1 and 2. John Worrall and Greg Currie (eds), Cambridge: Cambridge University Press.

Lakatos, Imre and Alan Musgrave (eds) 1970. *Criticism and The Growth of Scientific Knowledge*, Cambridge: Cambridge University Press.

Nagel, Ernst, 1961. *The Structure of Science*, New York: Harcourt, Brace and World.

Nagel, Ernst. Patrick Suppes and Alfred Tarski (eds). 1962. *Logic, Methodology and Philosophy of Science*, Stanford, CA: Stanford University Press.

O'Hear, Anthony. 1980. *Karl Popper*, London: Routledge and Kegan Paul.

Phillips, Derek L. 1975. 'Paradigms, Falsification, and Sociology', in *Acta Sociologica*, vol. 16, pp. 15–51.

Poincaré, Henri. 1946. *The Foundations of Science*, Lancaster: The Science Press.

Popper, Karl R. 1959. *The Logic of Scientific Discovery*, New York: Harper and Row.

Popper, Karl R. 1965. *Conjectures and Refutations*, New York: Basic Books.

Popper, Karl R. 1974. 'Replies to my Critics', in P. A. Schilpp (ed.), *The Philosophy of Karl Popper*, vol. II, Library of Living Philosophers, La Salle, IL: Open Court, pp. 961–1197.

Popper, Karl R. 1979. *Objective Knowledge*, Oxford: Oxford University Press.

Quine, Willard van Orman. 1976. 'Two Dogmas of Empiricism', in Sandra G. Harding (ed.), *Can Theories Be Refuted?* Dordrecht: Reidel, pp. 41–64.

Quinton, Anthony. 1973. 'The Foundations of Knowledge', in Roderick M. Chisholm and Robert J. Swartz (eds), *Empirical Knowledge: Readings from Contemporary Sources*, Englewood Cliffs, NJ: Prentice-Hall, pp. 542–70.

Salmon, Wesley C. 1967. *The Foundations of Scientific Inference*, Pittsburgh, PA: University of Pittsburgh Press.

Scheffler, Israel. 1967. *Science and Subjectivity*, New York: The Bobbs-Merrill Company.

Schilpp, Paul Arthur (ed.). 1974. *The Philosophy of Karl Popper*, two volumes, Library of Living Philosophers, La Salle, IL: Open Court.

3

CONSTRUCTIVE CRITICISM

Philip Catton

Aristarchus, Harvey, Wegener, Newton and Einstein all made significant scientific progress in which they overturned the thinking of their predecessors. But Popper's model of conjectures and refutations is a poor guide to fathoming the accomplishment of these scientists. By now we have a better model, which I articulate. From its vantage point, I criticise Popper.

1 Aristarchus

Let us first consider the reasoning by which the ancient astronomer Aristarchus determined that the sun is much further away from Earth than the moon is. That the sun is much further away from Earth than the moon is unquestionably is a *theoretical* truth, both because it is a *generalisation* not only about all times in a given month or in a given year but also over the whole history of the astronomical system, and because we *cannot just by looking tell* which body, the moon or the sun, is further away. It is true that, once people had worked out theoretically that a solar eclipse is caused by the moon's occluding light from the sun, then the very fact that there are solar eclipses evidenced to them that, at least on those occasions, the moon is closer to Earth than the sun is. But *how much* closer it is, solar eclipses do not evidence. Nor do they evidence whether the moon is *at all times* closer. When Aristarchus determined an empirical way by which to infer that the moon is in fact consistently much closer to Earth than is the sun, this significantly altered the fabric of people's thinking. Aristarchus empirically refuted the ready but false understanding that the distances from Earth of those two bodies are roughly the same. Yet the value of Aristarchus's argument was not merely that it refuted that ready understanding. It also cemented a new understanding, that the sun is consistently many times further away than the moon is. Indeed if we grant Aristarchus some pretty innocuous-seeming background assumptions, we will make him out as having empirically *demonstrated* this new conclusion. In short, Aristarchus's contribution was not merely critical; it was also constructive. It itself sharply delimited the needed new understanding. This illustrates a kind of accomplishment in science which (I shall argue) in fact often obtains; yet, to this kind of scientific accomplishment Popper's philosophy is totally blind.

Aristarchus's reasoning concerns the sphericity of the moon and the way that the moon shows phases. The phases of the moon depend on its angular separation from the sun. When the moon is 180° away from the sun relative to Earth it appears 'full', because in that configuration the sun illuminates the entire side of the moon that faces Earth. Thus a full moon always both rises at sunset and sets at sunrise. (Moreover, a moon that rises at sunset will set at sunrise, and on that particular day of the month is always full.) By contrast, when the moon is angularly close to the sun it appears crescent-shaped, because in that configuration the sun illuminates a side of the moon that mostly, although not quite completely, faces away from Earth. (And conversely, whenever the moon appears crescent-shaped, so that from our perspective the sun is illuminating a side of the moon that mostly, although not quite completely, faces away from us, the moon will be angularly close to the sun.) Aristarchus realised that if the sun were nearer to Earth than the moon, then the facts just mentioned would be otherwise. In that case the moon would always appear more than half full, and would appear full twice per lunar cycle rather than only once: both when it was 180° away from the sun, and when it was 0° away (but beyond) the sun. Were the moon and the sun nearly equidistant from Earth, with the sun only slightly further away, then the angle relative to the sun at which the moon appears to us to be half full would be exceedingly small, close to 0°, and the lunar cycle would be very lop-sided; the moon would spend almost the whole time being more than half full. In the face of this realisation, Aristarchus asked himself the following brilliant question. At what angle relative to the sun does the moon appear to us to be half full? In other words, how evenly is the lunar cycle split between the moon's being more than half full, and its being less than half full? One significant point about this I have just mentioned: that if the moon and the sun were roughly equidistant from Earth, then this angle (the angle relative to the sun at which the moon appears to us to be half full) would be appreciably less than a right angle. Another significant point is that the moon advances through its phases at a remarkably constant rate, which it would do neither if the relative distances Earth-to-moon and Earth-to-sun were significantly varying within the course of each month, nor if the moon and the sun were even roughly equidistant from Earth. Now Aristarchus could easily determine that the angle relative to the sun at which the moon is half full is rather close to 90°, implying that the sun is considerably further away than the moon. Aristarchus estimated the angle to be 87°, and by determining that what we would call the sine of the complement of this angle lies between 1/18 and 1/20, he concluded that the sun is at least eighteen times further away from Earth than is the moon. This was a momentous astronomical measurement, and a step along the way to Aristarchus's determining (from still further theoretical reflection pertaining to still further phenomena) that the sun is very much larger than is the Earth.

In fact Aristarchus underestimated the moon–Earth–sun angle when from Earth's perspective the moon is exactly half full. That angle is still closer to 90° than Aristarchus realised. And so, in his ensuing calculation, Aristarchus severely underestimated the ratio of distances. The moon–Earth–sun angle when the moon is exactly half illuminated from the perspective of the earth is 89°50′, implying that the sun is roughly 400 times more distant than the moon.[1] Aristarchus is often castigated for the apparent carelessness with which he estimated the angle in question. Surely he could have done better, modern people are disposed to think. There is both something silly and also something right in the accusation. What is silly is how it misses Aristarchus's insight that the angle is much closer to 90° than to 0°, and that this fact is telling about the relative astronomical distances. That was a momentous accomplishment, never mind about the exact figures. What is right in this criticism is that despite Aristarchus's brilliance as a measurer, his carelessness about the exact figures shows that he was a measurer in only a limited way. Quite without getting his hands dirty Aristarchus could tell that the relevant angle is a lot closer to 90° than to 0°. That much he could tell quite without the use of instruments. Theoretical activity in his time was not set into a practical connection; it used neither instruments nor experiments. The Greeks were wont to fashion theoretical science a contemplative activity, and to think its practitioners too lofty to bother with merely practical activities of almost any sort. This attitude is apparent in Plato's disdain for the body and for the senses. It comes through in Aristotle in his fateful three-fold division of the sciences, by which Aristotle *segregated* the 'theoretical', the 'practical' and the 'productive' (*Top.* VI.6.145a14–16; *Met.* VI.1.1025b24, XI.7.1064a16–19; *EN* VI.2.1139a26–8). It is obvious to us now that science could not grow its experimental methodology until those divisions had all been surmounted.

Part of the significance of Aristarchus's reasoning is how it pointed past those stultifying prejudices. This it did quite without Aristarchus ever himself realising that it did so. Since Aristarchus had grasped how to deduce his theoretical conclusion from a phenomenon, it seems to us that Aristarchus quite clearly had reason to go on and study the phenomenon closely, using instruments as needs be, in order to estimate the relevant moon–Earth–sun angle quantitatively well. That he himself did no such thing in one way detracts from his accomplishment, but in another detracts little from the lesson that he taught. For when science truly got going it had simply to heed the call that Aristarchus had himself not so fully heeded. It had to tie theory into a more thoroughgoing practical connection. It had to do this in order to make all the more *measured* the theories with which it proceeded. Yet that great change amounted simply to lifting to a still higher pitch and intensity Aristarchus's own evident aspiration for a measured understanding.

My complaint against Popper is that he repeats the ancients' mistake. His orientation is highly intellectualist; he makes out science as pre-eminently theoretical. Since Popper was a philosopher, and philosophy is a supremely theoretical activity, it is easy to understand how he might have made that old mistake. Philosophy itself inclines philosophers to be far less practically oriented than they otherwise might be. On average you would say that philosophers are not very practical. So it is perhaps especially easy for philosophers to make the ancients' mistake. But there is a good deal less excuse for it in the modern era, after the inception of up-and-running science. For when science ignited in the seventeenth century, it did so precisely by bridging the former gaps between the theoretical, the practical and the productive. Some natural philosophers adopted an *experimental* approach in inquiry, oriented to measurement. That made an immediate and lasting difference to inquiry's success. Philosophy perhaps disposes philosophers not to understand these events, but truly, with the events so clear, so recent, and so resoundingly echoed in the characteristics of present-day science, the confusion should not happen.

I have said that Popper was confused about measurement, and apt to repeat the mistake of the ancients, of fashioning science as a purely contemplative activity. Of course Popper applauded the making of measurements for the purpose of *testing* a theory. But that is not even remotely to do justice to the connection between theory and practice that is cemented in the making of measurements. It is to understand measurements in only a negative respect, when their function is actually more significantly positive. That measurements do not principally perform the negative function of *testing* a theory can be seen in our present example. Aristarchus did not merely show how his newfound theory of astronomical distances *checks out* with empirical facts. On the contrary, Aristarchus started from the empirical fact that when the moon appears half full the moon–Earth–sun angle closely approaches 90°, and he outright *deduced* from that that the sun is far further away from Earth than the moon is. (To see this deduction as such, we need only grant to Aristarchus some pretty innocuous seeming background assumptions concerning the cause of the phases of the moon. These assumptions include explicit or tacit convictions about the sun shining by its own light, the moon's shining by reflecting sunlight, the moon's being a sphere, light's propagating rectilinearly, and Euclidean geometry's being applicable on the scale of those astronomical distances. Note that the *generality* of Aristarchus's conclusion concerning relative distances to the moon and the sun merely matches the generality of the phenomenon, of the moon's running through its phases in a regular way, and running about the ecliptic in a regular way much more quickly than does the sun.)

As this example illustrates, measurements standardly perform a *positive* function, of proving why a theory is true. Of course the proof will be at least somewhat fallible, because of the fallibility of background assumptions that it employs. Aristarchus did not know for sure, for example, that you can write Euclidean geometry up onto the heavens and be right to do so (and we now know that you can't entirely, yet you can well enough for Aristarchus's reasonings to be cogent). Aristarchus did not know for sure (though the evidence in front of him for this conclusion was itself extraordinarily good) that the phenomena of the moon's phases are from a spherical moon's being illuminated from different angles by the sun. None the less it would be churlish to exaggerate the fallibility of Aristarchus's inference. As inferences go, it was very cogent. Little is to be gained even by calling Aristarchus's new theory a *conjecture*. He had roundly refuted the predecessor theory by *deducing from phenomena* that his new theory is true.

2 Harvey

William Harvey helped to topple a traditional understanding of the heart. According to the traditional understanding, the heart has an *emanative* function, emanating one of the four humours (blood, phlegm, black bile and yellow bile) to the furthest reaches of the body. Yet Harvey's breakthrough was not just to level criticism against that traditional theory. It was to deduce from evidence the required form for its replacement. For Harvey succeeded in showing that the heart's influence is not emanative, by empirically demonstrating that it is instead circulatory.

Harvey benefited from key discoveries by several of his predecessors. That the heart's septum is too dense to be permeable to blood, as was required by Galenic theory, that the valves both in the heart and in the venous system function mechanically to guarantee a one-way flow of blood, and even that there is a cardio-pulmonary circulation of blood, all was known to Harvey because of the work of his predecessors. Harvey's accomplishment was to study the heart in its own mechanical affections, and to relate those findings to the question of the heart's relation to the body as a whole. By brutal vivisections Harvey carefully determined that the heart moves blood precisely when it contracts, rather than when it expands as had been the traditional view. He thus perfected an understanding of the heart as a pump. And he determined how much blood is thus mechanically advanced out of the left side of the heart into the arterial system with each contractive beat. Thus by considering the number of beats per minute Harvey could calculate the quantity of blood that passes out of the heart towards the body each hour. In weight, this is many times the weight of the whole body. Thus by complete necessity he 'began to think whether there might not be a MOTION, AS IT WERE, IN A CIRCLE' (1628; ch. VIII). Such a prodigious passage of blood from the heart seemed to him surely impossible unless 'the blood should somehow find its way from the arteries into the veins, and so return to the right side of the heart' (ibid.) from whence it was already known to proceed out to the lungs, and then back to the left side. In other words, Harvey thought he had sound deductive grounds for thinking that the heart pumps blood in a double circulation.

Clearly the background assumptions in which this inference trades are fairly innocuous. You just have to suppose that matter is conserved, or at least that there is no way that such amounts of matter as exit the heart per hour along the arteries could either be created in the heart or for that matter consumed without trace by the body. With these assumptions and the experimental evidence about the quantity of blood pumped, the blood's 'MOTION, AS IT WERE, IN A CIRCLE' cannot but be inferred.

Once again, the theory is not advanced as a conjecture, and shown simply to check out with the known evidence. Rather it comes into Harvey's possession by a deduction from phenomena. The situation is not merely that if the heart circulates the blood, then the quantity of blood advancing through the heart per hour could without paradox greatly outweigh the entire body. Rather the situation is that since the quantity of blood advancing through the heart per hour greatly outweighs the entire body, we cannot without paradox deny that the heart circulates the blood.

Has Popper prepared us in any way to recognise inferences of this form in the history of science? The answer is clear: he has not. Yet, as I hope to show both by some further illustration and then by some general considerations, it very much impairs our overall understanding of science not to do so.

3 Wegener

The geologist Alfred Wegener marshalled on the basis of empirical evidence a number of very impressive arguments that the continents have moved. My purposes will be well served if I pause here to discuss not only some of the arguments that Wegener used, but also the upshot of his discussion later in the twentieth century, when theoretical geologists finally achieved closure, in plate tectonic theory, on the former debate about the reality of continental drift. Both these developments, Wegener's own contribution, and the eventual closure, were rational in ways that Popper ill equips us to fathom.

Wegener marshalled many empirical arguments that the continents have moved. He organised these under the headings geodetic, geophysical, geological, palaeontological and biological, and palaeoclimatic. Under each heading he provided an array of impressively mutually supporting empirical considerations. I shall focus on just one geological argument that Wegener gives. Of course, the empirical findings on which he drew were secured by geologists using their considerable practical knowledge about how to interpret natural landscapes and their features. Their findings were 'theory laden'. Yet as I will shortly remark, the respects in which they were so were innocuous. Wegener notes for us that in North America, geologists had recognised stretches of old moraine. That is, they had recognised certain extant features of a landscape as expressing the past action of glaciers that had once existed but had later long ago receded and disappeared. It is within the practical wherewithal of almost every geologist to be able to recognise a moraine as a moraine. Moreover, it is within the practical wherewithal of almost every geologist carefully to analyse the composition of old moraines if they wish to. A geologist can quantitatively assess the proportions of various types of rock, the incidence of various kinds of fossils in those rocks, and so on, and say what the composition is of a given old moraine. In Europe, geologists had likewise recognised stretches of old moraine. There too, they analysed their composition. Astoundingly, they found that some bits of old moraines in North America were utterly alike in constitution to some bits of old moraines in Europe (Wegener 1966 [1929], pp. 76 ff.). Such pairings existed also between South America and Africa. The moraines in question had identical proportions of various kinds of rock, identical incidences of various kinds of fossils in those rocks, and so on. Now, as a geologist Wegener knew to expect no two moraines to be alike in constitution unless they were created by one and the same glacier. Geological variety, Wegener well knew, makes it utterly unlikely that two moraines, created by two different glaciers in two different places, should end up indiscernible from one another in constitution. Wegener also knew as a geologist that no single glacier could create moraines on opposite sides of the Atlantic Ocean. And he also knew, as a matter of commonsense knowledge rather than geological knowledge of the possible behaviours of piles of rocks, that moraines do not get up and walk. If bits of one and the same moraine are found in two very different locations, so that one or the other or both of the bits of moraine have moved, then the ground underneath those two bits of moraines has moved. Thus Wegener could offer a reason for thinking that North America and Europe had moved apart. Similarly he could offer a reason for thinking that South America and Africa had moved apart. Moreover, when Wegener used one old moraine to determine how North America and Europe had formerly touched, his conclusion matched the conclusion he could reach in a similar fashion by appeal to other, quite separate, old moraines, and indeed by examining moraines with information about how South America and Africa once had touched (ibid.). Moreover, as Wegener details at length, the agreement extended to other kinds of evidence that likewise suggested continental drift, for example geological evidence concerning features other than moraines, palaeobotanic, palaeozoological, and palaeoclimatic evidence, and also evidence concerning present-day distributions of plants and animals.

In the 1966 Dover English language version of the 1929 fourth edition of Wegener's *Die Entstehung der Kontinente und Ozeane*, Wegener is translated as follows:

> It is just as if we were to refit the torn pieces of a newspaper by matching their edges and then check whether the lines of print run smoothly across. If they do, there is nothing left but to conclude that the pieces were in fact joined in this way. If only one line was available for the test, we would still have found a high probability [p] for the accuracy of fit, but if we have n lines, then [the smallish] probability [$1-p$, that the match is mere coincidence] is raised to the nth power [and thus becomes very small indeed, so that the probability that we infer correctly becomes correspondingly close to 1].
>
> (p. 77)

> This evidence for the correctness of our synthesis is very remarkable, and one is reminded of a torn visiting card used as a means of recognition.
>
> (p. 62)

How, then, was it reasonable for Wegener to infer as he did that the continents have moved? I think it is clear that Wegener *deduced* it.[2] In fact he deduced it many times over. This is why his theory was rich with consilience features, the features he remarks in the above quote. With respect to each way Wegener could deduce his conclusion, the deduction left room for doubt, for it employed fallible assumptions, some of them themselves theoretical. But the way that the many deductions produced the one conclusion gave Wegener excellent reason overall to think that the continents have indeed moved.

Notoriously Wegener did not fully succeed with his arguments. He was not able to convince the geological community as a whole to accept the reality of continental drift. An outstanding puzzle concerned how the lighter-weight, physically weaker materials that predominate within the continental landmasses could possibly drift within the far denser, physically harder rock of which the oceanic crust is chiefly comprised. Ultimately this puzzle was resolved when, in the 1960s, geologists began to explore and interpret a new kind of data, specifically palaeo-magnetic data concerning the 'magnetic anomaly' in rocks on the sea floor. Under a then quite speculative understanding that the polarity of the earth's magnetic field periodically reverses, and that the sea floor freezes the local magnetic orientation at the time when it is volcanically formed, geologists swept the ocean floors with magnetometers. Their object was to discover patterns in the magnetic anomaly in the rocks. Patterns were certainly there, so much so that the regions of like magnetic anomaly proved, on inspection, to be organised in very telling ways. In many regions of the sea floor, bands of positive and negative anomaly were organised, with appreciable clarity, symmetrically on either side of the deep ocean trenches, suggesting that in such a trench new seabed is actually formed and then shunted by new formation behind it laterally outwards in either of two opposing directions at right angles to the ocean trench. Elsewhere, the palaeomagnetic evidence revealed clear indications of subduction of one part of the sea floor under another, or of two facing parts together, or of a part of the sea floor under continental land mass, and so on. Geologists quickly worked out ways to read the patterns for understanding of how the land masses, now conceived to be shunted around by the activity of the sea floor, had moved through ages past. The data, when used in this way, initially seemed good out to 200 million years to the past, and by now are read in some places out to 750 million years. Beyond then, the lines of seafloor magnetic anomaly that could tell a further story would mostly have already been subducted somewhere. The remarkable thing was that the reconstructions steadily outwards to 100 million years ago agreed in detail with Wegener's findings about past positions of continents. The analysis of the further tracts of past time tells a story that accommodates Wegener's own very beautifully.

Through these developments, geology proceeded onto an especially sure path theoretically. In its present activities it is an evidently purposeful and intelligently directed activity. It would be pretty silly now, if it wasn't already silly long ago, to suggest that theoretical geology is an entirely tentative collection of conjectures. Thanks to major developments not four decades old, geologists have a very healthy discipline, theoretically speaking, and they know it. What they know is that, by the lights of the ideas now ascendant in their discipline, vast ensembles of seemingly utterly disparate kinds of data are in fact quite excellently well fitted to one another. For example, geologists can chase the continents about into remoter and remoter past historical configurations using inferences from seafloor palaeomagnetic evidence, and find them touching in ways and at times and at latitudes etc. which are required by the palaeoontological, palaeobotanic, palaeoclimatic etc. evidence which originally convinced Wegener and others of continental drift. These are powerfully important developments, and a philosopher's theory of science would be a poor one if it could not do justice to them.

The most significant pattern of inference in this development can aptly be characterised as a *measurement*. In a measurement, one employs background considerations to determine what salience something that one can empirically or practically establish has at the level of theory. One deduces a theoretical conclusion from a phenomenon (together with the background considerations). The phenomenon is one to which one's recourse is usually by practical means. It is helpful to think of a measurement as a kind of transcendental argument. In a transcendental argument, we infer something, A, from some known fact or phenomenon B, by noting that A is necessary for the very possibility of B. In that case since B obtains A must also obtain. This inference form allows us to go deeper than surface phenomena and that is why its form is known to us from metaphysics. Such a form of argument is of course fallible, because it depends on our fallible judgments concerning what is necessary for the possibility of what. But sometimes quite momentous conclusions A can come using known facts B, with the help only of very innocuous seeming judgments concerning what is necessary for the possibility of what. We have seen this already in the cases of Aristarchus and Harvey. We are now seeing it again in the case of Wegener. Aristarchus traded in geometrical assumptions concerning what is necessary for the very possibility of the moon's being half-full. Harvey traded in a physics-of-materials assumption concerning what is necessary for the very possibility that the heart should advance in an hour a weight of blood many times greater than the weight of the entire body. Wegener traded in low-level geological knowledge concerning what is necessary for the very possibility of a moraine, and for two moraines to be alike in constitution. Each of these figures reached a momentous new theoretical conclusion by a deduction from a phenomenon, in which all you need to grant is the innocuous-seeming background assumption concerning what is necessary for the possibility of what. Scientists regularly produce very cogent arguments for theoretical conclusions by finding a way to mobilise what seems most sure in their background conceptions in support of such transcendental arguments, or deductions from phenomena. In fact, Immanuel Kant, who first articulated this form for argumentation in metaphysics, first learned of it from Isaac Newton.

4 Newton

The activity of measuring is at one and the same time both practical and theoretical: in making a measurement, we establish *practically* something *theoretical*. Measurement is the practical activity of deducing something theoretical from a phenomenon. When we deduce something theoretical from a phenomenon, the deduction in question has, I am saying, the form of a so-called transcendental argument: from the phenomenon B, we infer what is necessary for the very possibility of B's obtaining as it does. We seek to discern from B some *moral* about things more generally – what, broadly speaking, things needed to have been like before B could ever have obtained as it does. Our conclusion, A, will be the more metaphysical the greater the breadth of our consideration about necessity and possibility. At one extreme it will concern what was *conceptually* necessary for the very *conceptual* possibility of what. For example, when Newton effectively measured what his doctrine of spacetime structure needed to be like, in order that the phenomenon of inertiality should even be possible, he was operating at this metaphysical extreme. At the other extreme, the relevant background judgments concerning what is necessary for what will be so very practical, so very concerned with given, purely causal forms of necessity and possibility, that they scarcely seem to us even to be theoretical. I shall discuss such an example fully in just a moment.

All measurements are formally transcendental, however mundane or metaphysical the conclusions reached by them may seem. There is not a difference in kind, but only a difference in degree, between even the most metaphysical of all conclusions to be reached in science, such as Newton's about space and time, on the one hand, and the most mundane and straightforward empirical determination by measurement, such as how long something is, on the other. Thus it is hardly surprising that there are cases in between the extremes. For example, when Newton reached his highly theoretical conclusions concerning the gravitational mechanics of the solar system, he did so by deducing them from phenomena, that is by making ingenious measurement inferences.[3] These conclusions were notably less metaphysical than were Newton's own conclusions concerning space and time, but notably more metaphysical than a conclusion concerning, say, the radius of the earth, let alone one concerning, say, the weight of a bag of apples.

Measurements at all levels are notably fallible, even if they are at all levels the best, or most improving, form of inference that there is. It is a practical matter to have knowledge by measurement and it is also best practice to garner such knowledge. We can be practically wise only if we can reason skilfully and with good empirical information concerning what is necessary for the possibility of what.

An everyday example of a measurement

If my daughter and I want to measure how tall my daughter is, we might do it as follows. I shall use this example to illustrate in a mundane way the above points. First, she slips off her shoes and stands vertically against a wall, shoulders square, head high and heels on the floor. Then I carefully mark on the wall the height to the top of her head. Then she steps aside and we place a measuring tape along the wall vertically from the floor to that mark. We then read a number off the tape measure.

When we do so, we declare that she is 159 centimetres tall. This is a theoretical conclusion. We have deduced it from the phenomenon in front of us, that a mark that I have made on the wall coincides with a certain number on the measuring tape. On the basis of various beliefs that my daughter and I have, we reason that it is – in the circumstances as we have contrived them to be – all things considered *necessary for the very possibility* of that phenomenon's being as it is, that my daughter is in fact 159 centimetres tall.

All measurement fallible

This reasoning about my daughter's height is of course fallible – both because she and I might be mistaken about the phenomenon in front of us, and more particularly because we might be mistaken somewhere in the assumptions that we have brought into our considerations about what is necessary for the possibility of what. Because of the latter kind of difficulty, transcendental argumentation is always at least somewhat problematic. Consequently, all measurement is fallible.

For example, my daughter and I might be mistaken in our belief that the tape measure was manufactured accurately and has not subsequently been stretched or shrunk or otherwise distorted. If we are thus mistaken, then in a particularly simple or mundane way we are almost certainly mistaken in what we think is necessary for the possibility of the phenomenon that is in front of us. A more interesting mistake is if we think that rather more *about my daughter* is necessary for the possibility of the phenomenon in front of us than in fact is necessary for this possibility. For example, we are likely not to have hedged around our conclusion that my daughter is 159 centimetres tall with the qualification 'in the morning' (if that is when we measured her). Or again, we are likely not to have hedged around our conclusion that my daughter is 159 centimetres tall with the qualification 'in the rest frame', i.e. the frame of reference in which my daughter and I, the wall, the tape measure etc. are all at rest rather than moving. Tacitly we have proceeded with what are arguably rash views, that if it is necessary for the possibility of the phenomenon in front of us that my daughter is 159 centimetres tall in the morning and in the frame of reference in which she is at rest then it is necessary for the possibility of the phenomenon in front of us that my daughter is 159 centimetres tall at any time of day and in any frame of reference whatsoever. These views are mistaken, since, as it happens, people often shrink by as much as a couple of centimetres over the course of a day, later regaining in the night by stretching in their sleep the height they lost the previous day, and moreover, in a suitably moving frame of reference, I, my daughter, the wall and the measuring tape all are 'length contracted' by an amount that is appreciable if our speed in that frame is appreciable with respect to the speed of light. It would be churlish however to place a greater weight on the fallibility of our judgment that my daughter is 159 centimetres tall than is due to it. This measuring inference, like many others, is, as inferences go, a very cogent one.

Mounting respect for 'deductions from phenomena'

It is only within the past three decades that philosophers of science have learned to respect the idea of deductions from phenomena and to place due emphasis on the practical activity of measurement. One must say that Popper himself inhibited this learning. For reasons that I shall address, philosophers of science such as Popper had in former times concerned themselves overmuch with a relatively unintelligent guess-and-test methodology for inferring theoretical conclusions. This methodology directed their attention overmuch to *observation* in science, and thus insufficiently much to the practical or *experimental* activity of measuring.

During the past thirty years, philosophers of science in increasing numbers have at long last accorded Newton the respect that he deserves for his claim to have deduced his theoretical conclusions from phenomena.[4] Philosophers of science have at last carefully examined the pattern of Newton's argumentation in *Principia* and elsewhere, and have come to appreciate Newton as a measurer extraordinaire – able to reach conclusions about the physics of the solar system, for example, with cogency comparable to my daughter's and mine about my daughter's height. Even the long, involved argument in *Principia* for universal gravitation – perhaps the most boldly theoretical conclusion ever drawn – is such a deduction, albeit a considerably ramified one. Many of its parts are wonderfully cogent relatively unramified deductions from phenomena – that is to say, really pure and sterling examples of clever acts of measurement.

Newton a fine methodologist

A still more impressive discovery about Newton from the past three decades or so is that Newton was a *methodologist* extraordinaire. That is to say, he really knew not just what to do but also what he was doing. Newton in fact had a rich and searching understanding of his method and its significance – including what was questionable about his method, what its strengths were and what its limits were. In particular, Newton well understood the *fallibility* for what it is of his deductions from phenomena. That Newton was in fact very knowing as regards methodology calls for some really full reconsideration of a number of prejudices in both history and philosophy of science.

As regards the deductions-from-phenomena inferences in *Principia* that Newton explicitly marks out as such, the remarkable fact is that he was, for carefully considered reasons about which he was completely explicit, fallibilist about the background assumptions on which he rested these inferences. And this is so despite the fact that all Newton's contemporaries would have been happy to permit Newton to claim to be absolutely certain of those assumptions. The assumptions were: that Euclidean geometry holds in the heavens, and that the three laws of motion are true. It was amazing but also prescient that Newton understood these assumptions to be fallible![5] Because he was thus explicitly fallibilist about his assumptions, Newton was also explicitly fallibilist about all the conclusions that he inductively reached. (Why I say that Newton reached his theoretical conclusions inductively is that, while he inferred by *deduction* from phenomena the form for, for example, a force law, he then rendered that conclusion general by *induction*. This is why Newton himself talks both of induction, and of deductions from phenomena. He was explicitly fallibilist about both.) *Pace* Duhem (cf. his 1954 [1914], pp. 190–5), Popper (see note 3), Lakatos (cf. his 1977, p. 2), Einstein (1954, p. 273; 1991 [1950], p. 72), and many others, there is no basis whatever for thinking that Newton meant by 'induction' or 'deductions from phenomena' an infallible method in science.

Newton deduced his doctrine of spacetime structure from phenomena of inertiality

The following contention about Newton's use of his method is important for my purposes (for the way in which I wish to connect Newton with Einstein). I shall say that *Newton deduced from phenomena his whole doctrine of spacetime structure*. That is to say, the views about absolute space and absolute time that Newton laid out for us at the beginning of Book I of his *Principia* proceed in effect from a *measurement* that Newton made. That is not how Newton himself introduces them in his *Principia*, but the following consideration points to why I say that is how he reached them. To reach the views there laid down, Newton in effect said, 'let the symmetries of spacetime be no more than the symmetries of the phenomena of inertiality – otherwise it is a nonsense that there should be such phenomena'. (This form of argument is there to see in Newton's *De Gravitatione et aequipondo Fluidorum* or 'On the Gravity and Equilibrium of Fluids', familiarly known as *De Grav*, 1962 [n.d.].) That is, from the phenomena of inertiality Newton deduced what (so far as he could see) is necessary concerning spacetime structure for the very possibility of such phenomena. In this way he measured (as well as he might) what his spacetime doctrine needed to be like.

It was, as it happens, beyond Newton, given the state of mathematics in his day, to accomplish this deduction perfectly. After all, in order to identify the truly necessary conditions concerning spacetime structure for the possibility of the phenomena of inertiality as he recognised them, Newton ought to have said (in effect): 'let the symmetries of spacetime be *neither more nor less than* the symmetries of the phenomena of inertiality'. The structural insight is difficult, however, and was just beyond Newton's reach, which clarifies how we can *have* the symmetries in spacetime be neither more nor less than those in the phenomena of inertiality. Because the relevant structural insight was beyond Newton, Newton was notably mistaken in his judgment about what was necessary for the possibility of what. Newton set forth a doctrine of spacetime structure which implied in effect that the symmetries of spacetime structure are rather less than the symmetries inherent in inertial phenomena. Newton simply could see no alternative to this. He recognised perfectly well himself – indeed, explicitly stated as corollaries to his laws of motion – the respects in which his spacetime structure carried an excess of richness relative to the symmetries inherent in inertial phenomena. But he could not see how to pull back from that structure, without reaching a spacetime structure that was less rich than the phenomena required and thus would violate the necessary conditions for the very possibility of those phenomena.

Newton's adversaries philosophically confused

Some of Newton's contemporaries roundly criticised him in effect for his having advanced a doctrine of spacetime structure that was richer than the phenomena warranted. However, Newton in fact achieved a higher methodological standard than did his contemporaries who criticised him, and by doing so achieved greater insight about spacetime structure than they ever did. The difficulty for him was also a difficulty for them, so that no-one in that day was able to point to the actual defect in Newton's reasoning. His detractors, moreover, set forth doctrines of spacetime structure that were in fact disastrously *less* rich than they needed to be, in order for the phenomena of inertiality to be possible at all. Newton sharply demonstrated this, for example using his thought experiment about the spinning bucket. Not one of Newton's adversaries replied adequately to Newton about this – an historical point that Howard Stein roundly demonstrated more than three decades ago. So we should regard Newton as substantially having won the debates in his day that were in effect about spacetime structure. In short, Newton had altogether the right method and was only slightly frustrated in the exercise of it. He had a deep understanding of what he was about. We should look to his own understanding of the status of spacetime with all due respect and attention.

5 Einstein

I believe, moreover, that Einstein – the darling of philosophers, as I am sure you are aware, and therefore by far the much more admired and studied by philosophers than Newton – himself essentially adhered to Newton's method. However, philosophers were until recently unaware of this, and indeed were confused by Einstein's own proclamations about the true methodological character of Einstein's own work. For Einstein did not *say* that he adhered to Newton's method, and in fact he said quite the opposite. Unfortunately, and unlike Newton, Einstein was actually rather muddled in himself concerning the methodological character of his own researches. And moreover he was not at all insightful concerning the methodological character of Newton's researches. Einstein never understood what Newton had meant by 'deductions from phenomena'. Einstein simply inferred from the label 'deductions from phenomena' that Newton had meant a method that rendered theoretical conclusions infallible. Einstein argued that it is impossible for science to achieve infallibility, and on this ground officially denounced the idea of 'deductions from phenomena'. Thus Einstein attacked a straw man. Because he wanted to state his fallibilism officially, he officially committed himself to hypothetico-deductivism since that is a notably fallible method. Yet Einstein, despite his official hypothetico-deductivism, in the actual course of his work employed always the method that would deliver the most cogent conclusions. And for this reason he adhered (unknowingly) to Newton's method, for that is the method that is best – provided it can be made to work at all. Newton's method is both far more challenging to the researcher and also (if it can be made to work) far more cogent than the method of guess and test.

To all intents and purposes, Einstein's work within spacetime physics consists, like Newton's, in carefully measuring what the doctrine of spacetime structure needs to be like. The key question that exercises Einstein is Newton's question, concerning what is necessary for the very possibility of the phenomena of inertiality being as they are. But Einstein took a broader view than Newton of the phenomena of inertiality. For by Einstein's day, rather more about the physics of inertia had been learned.

In short, Einstein assembled rather more than Newton had done into his understanding of inertiality. With the phenomena of inertiality appropriately recolligated, Einstein made Newton-style inferences concerning spacetime structure. Of course these inferences took Einstein well beyond the understanding of spacetime structure that Newton had had. But the method was the same.

Einstein twice recolligated phenomena of inertiality, and twice deduced new doctrines of spacetime structure

Whereas Newton colligated the phenomena of inertiality by his three laws of motion, Einstein was working in the context of a fully developed theory of electromagnetism and therefore right from the start had rather more than Newton's three dynamical principles to think about. In the decades leading up to Einstein's work, some physicists (the proponents of the so-called 'electromagnetic world picture') had endeavoured to understand the concept of inertiality that came from Newtonian mechanics strictly in electromagnetic terms as met with in Maxwell's theory. That is to say, they had sought to make out how the mass or resistivity to acceleration of bodies is but an electromagnetic effect. Despite attempts to overcome the mechanical world conception and replace it with an altogether electromagnetical one, these physicists failed to make out the mass or resistivity to acceleration of bodies as nothing but an electromagnetic effect. Nevertheless, their work did establish that there are robust connections between electromagnetism and inertiality. They showed experimentally, for example, that there can be an increase in the resistivity to acceleration or mass of a body precisely for electromagnetical reasons.

By appropriately broadening his view of the phenomena of inertiality to embrace their connection with electromagnetism, Einstein was led to rethink the fundamentals of kinematics. After some struggles he found how to deduce the kinematics of special relativity theory, not from any considerable part of electromagnetic theory – for that theory was by his own lights suspect, standing in need of correction at least for the reasons that had been pointed to by Planck – but deducing it rather from a single electromagnetical phenomenon, the phenomenon of relativity, or thus of a symmetry in electromagnetic phenomena generally that he insisted should also inhere in electromagnetic theory. Einstein made his deduction through the joint use of his principle of relativity, and a principle that he called 'the light postulate', the so-called constancy of the speed of light. The deduction that Einstein delivered essentially gave us Minkowski's doctrine of spacetime structure as a replacement to Newton's, although it took three years and the independent work by Minkowski to show how theories of kinematics are aptly presented as doctrines of spacetime structure.

Of course this reconstruction skirts around many complexities of what was a bold innovation. (An excellent recent collection in which this and other early innovations by Einstein are more fully discussed and illuminated is Don Howard and John Stachel, eds, 1998.) Bold innovations are seldom viewed at the time with the clarity with which they can best be viewed in hindsight. But in essence, viewed in what I believe to be the best way available to us today, Einstein's inference was as follows. Einstein revisited the whole question of what the symmetries of spacetime should be, because his understanding of inertiality was more encompassing than Newton's had been. In order to hold the symmetries of spacetime to be neither more nor less than the symmetries of the phenomena of inertiality, it was necessary, Einstein realised, to consider the symmetries that are inherent in electromagnetic phenomena. Einstein discovered a particularly pure way to attend to these symmetries when he hit upon his so-called light postulate, concerning the constancy across all frames of reference of the velocity of light. From the light postulate, plus relativity treated as a phenomenon, Einstein without any question did actually outright deduce the kinematics of special relativity theory. In other words, it was possible for Einstein to use the light postulate to establish as necessary for the possibility of the truth of the principle of relativity that special relativistic kinematics obtain. That is to say, Einstein *measured* what we must say concerning spacetime structure, using the relativity principle as his phenomenonal basis for this act of measurement.

Later, Einstein recolligated inertial phenomena yet again, so as to comprehend gravity wholly as inertia. (This, incidentally, was a move that Newton in fact might also have made had he thought of it. Newton had actually remarked and even experimentally investigated the equivalence of gravitational and inertial mass, which invites one to comprehend gravity wholly as inertia. Elie Cartan – see his 1923 – delivered the mathematics by which Newton, within the context of his own gravitational theory, might have comprehended gravity as inertia no less surely than is possible within the context of Einstein's 'relativistic' correction of that theory.) As is well known, this recolligation of inertial phenomena takes the following form. Instead of treating me, for example, as at present in a nearly inertial state of motion, with a force from gravity upon me exactly compensated by the automatic electromagnetic forces pressing on my feet and seat, I may be treated instead as in a non-inertial motion, with the automatic electromagnetic forces that are pressing on my feet and seat accelerating me or thus nudging me from what would have been the straightest trajectory. Proceeding in this way with all bodies whatsoever, I change what motions I regard as inertial and what not precisely so that gravity – as a force, or thus as a separate phenomenon from inertia – simply disappears. On the basis of the thus recolligated phenomena of inertiality, Einstein, through relentless searching investigation and rumination over many years, found how to deduce the doctrine of spacetime structure that is called the theory of general relativity. This doctrine is boldly different from any earlier doctrine of spacetime structure in that it employs an inhomogeneous, non-Euclidean geometry in a way that collapses the traditional division between kinematics and dynamics.

Einstein's accomplishments best viewed as extensions of Newton's

The description that I have just given hugely simplifies upon Einstein's own understanding of what he was up to, and quite fails to elaborate upon many crucial steps Einstein took to accomplish what he did. (The detailed story is ever more fully in scholars' grasp by now. See for example Norton 1984 and Stachel 1987 and 1989.) Complexities aside, however, I believe that the way to view Einstein's accomplishment which best illuminates its significance and warrant is thus as an extension of Newton's. And that is why I uphold the description that I have just given.

In essence my view is that philosophers of science should be willing to be charitable about method or warrant in somewhat the same way that they have chosen to be about meaning. We say, with good purpose, that the word 'gold', out of the mouths of people even several centuries ago, referred to the element with atomic number 79, even though no-one then could possibly have held the relevant belief. Of course there do have to be certain pretty robust features of their general use of the word 'gold' to support such a charitable construal. It is not to the present purpose to discuss what these conditions are, but rather to remark that, provided that they are satisfied, people's terms are best construed as deriving their meaning from ideals for thought and practice which may need to be much better worked out than they have managed for themselves. An ideal which may not be well worked out until much later is actually implicated by what they do, and it conditions the meanings of what they say and are about. As it is with meanings, so it is also with warrants, or so I believe. I want to say that, provided some pretty robust features of actual practice suggest it, a methodological ideal may be invoked in the reconstruction of scientists' reasoning that is at least somewhat better worked out than the scientists had managed for themselves. Newton I believe requires no such assistance, but Einstein does, and I see no difficulty about giving it to him given the robust basis there is for thinking that he genuinely deserves it.

Significantly, some of the key epistemological pronouncements by Einstein which in his own mind set him apart from Newton in fact underline the similarities in their positions. I shall illustrate this shortly.

Einstein officially viewed Newton as a bad methodologist, but was wrong to do so

As is well known, Einstein's official view was that Newton was a bad methodologist. Moreover, Einstein officially held that Newton was excessive in the commitments that he assumed concerning spacetime. Supposedly Einstein was the better epistemologist, and by dint of a superior philosophy helped to sort out all the mistakes that Newton had made. Years ago Howard Stein challenged this whole view, cogently arguing that it is riddled with confusions. Subsequently many philosophers have worked to sort these confusions out, i.e. to capture in a well considered way the nature of Einstein's contribution, its relation to Newton's, why Einstein thought what he did about the nature of his and Newton's contributions, why he was right in some respects and wrong in others, and so on. The task has been enormous, and the earlier efforts by the philosophers who have worked on this have themselves required correction in ensuing further studies.

Einstein's errors can probably be blamed on the inevitable headiness of his situation. He had after all overturned Newton's theory. This promoted him to the attention of all the world. Philosophers beat a path to his door, to learn from him what knowledge-making is all about. It is as though Einstein's office sported a sign reading 'EPISTEMOLOGICAL ADVICE AVAILABLE ON REQUEST'. These are poor conditions for issuing always sober, carefully considered pronouncements. And this is especially so given how difficult the going had been for Einstein. He was pushing the very limits of what a human can do, and was inevitably not always immediately clear in himself about the nature of his own accomplishment. Newton by contrast was an enormously solitary and careful worker. How he brought order to his situation shows singular genius, in among other way,s in his developing needed new mathematics. But none of the mathematics was as difficult as that which Einstein was forced into using. Newton had been deeply influenced by what he regarded as the negative example of Descartes, a philosopher supremely confident that he knew what he was about, yet deeply confused in his scientific conclusions (as Newton well recognised). On matters of methodology, no less than of science, Newton was determined not to repeat Descartes' mistake. So, Newton's pronouncements were careful in the extreme. What Newton says about his own methodology is considered with utmost thoroughness and reliability.

Einstein's freedom

Einstein had produced both special and then general relativity theory by the time he was thirty-seven, along with a number of other almost equally breathtaking contributions to theoretical physics. When we consider the early years of his life therefore we confront the flowering of a prodigious scientific imagination. Indeed it was so prodigious that for a while it remained doubtful not only whether Einstein would eventually secure a place in the profession of theoretical physics but even whether he would produce a doctoral thesis that that profession would pass. Einstein's remarkable independence of mind and deed in his early years underlines for us that he was one of the freest human beings ever to have lived. Yet it is vitally important to understand correctly the nature of this freedom. Einstein's example communicates to us the following philosophical lesson. *The highest spontaneity of the understanding is also the most responsible, and so produces concepts that are already richly supported by evidence.* The imagination is free, but the deliverances of the *freest* imagination are in fact the *least* conjectural.

What is freedom? If I pursue this question briefly then this will allow me to frame as best I might why I think that Einstein's example teaches an almost opposite lesson from the one that Popper extracted from it. When asked what freedom is, many are tempted by the frivolous, 'negative', view, that to be free is to be able to do simply as one pleases. Freedom is on this conception an absence of constraint. There is, however, an opposing, 'positive', more serious and demanding, view. According to it, to be free is to act from a rationally deeply measured conviction, in light of which one synthetically sees the necessity to act in the given way rather than any other. On this conception, the highest freedom is simply to do as one determines for oneself by synthetic rational insight that one intuitively must. Freedom is in that case from liking what is right. Socrates, Hypatia and Ghandi evince this kind of freedom in apparently unearthly degree. In circumstances fraught with forces against which your or my will to maintain our integrity would snap like a matchstick, these figures neither flinched nor wavered, their simplicity and insight overmatching all calls on them to compromise their own integrity. In their own utterly creative ways of being human, these thinkers cleaved always to what they could remark as necessary. It seems impossible in their circumstances that any human being should have accomplished this and yet they did. Indeed that is why we all know something about these figures. We seem to need Socrates, Hypatia and Gandhi to be heroes in our eyes. The function this serves seems to be to prove the possibility that life can be reckoned with truly rationally – that reason can confront the tangle of competing demands and pulls that life presents it with and reduce what we should do to a form that manifests complete coherence.

Einstein was a free spirit in science in precisely the same way as Ghandi was in the sphere of practical action. Yet philosophers of science have been very slow off the mark to admire him for this. The positivists, Popper, and Kuhn, all, it is true, were tremendously impressed by Einstein, but they did not understand the freedom that he evinced. They one and all treated Einstein's theoretical imagination as though it lay beyond the purview of reason. Thus, they treated his freedom as though it were of the negative sort. The positivists proposed that the 'context of discovery' within which imagination plays a role be distinguished from the 'context of justification' which concerns how a theory connects with evidence. They lauded Einstein for ostensibly bringing into the open a kind of deep-lying conventionality or partial arbitrariness in all theoretical thought. Popper treated Einstein's prodigious imagination as a pure form of negative freedom – a power to 'conjecture'. Popper insisted that the defining strength of Einstein's theoretical proclamations was that they could be empirically tested. Only when a quest for empirical refutation of a conjecture instead turned up novel empirical agreement with it was such an imagining in any way 'corroborated'. Even if endlessly corroborated, however, its status would forever remain that of a conjecture. To insist otherwise, Popper insisted, is 'inductivist', whereas when Einstein helped us to see that no less a figure than Newton had erred, Einstein had in Popper's view helped to demonstrate the hopelessness of 'inductivism'. Popper's anti-inductivist stance essentially deprives us of the very category of evidence for a theory. Certainly it implies that no evidence at all can support an imaginative 'leap', i.e. the act of 'conjecture'. Kuhn, for his part, did acknowledge that Einstein's acts of imagination were synthetic. But Kuhn suggested that, for this very reason, Einstein's theories could neither engage rationally with predecessor conceptions nor claim in their favour any of the evidence that the predecessor conceptions enjoyed in their support. Like the positivists and like Popper, Kuhn in effect recognised in Einstein only a negative kind of spontaneity or imaginative freedom.

When addressing themselves thus to the spectacular example that Einstein set, the positivists, Popper, and Kuhn, simply did not know what they were talking about. They are, however, scarcely to be blamed for their ignorance. To know what they were talking about they would have needed to fathom Einstein's scientific imagination. And that is a large and difficult task. Indeed with the best will in the world even Einstein scholars were largely at sea with respect to it for the longest while. This was so partly because the primary source materials, which are far from complete, had long remained in disarray and largely inaccessible to most. There is also so very much that Einstein scholars must know about, much of it difficult, if they are to achieve needed insights into their chosen subject. No wonder then that, in the absence of any published Collected Works, the scholars that there were worked largely alone and seldom achieved definitive conclusions.

Fortunately in Einstein scholarship the tide has now turned. Contemporary workers in the field evince not only unsurpassed historical acumen and knowledgeability, but also a salutary and well deserved *esprit de corps*. (See for example Howard and Stachel (eds) 1998.) They work within an elite scholarly community that is making long awaited but outstanding progress, and they know it. What they know, with palpable clarity, is the mind of a scientific genius. And they know that in order to have achieved this they have needed to combine their own many strengths, for it has been a many-sided task for them to get their heads ever more deeply into the science as well as the wider circumstances in which Einstein was immersed and thus into the activity of his own mind. The Collected Works so far published (commencing with Volume I, published in 1987), and the wisdom accumulated by the massive editorial enterprise that those publications represent, stands clearly as a necessary condition for the excellent work now being produced.

I believe that the greatest contribution from all this recent scholarly advancement is in what it shows us about Einstein's almost unearthly freedom of thought.

We learn much both about the provenance of this spirit of his, and about how it expressed itself scientifically. Most importantly, we see in detail how *positive*, that is to say, how emphatically rationally *responsible* his freedom was. Einstein gathered to himself a prodigious body of received thought and evidence in physics and knew from the outset that it failed to hold together as well as it might. He sought to limn what was most sure in the extant facets of his field, and to employ just such insights in order to probe what was either most sure or most problematic in other of its extant facets. Such efforts were supremely creative, but that is not to say that they were supremely conjectural. On the contrary, all such efforts engaged with extant evidence in the most responsible way possible. Not many even in Einstein's field and in Einstein's day could fathom this or thus appreciate his genius. It is little wonder then that philosophers of science such as Popper could be so wrong concerning Einstein.

6 Popper

Popper lauds the example of Einstein (perhaps most famously in his 'Science: Conjectures and Refutations', in 1972b, pp. 33–65, but also at numerous other places throughout Popper's writings). Yet Popper is more or less bound by his conception of science to say that Einstein was without any evidence for his general theory of relativity between the time when he first enunciated it (late in 1915) and when it received its first empirical corroboration (in Eddington's eclipse observations of 1919). Or at least, for Popper to say otherwise he would need to take the known anomalous perihelion precession of Mercury as a relevant phenomenon against which to 'test' Einstein's theory. If Popper were to take the historical facts this way, then he could construe Einstein's 1916 explaining of the anomaly as a first empirical corroboration of Einstein's theory. So he could say that that first empirical corroboration came in 1916 rather than 1919. But Popper would still have to say that at the theory's inception Einstein as yet had no evidence for it. Should we agree with Popper about this? Most certainly not. Thanks to the recent scholarship that I briefly discussed above, we now know enough about Einstein's work leading up to 1915 to be able to dismiss such a suggestion as an outright howler. To appreciate Einstein's work at all well, is to see that when he advanced the general theory of relativity it was *already* richly supported by evidence. The theory Einstein enunciated in late 1915 was the culmination of years of arduous work. At every step of the way, Einstein had shown the utmost concern about evidence – about how it stacked up for various parts of existing theory, and thus about which parts of existing theory were the most sure and which were not. Consequently evidence spoke richly in all the considerations that shaped his new theory and that dictated its final form. This is not to say that in late 1915 Einstein knew his new theory infallibly, but it is to say that in relation to its predecessor, Newton's theory, it already had very much the upper hand. (For, in ways spearheaded by Einstein, the physics community already at this time possessed clear knowledge that Newton's gravitational theory is false, in among other ways by contravening the limitations on the speed of causal signalling implied by Einstein's special theory of relativity.) One can put the point about the evidence facing Einstein in late 1915 more graphically by considering that it is only happenstance that the solar system contains an inner planet like Mercury, and only happenstance that Earth has a moon that nicely eclipses the sun. Suppose that neither of these things had been the case. This would not have precluded Einstein's doing all the work he did. He could still have enunciated his theory. And moreover, that theory would have gradually been accepted as an appropriate replacement for Newton's. Such acceptance would have come as a widening circle of physicists came to understand what had compelled Einstein to formulate it as he did.

Popper is best known for his attempt to demarcate science from non-science in terms of the criterion of falsifiability. Thus, *criticism* is central to his conception of science. But part and parcel of his emphasis in effect upon a scientist's *negative* freedom of theoretical imagination, is a kind of programmatic blindness to the *constructive* aspects of criticism that I have sought to emphasise above. The examples above, by which I have illustrated that these aspects are important in science, also illustrate that, in order to appreciate these aspects, you need to get your head well and truly into the science. This can be an enormously demanding task, as the tremendous effort that is required in order to bring Einstein scholarship to a state of reasonable maturity and clarity helps to illustrate. Philosophy of science tends of course to look for topic-neutral methodological understanding of science. In the early days of analytic philosophy of science, philosophers would illustrate their ostensibly topic-neutral views about the very nature of science with all-swans-are-white type examples that have nothing to do with the actual working of any science. Popper, for example, often wrote this way (e.g. 1972a pp. 68–9; 422ff.). Popper sought to supply a topic-neutral understanding of the demarcation between science and non-science. I believe that it is important to question whether this is the right approach.

As a consequence perhaps of his quest for a topic-neutral understanding of what makes a science a science, Popper cleaves to relatively simple units of analysis in his thinking about science and its method. Popper holds that insofar as a theory is *scientific* and *true*, it *accurately predicts what we observe*. Thus Popper adopts as his units of analysis for investigating science principally *theory*, *observation* and *prediction*. (Thus at 1972a pp. 42–3 previously cited, Popper introduces the example 'All ravens are black' and writes that the 'theories of natural science, and especially what we call natural laws, have the logical form of strictly universal statements'. At 1972a pp. 422 ff. previously cited, he uses 'All swans are white' to illustrate his frequently made point about the theory-ladenness of observation. Notice, incidentally, that, *pace* Popper, the logical form of many actual scientific laws is vastly richer than that of a simple generalisation. Newton's second law of motion, $F = ma$, for example, states that the respective, continuously variable quantities F, m and a stand in a steadfast functional relationship to one another. To unpack the logical burden of this would require many quantifiers and much nesting of quantifiers, a fact that is well known to us ever since a very rich logical analysis proved to be required of the concept of a continuum. To reckon by empirical means with the phenomena that we colligate under concepts such as F, m and a, is likewise something vastly richer practically and more sophisticated logically than 'observation', theory-laden or no.)

I should say on the basis of the examples I have discussed in preceding sections that in order to make Popper's views about science properly serviceable we need at least to replace 'accurately predicts' by 'concertedly harmonises' and 'what we observe' by 'phenomena'. A theory, insofar as it is *scientific* and *true*, *concertedly harmonises phenomena*. In saying this I have in mind both that a phenomenon is as far different from what we might observe as concerted harmonisation is from mere accuracy of prediction, and that the differences are very similar. Phenomena often have a richness far and away beyond what can be brought under simple observation, yet phenomena also possess robust consilience features which remark a kind of harmony in what they draw together. A good example of a very low-level phenomenon is *that this (something) is a moraine*. Somewhat higher-level is *that two (specific) far-separated moraines are quite utterly alike in constitution*. Still higher-level again is the phenomenon *that there is consilience among the morainal phenomena* of the second mentioned sort: they point to identical conclusions about the former juxtaposition of two now separated land masses. Colligating a phenomenon in the first place and concertedly harmonising phenomena with other phenomena and thereby explaining them are highly related activities. And were we to cleave in our thinking about science solely to the ideas of theory, observation and prediction, we should be able to make out well neither what it is to detect a phenomenon nor what it is to harmonise phenomena. Key to the understanding of consilience and thus harmonisation is the Newtonian notion of deductions from phenomena.

(Notice that unless the logical form of principles with which one is dealing is richer than that of singly quantified universal generalisations, deductions from phenomena will not be possible. To take a trivial example, in order to deduce from the phenomenon of this F's being G that all Fs are Gs, we need some such background principle as that if any F is G then they all are. Such a background principle involves two quantifiers rather than one – namely, $\exists x(Fx \wedge Gx) \rightarrow \forall y(Fy \rightarrow Gy)$. Our thinking is always already brimming with principles of the requisite logical richness for deductions from phenomena to be made; but this fact is obscured completely by philosophers' concentration on 'All swans are white' examples. For if all background principles were of no greater logical richness than a simple generalisation, deductions from phenomena could never be made.)

Most phenomena for which science seeks systematic explanation are delineated by experimental means. Measurement, the practical activity of deducing a theoretical conclusion from empirical data, typically enters into the experimental work through which a phenomenon is delineated. And similar deductive linkages running upwards to theory from empirical considerations (rather than the other way around as in prediction-making) are to be found even in the highest reaches of scientific theory. I have illustrated this above by briefly discussing the work of Aristarchus, Harvey, Wegener, Newton and Einstein.

In order to comprehend scientific activity we therefore need a robust understanding of the relation between theory and practice. To have too intellectualist a leaning, that is, too singular an interest in theory rather than practice, would quite prevent our adequately comprehending what science is or how it works. Science is crucially about doing and making, not only thinking, because it is crucially an experimental activity, directed to measurement. The rationality of scientific theorising ineluctably connects with that of a wider kind of scientific agency.

Popper's notorious anti-inductivism epitomises his own highly intellectualist stance. He solves to his own satisfaction the problem of induction by suggesting that our inferences are never inductive. We are to hold theories always tentatively. Their successful 'corroboration' simply remarks their *past* success. But as has been pointed out by many critics of Popper, Popper cannot extract from this conception a defensible account of why we depend on science to inform our practical decision-making. Yet my point very much is that this directly indicts the account of science in itself. For science is an enormously practically directed activity, based as it is on measurement and experiment.

A science that is flourishing is like an agent who is together. Popper's anti-inductivism makes it impossible to understand how an agent could count as rationally well sorted out, in acting one rather than another way towards future contingencies based on past experience. Thus Popper is at a loss to say what it would be for an agent to be together. For related reasons he cannot tell us well what it is for a science to flourish.

Science flourishes under the influence of responsible people. In science, similarly to the wider practical sphere, responsible people seek the most measured way to understand their situation. A truly measured understanding is thick with arguments in support of every last belief. To achieve such an understanding is richly synthetic – and science has become systematically good at progressing towards this aim. I have examined some of those successes in my discussion of Aristarchus, Harvey, Wegener, Newton and Einstein. Yet when Popper considered the nature of science, he was predisposed by his overly intellectualist orientation to misunderstand the nature of measurement, and thus to fall into confusion about what makes science reasonable. Measurement is not, as Popper invites us to think, merely a way to bring theory face-to-face with a potentially falsifying 'observation'.

The epitome of this confusion about science is the infamous 'problem of induction' which Popper made so central to his account. I have here endeavoured to deflate this problem by discussing science in action. Such action involves always a rich background of already theoretical thinking. The supposed problem of induction takes hold, however, only when one artificially considers what might be the route rationally to one's first-ever theoretical belief. In active settings in

science where there inevitably is a rich background of already theoretical thinking, inferences to new theories proceed often under the support of deductions, as
my examples have shown. The deductions are of a sort that Popper considered
impossible: deductions from phenomena. *Pace* Popper, scientists must, as a matter
of their measurement-oriented practice, consider what aspects of their background thinking are most sure, and what are not. They cannot treat the whole
edifice as equally tentative, as all a conjecture. A telling measurement will
employ only the surest elements of the background to help deduce a new theoretical conclusion from the phenomena. Thus in all the examples I have considered
above, the virtue of the inference lay in part in how innocuous seeming were the
background assumptions which allowed the deduction to proceed. If all aspects
of theory were forever totally tentative there could be nothing like a telling
measurement. Yet my examples from science show that this is not the case, and
in this way they impugn the anti-inductivist conception of science that Popper
advanced.

Notes

1 I suspect, but do not know for sure, that this way of putting the figures is apocryphal.
What I suspect is that we moderns know that the angle is 89°50′ only because we have
worked back to that from our knowledge from other sources that the sun is roughly
400 times further away from Earth than the moon is. (I do know that it was only by
careful eighteenth-century observations simultaneously from opposite hemispheres of
the earth of a transit of Venus that astronomers first estimated well the absolute distance to the sun. Yet the absolute distance to the moon had been estimated well even
in ancient times, by the use of parallax. Taken together these facts imply that the relative distances of the moon and sun are better known by first determining the
respective absolute distances, than by considering as Aristarchus did the phases of the
moon.) There is of course no great technical difficulty in the way of precisely determining an astronomical angle to be 89°50′; what is difficult, however, is determining
with the requisite precision when it is that the moon is exactly half full. To the
unaided eye there is, I suspect, no picking between degrees of fulness of the moon half
a percentage or so around the 50 per cent mark, especially given the roughness of the
terminator (the line between light and dark) due to cratering. If I were sure that a
human observer could not with precision determine that the moon becomes half full
when it is at an angle of 89°50′ to the sun, then I would have still another complaint
to make against the typical castigation of Aristarchus for his allegedly uncareful estimation of this angle. I none the less concede that had Aristarchus put his mind to it
he might have determined the angle more accurately than he did.
2 It was not on the basis of such a deduction that Wegener initially formed the view that
the continents have moved. But the question in front of us is not how Wegener initially formed this conception, but rather how he inferred that it is true. For what it is
worth, Wegener himself reports (see the Introduction to his 1966 [1929]) that he initially formed this view by inspection of the apparent conformity of the coastlines on
opposite sides of the Atlantic Ocean. It was not until years later that he felt he had
good evidence to believe that it is true. When I say that Wegener deduced this conception from evidence (by the aid of various very innocuous seeming background
theoretical assumptions), I do not mean to imply that this was how he 'discovered'
or first formed that conception. Rather I am concerned with how he warranted that

conception, and I say that he did so by a variety of mutually supporting deductions from phenomena.

3 This assertion is pace Popper, who with Pierre Duhem, Albert Einstein and others, claims that Newton had a mistaken understanding of his own methodology, and in particular was wrong to suppose that he had performed deductions from phenomena. See, for example, Popper's 1972b, p. 185; or his 1979, p. 357.

4 Workers on Newton's methodology who have championed the view that he did indeed deduce his conclusions from phenomena include Jon Dorling, Clark Glymour, William Harper, George Smith, and (with qualifications) Howard Stein.

5 The basis on which I say that Newton was clearly and explicitly fallibilist about his method and the assumptions, including Euclidean geometry, underwriting it, is the following. We know (from William Harper and others) that, by wielding these assumptions, Newton showed, by geometrical demonstration, how (holding fixed, as assumptions, both Euclidean geometry and the laws of motion) phenomena such as those embraced within Kepler's Laws can measure the value of some theoretical parameter, thus constraining the form of some high-level theoretical principle. The laws of motion that help to underwrite these deductions of bits of theory from phenomena or complexes of empirical evidence, Newton calls 'axioms' of his system, fully recognising their role as background assumptions in all his reasoning. For Newton their basis is, in part, in experiments, but remains as well in a much broader aspect empirical. The generality and successes of the investigations that may proceed from them are, for Newton, the proper measure of their warrant. It is remarkable that for Newton not just his mechanical axioms are empirical. Even geometry is based on principles that are 'brought from without', 'founded in mechanical practice', and presumably always subject to revision if ever that proves to be a condition for advancing to 'some truer method' in physics or natural philosophy (see the Preface to the *Principia* – Newton 1934 [1687], pp. xvii–xviii). For Newton, all items of presumed knowledge are thus tentative and subject to the demand to give ever improved results. Even the most basic assumptions or highly prized forms of argumentation are subject to revision with the advance of knowledge. From the vantage point provided by his own successes, Newton says (ibid.) that 'the whole burden of philosophy seems to consist in this – from the phenomena of motions to investigate the forces of nature, and then from the forces to demonstrate the other phenomena.' But this prescription for philosophy (or, as we would say, physics) with its attendant commitments to geometrical principles, definitions and axioms of motion, is not and can never be something settled. The method thus prescribed 'seems' from its success so far to be 'the best way of arguing which the Nature of Things admits of' (Newton 1979 [1704], p. 404), but Newton is tentative about this. That 'the best way of arguing' depends on 'the Nature of Things' means that method itself must be empirically learned. Newton has reasons to recommend his method, but is well aware that further discovery may bring about its improvement or replacement. 'I hope,' Newton writes (1934 [1687], p. xviii), that 'the principles here laid down will afford light either to this or some truer method of philosophy'. We see, then, that Newton is in these respects an empiricist so radical that he sees geometry, and even method itself, as ultimately empirically based. If by his preferred method nature proves comprehensible, that fact is incomprehensible, because brute, because contingent and discoverable only empirically.

References

Aristarchus. 1981 [1913; c. 270 BCE] *On the Sizes and Distances of the Sun and the Moon*, Thomas Heath (trans.), in Thomas Heath, *Aristarchus of Samos, the Ancient Copernicus*, New York: Dover.

Aristotle. 1984. *The Complete Works of Aristotle: the Revised Oxford Translation*. Jonathan Barnes (ed.), two volumes, Princeton, NJ: Princeton University Press.

Cartan, Elie. 1923. 'Sur les veriétés à connexion affine et la théorie de la relativité generalisée', in *Annales Ecole Normal Superieure*, vol. 40, pp. 325–412, and vol. 41, pp. 1–25.

Cartwright, Nancy. 1983. *Nature's Capacities and Their Measurement*, Oxford: Clarendon Press.

Dorling, Jon. 1995 [1987]. 'Einstein's Methodology of Discovery was Newtonian Deduction from Phenomena', in Jarrett Leplin (ed.), *The Creation of Ideas in Physics: Studies for a Methodology of Theory Construction*, The University of Western Ontario Series in Philosophy of Science, vol. 55, Dordrecht, Boston: Kluwer Academic Publishers.

Duhem, Pierre. 1954. *The Aim and Structure of Physical Theory*. P. P. Wiener (trans.), Princeton, NJ: Princeton University Press.

Einstein, Albert. 1923 [1905]. 'On the Electrodynamics of Moving Bodies', in H. A. Lorentz, A. Einstein, H. Minkowski and H. Weyl (with notes by A. Sommerfeld), *The Principle of Relativity: A Collection of Original Papers on the Special and General Theory of Relativity*, W. Perrett and G. B. Jeffery (trans.), London: Methuen.

Einstein, Albert. 1954. *Ideas and Opinions*, New York: Bonanza Books.

Einstein, Albert. 1959. 'Autobiographical Notes', in P. A. Schilpp (ed.), *Albert Einstein: Philosopher-Scientist*, New York: Harper Torchbooks.

Einstein, Albert. 1991 [1950]. *Out of My Later Years*, Don Mills, Ontario: Citadel Press.

Einstein, Albert and Infeld, L. 1938. *The Evolution of Physics*, New York: Simon and Schuster.

Glymour, C. 1980. *Theory and Evidence*, Princeton, NJ: Princeton University Press.

Hacking, I. 1983. *Representing and Intervening*, Cambridge: Cambridge University Press.

Harper, William. 1991. 'Newton's Classic Deductions from Phenomena', in *PSA 1990*, vol. 2, East Lansing, MI: Philosophy of Science Association.

Harper, William. 2002. 'Newton's Argument for Universal Gravitation', in I. Bernard Cohen and George E. Smith (eds), *The Cambridge Companion to Newton*, Cambridge: Cambridge University Press, pp. 174–201.

Harvey, William. 2001 [1628]. On the Motion of the Heart and Blood in Animals, vol. XXXVIII, Part 3, The Harvard Classics. New York: P. F. Collier and Son, 1909–14; Bartleby.com, 2001. http://www.bartleby.com/38/3/

Howard, Don and John Stachel (eds). 1998. *Einstein: The Formative Years, 1879–1909*, Boston, Basel, Berlin: Birkhäuser.

Kant, Immanuel. 1996 [1781, 1787]. *Critique of Pure Reason*, Werner S. Pluhar (trans.), Indianapolis: Hackett Publishing Company.

Kuhn, Thomas S. 1996 [1962]. *The Structure of Scientific Revolutions*, Chicago and London: The University of Chicago Press.

Lakatos, Imre. 1970. 'Falsification and the Methodology of Scientific Research Programmes', in I. Lakatos and A. Musgrave (eds), *Criticism and the Growth of Knowledge*, Cambridge: Cambridge University Press, pp. 91–196.

Lakatos, Imre. 1977 [1973]. 'Science and Pseudo-science', in I. Lakatos, *Philosophical Papers*, vol. 1. Cambridge: Cambridge University Press, pp. 1–7.

Laymon, Ronald. 1983. 'Newton's Demonstration of Universal Gravitation and Philosophical Theories of Confirmation', in J. Earman (ed.), *Testing Scientific Theories*, vol. X of the Minnesota Studies in the Philosophy of Science, Minneapolis: University of Minnesota Press.

Newton, Isaac. 1934 [1687]. *Philosophiae Naturalis Principia Mathematica*, F. Cajori's revision of the A. Motte translation, Berkeley, CA: University of California Press.

Newton, Isaac. 1962 [n.d.]. 'De Gravitatione et aequipondio fluidorum et solidorum'; original Latin and English translation in A. Rupert Hall and Marie Boas Hall (eds), *Unpublished Scientific Papers of Isaac Newton*, Cambridge: Cambridge University Press.

Newton, Isaac. 1979 [1704]. *Opticks*, New York: Dover.

Norton, John. 1984. 'How Einstein Found His Field Equations: 1912–1915', in J. L. Heilbron (ed.), *Historical Studies in the Physical Sciences*, Berkeley, CA: University of California Press, vol. 14, pp. 253–316.

Pais, Abraham. 1982. *Subtle is the Lord: The Science and Life of Albert Einstein*, Oxford: Oxford University Press.

Popper, Karl R. 1972a [1934]. *The Logic of Scientific Discovery*, London: Hutchinson and Co.

Popper, Karl R. 1972b [1963]. *Conjectures and Refutations: The Growth of Scientific Knowledge*, London and Henley: Routledge and Kegan Paul.

Popper, Karl R. 1979 [1972]. *Objective Knowledge: An Evolutionary Approach*, revised edition, Oxford: The Clarendon Press.

Smith, George E. 2002. 'The Methodology of the *Principia*', in I. Bernard Cohen and George E. Smith (eds), *The Cambridge Companion to Newton*, Cambridge: Cambridge University Press, pp. 138–73.

Stachel, John. 1987. 'How Einstein Discovered General Relativity: a Historical Tale with Some Contemporary Morals', in John Stachel, *Einstein from 'B' to 'Z'*, Boston, Basel, Berlin: Birkhäuser, 2001, pp. 293–9.

Stachel, John. 1989. 'Einstein's Search for General Covariance', in John Stachel, *Einstein from 'B' to 'Z'*, Boston, Basel, Berlin: Birkhäuser, 2001, pp. 301–37.

Stein, Howard. 1967. 'Newtonian Space-Time', in *Texas Quarterly*, vol. 10, pp. 175–200, reprinted in R. Palter (ed.), *The Annus Mirabilis of Sir Isaac Newton*, Cambridge, MA: MIT Press, pp. 258–84.

Stein, Howard. 1970. 'On the Notion of Field in Newton, Maxwell, and Beyond', in R. Stuewer (ed.), *Historical and Philosophical Perspectives on Science*, Minnesota Studies in the Philosophy of Science, vol. V, Minneapolis: University of Minnesota Press, pp. 264–87.

Stein, Howard. 1990. 'On Locke, "the great Huygenius, and the incomparable Mr. Newton"', in R. I. G. Hughes and Phillip Barker (eds), *Philosophical Perspectives on Newtonian Science*, Cambridge, MA: MIT Press, pp. 17–47.

Stein, Howard. 1991. '"From the Phenomena of Motions to the Forces of Nature": Hypothesis or Deduction?', in *PSA 1990*, vol. 2, East Lansing, MI: Philosophy of Science Association, pp. 209–22.

Wegener, Alfred. 1966 [1929]. *The Origin of Continents and Oceans*, John Biram (trans.), New York: Dover.

4

THE MANY FACES OF POPPER'S METHODOLOGICAL APPROACH TO PREDICTION

Wenceslao J. Gonzalez

Karl Popper is presumably the most influential author in methodology of science in the second half of the twentieth century. In particular, his views on scientific prediction, both in natural sciences and in social sciences, have had a wide influence. Moreover, his thought has directly affected the methodology of economics, due to his influence upon very well known specialists, such as Mark Blaug. Given these factors, the analysis in this chapter will follow four steps in order to clarify Popper's conception of scientific prediction. It will examine: (i) the three methodological levels of his approach regarding prediction; (ii) the role of prediction in his general methodology of science; (iii) prediction in his methodology of social sciences: the problem of historicism; and (iv) his methodological conception of prediction and economics.

* * *

Methodology is the crucial subject in Popper's studies of science: he always puts special weight on the analysis of the growth of scientific knowledge. But, generally, the methodological component is connected with other elements of science (language, structure, knowledge, activity, aims, . . .). Therefore, it is convenient to start with an *initial characterisation* of Popper's views on *scientific prediction*: semantically, he distinguishes 'prediction' and 'prophecy', especially in social sciences (Popper 1959); logically, prediction appears always in a deductivist sphere (i.e., a theory can have a predictive content and is structured in a deductive way), because he does not accept the scientific character of induction; epistemologically, prediction is linked to future knowledge – for this reason corroboration has no predictive import;[1] methodologically, prediction is a feature of the growth of scientific knowledge (a mark of scientific progress); and axiologically, prediction is a characteristic aim of science. Here the analysis will emphasise the methodological aspects of prediction.

1 Three different methodological levels

There are at least three different *methodological levels* that can be analysed in Popper's approach: (1) the general methodology of science, where prediction appears as a usual element of scientific theories and one that is relevant for testing theories; (2) the methodology of social sciences as a whole, where he develops a strong criticism of the tendency articulated around the key role of prediction, which he calls 'historicism' (and which has two different kinds: dualistic and monistic); and (3) the methodology of economics, a field that was not in the front line of his research (even though he was Professor of a university centre devoted to that realm: the London School of Economics[2]).

Prima facie, the analysis of Popper's approach to prediction seems to offer a paradoxical status: on the one hand, he stresses the role of prediction within the general methodology of science, because he considers that it is a relevant element for the progress of scientific knowledge (i.e., it can be used to test scientific theories); and, on the other hand, he criticises the role of historical prediction as a scientific element within social sciences, as can be seen in his writings on 'historicism', in which he rejects the existence of a logical basis for scientific prediction in historical settings. (Cf. Popper 1991 [1957], p. vi.) Consequently, this latter aspect affects economics, because this subject only can be seen within the realm of social sciences (even though some authors, such as Philip Mirowski, think that classical economics is built up following the schemes of Newtonian physics – cf. his 1989).

This tension between prediction in the general methodology of science and prediction in the methodology of social sciences can be seen also in the *wider framework* that underlies Popper's approach. In effect, he offers two different perspectives for the methodological problems: on the one hand, he holds the very well known position of *falsificationism*,[3] which is conceived to grasp the growth of scientific knowledge – the method of science in general, although it is frequently focused on the case of natural science; and, on the other hand, he defends a specific method for social science: the *logic of situation*, because he thinks that the proper method for the social sciences is based on rational decision-making in situation.

Among the elements to show the *divergence* in Popper between the general methodological framework – falsificationism – and the specific methodological approach to social sciences – the logic of situation – are two important features which he attributes to the latter: (i) that the method of explanation of the logic of situation is *unique* in the social sciences insofar as it is the way to grasp social events;[4] and (ii) that the situational analysis comes from a specific field, because it is the *method of economic analysis*: 'the analysis of situations, the situational logic, plays a very important part in social life as well as in the social sciences. It is, in fact, the method of economic analysis' (Popper 1992a [1945], p. 97).

To accept the existence of that *dualistic* wider framework in Popper's methodological approach – falsificationism versus the logic of situation – is very damaging for his conception of the *unity of method* in science. In effect, accepting such a divergence between the falsificationism and the logic of situation, it seems rather obvious that *de facto* natural sciences and social sciences will adopt different methodologies. In the case of falsificationism, there is no general principle which can be accepted always and by all, because *fallibilism* is essential to the growth of scientific knowledge; whereas in the case of logic of situation there is a *principle of rationality* which cannot be removed and which throws light on what happens in society.[5]

2 The role of prediction in Popper's general methodology

Within the general methodology of science, Popper pays attention to prediction from his first book – *Die beiden Grundprobleme der Erkenntnistheorie* (1979 [1932–3]) – through to his later writings. Specifically, it is a topic which appears in his main works: *The Logic of Scientific Discovery* (1968 [1959/1935]), *Conjectures and Refutations* (1989a [1963]), and *Objective Knowledge* (1989b [1979]), the books which reveal turning points in his career. These changes show that he does not offer a single conception of falsificationism. Moreover, there are – in my judgment – three successive conceptions of *falsificationism* in Popper: (a) a logico-methodological approach, which is clear in the first period (from the 1930s to the 1950s); (b) a methodological view in tune with an evolutionary epistemology, which is pre-eminent in the second period (during the 1960s); and (c) a methodological perspective more open to the ontological component, which is dominant in the third period (from the 1970s to the 1990s).

Each one of these conceptions can be seen in those important books. *The Logic of Scientific Discovery* represents the methodological approach rooted in logic (putting special emphasis in logical procedures such as the *modus tollens*);[6] *Conjectures and Refutations* offers an epistemological view of an evolutionary kind (an adaptive procedure of human knowledge) linked to methodology of falsificationism;[7] and *Objective Knowledge* shows a clear ontological perspective of science.[8] These successive conceptions of falsificationism – the logico-methodological approach, the position linked to an epistemological evolutionary view, and the perspective more ontological – have repercussions on his characterisation of prediction.

Falsificationism – Popper's general methodology of science – is then connected with logic of science, epistemology (i.e., critical rationalism), ontology of science and axiology of science, both in his main books and in other publications of the three main periods of his thought. *De facto*, the problem of scientific prediction appears – in one way or another – throughout all his writings. It can be found in those publications other than his main methodological books or his writings on historicism: 'Indeterminism in Quantum Physics and in Classical Physics' (1950, pp. 117–33 and 173–95), *Unended Quest* (1992b, pp. 24–5, 35, 37–8, 43, 103–4, 117, 121–2, 158, 171–2 and 238 (note 283)), 'Replies to my Critics' (1974, especially pp. 979–80, 997–8, and 1029–30), *The Open Universe: An Argument for*

Indeterminism (1982a, pp. 2, 6–7, 9, 11–12, 14–16, 32, 42, 62–78 and 129), *In Search of a Better World* (1992d, pp. 143–4), *The Myth of the Framework: In Defense of Science and Rationality* (1994, pp. 89, 94, 133, 162–5, 168–9, 173 and 182), or *All Life is Problem Solving* (1999 [1994], pp. 14, 106, 131 and 135).

As is well known, Popper's main book – *The Logic of Scientific Discovery* – offers a deductive method for science. He thinks that basic sentences (such as predictions) are *deducible* from theories: it is from universal statements in conjunction with initial conditions that we *deduce* the singular statement called 'prediction'.[9] Prediction appears as a *test* of a theory: it could be used after the explanations and for theoretical reasons. In effect, 'the theorist is interested in explanations as such, that is to say, in testable explanatory theories: applications and predictions interest him only for theoretical reasons – because they may be used as *tests* of theories' (Popper 1968 [1959/1935], p. 59, note 1). He offers a logico-methodological scheme with a theory–prediction link.

Hilary Putnam maintains that this view is not far from the 'inductivist' account of confirmation. In addition, he considers that the theory–prediction link is not the decisive feature of a scientific theory:

> it is because theories imply basic sentences in the sense of 'imply' associated with deductive logic . . . that, according to Popper, theories and general laws can be falsifiable by basic sentences. And this same link is the heart of the 'inductivist' schema. Both schemes say: *look at the predictions that a theory implies; see if those predictions are true.* My criticism is . . . a criticism of this link, of this point on which Popper and the 'inductivist' agree. I claim: in a great many important cases, scientific theories do not imply predictions at all.
>
> (Putnam 1974, p. 225)

Conjectures and Refutations combines an evolutionary epistemology and a falsificationist methodology. Thus, if the progress of science is to continue, we need positive successes in addition to successful refutations:

> we must . . . produce theories that entail new predictions, especially predictions of new effects, new testable consequences, suggested by the new theory and never thought of before. Such a new prediction was that planets would under certain circumstances deviate from Kepler's laws; or that light, in spite of its zero mass, would prove to be subject to gravitational attraction (that is, Einstein's eclipse-effect). Another example is Dirac's prediction that there will be an anti-particle for every elementary particle. New predictions of these kinds must not only be produced, but they must also be reasonably often corroborated by experimental evidence, I contend, if scientific progress is to continue.
>
> (Popper 1989a [1963], p. 243)

Objective Knowledge stresses the indeterministic status of both natural and social reality, which directly affects the problem of scientific prediction:

> evolutionary processes or major evolutionary changes are as unpredict-able as historical processes or major historical changes. I hold this view because I am strongly inclined towards an indeterministic view of the world, somewhat more radical than Heisenberg's: my indeterminism includes the thesis that even classical physics is indeterministic, and is thus more like that of Charles Sanders Peirce, or that of Alfred Landé. And I think that evolution proceeds largely probabilistically, under constantly changing conditions or problem situations, and that every tentative solution, whether more successful or less successful or even completely unsuccessful, creates a new problem situation.
>
> (Popper 1989b [1979], p. 296)

Common ground for theses successive conceptions of *falsificationism* – the logico-methodological approach, the position link to an epistemological evolutionary view, and the perspective more ontological – is the idea of elimination of error. Falsificationism is a general approach that systematises the method of learning from our mistakes. Popper thinks that his whole view of scientific method

> consists of these four steps:
>
> 1 We select some *problem* – perhaps by stumbling over it.
> 2 We try to *solve* it by proposing a *theory* as a tentative solution.
> 3 Through the *critical discussion of our theories* our knowledge grows by the elimination of some of our errors, and in this way we learn to under-stand our problems, and our theories, and the need for new solutions.
> 4 The critical discussion of even our best theories always reveals new problems.
>
> Or to put these four steps into four words: *problems – theories – criticisms – new problems.*
>
> (Popper 1994, p. 159)

Falsificationism is then set by four main categories, and the one which is most relevant to science is that of error-elimination through criticism: we learn from our mistakes through critical discussion (which includes testability). It is a deduc-tive procedure which uses experience as a negative test (as a means for refutation).

Emphasis on deduction and rejection of induction are two constant features of Popper's general methodology of science. This affects prediction directly, because he does not want to give elbow room to a predictive method based on *induction*:

> Corroboration has no inductive aspect; and the logic of prediction consists, simply, in deducting predictions from hypotheses plus initial

conditions. In other words, the logic of prediction is the ordinary deductive logic and nothing else.

(Popper 1974, p. 1030)

This position assumes that, among the array of generalisations which are compatible with the available observational evidence, there is a *rational basis in favour of
one unrefuted generalisation* (conjecture, hypothesis, . . .) instead of others for use
in a predictive argument.

However, this claim gives rise to some problems, as W. Salmon has pointed out
(1988 [1981]). Predictions are made for various purposes, such as to gain information in the theoretical context, which is useful in the *evaluation* of scientific
theories – to test a theory – or to *make a decision* regarding a practical action
(when the choice of an optimal decision requires the foreknowledge of future
occurrences). This means that prediction is involved in a distinction between
the *theoretical preference* and the *practical preference*. Salmon's emphasis is in the
second case, and he analyses the role of 'corroboration' in it. He considers that
the preferences between generalisations which are to be used in the practical
decision-making context are not as Popper has maintained, because corroboration has not the role which he gives in the practical preference. In other words, it
would be a mistake to defend, as Popper does, that corroboration reports past performance but that '*it could not be used to predict future performance*' (Popper 1992b
[1976], p. 103).

Popper's idea is that statements of *corroboration* of conjectures have no predictive content as such, whereas *general statements* (conjectures, hypotheses, . . .) do
have predictive content. Analysing this view, Salmon holds that the problem is
that there are many general statements (conjectures, hypotheses, . . .)

> which make incompatible predictive claims when conjoined with true
> statements about past and present occurrences. The fact that a general
> statement has predictive content does not mean that what it says is true.
> In order to make a prediction, one must choose a conjecture which has
> predictive content to serve as a premise in a predictive argument. In
> order to make a *rational* prediction . . . one must make a *rational* choice
> of a premise for such an argument. But from our observational evidence
> and from the statements about the corroboration of a given conjecture,
> no predictive appraisal follows.

(Salmon 1988 [1981], p. 119)

Therefore, for the purposes of *practical prediction*, corroboration does not furnish
the rational basis for preference of one conjecture to another.

Induction and prediction appear here as connected problems: if Popper
cannot provide a tenable account of rational prediction, then – despite his
emphasis upon objectivity and rationality of science – we cannot credit him with
having solved the problem of induction. He maintains that 'our corroboration

statements have no predictive import, although they motivate and justify our *preference* for some theory over another' (Popper 1974, pp. 1029–30).

But, in order to have a viable conception of *rational prediction* and an adequate solution to the problem of induction, the point is how corroboration can *justify* such preference of one theory over another.

When the question arises on how to select for the purposes of rational prediction in Popper's theories, his solution is 'we should *prefer* the best tested theory . . . it will be "rational" to choose the best tested theory . . . the best tested theory is one which, in the light of our *critical discussion*, appears to be the best so far' (Popper 1974, p. 1025).

However, he explicitly assures that testing has no *predictive import*. Thus, according to Salmon, it is difficult to see 'how it could be rational to judge theories *for purposes of prediction* in terms of a criterion which is emphatically claimed to be lacking in predictive import' (Salmon 1989 [1981], p. 122).

It seems that we need to distinguish *predictive content* and *predictive import*: even though corroboration statements have no predictive *content*, it does not mean that corroboration has no predictive *import*. For Salmon,

> statements whose consequences refer to future occurrences may be said to have predictive content; rules, imperatives, and directives are totally lacking in predictive content because they do not entail any statements at all. Nevertheless, an imperative – such as 'No smoking, please' – may have considerable predictive import, for it may effectively achieve the goal of preventing the occurrence of smoking in a particular room in the immediate future.
>
> (p. 123)

Continuing with this distinction, even if corroboration is lacking in predictive content, it does have *predictive import* (i.e., corroboration in some cases can provide the basis for deciding which theory – with its predictive content – is to be used to make practical predictions).

Therefore, there is a limit in Popper's general methodology of science: pure deductivism can hardly resolve the problem of rational prediction in contexts of *practical* decision making. Salmon maintains that science is inductive in matters of intellectual curiosity as well as of practical prediction. Moreover, he considers that 'Popper's adherence to the thesis that corroboration can provide a basis for rational prediction rests upon his realism, which embodies a version of a principle of uniformity of nature' (p. 124). If this suggestion is correct, we can still legitimately wonder whether Popper's methodology is as far from inductivism as he would have us believe.

After this analysis on prediction in his general methodology of science, it seems that he needs *induction* in order to have a consistent approach (a methodology in tune with his realist ontology) and, in addition, he must alter his view so that it now is that all prediction, aside from that involved in the testing of theories, is restricted to contexts in which practical action is at stake. Science is richer than that, because science gives explanations as well as predictions, and some of the predictions of theoretical science have practical consequences whereas others do not (i.e., in scientific theories predictions can have both theoretical and practical interest, not only in natural sciences but also in social sciences).

3 Prediction in Popper's methodology of social sciences: the problem of historicism

In spite of Popper's well known general methodology of science – falsificationism, which he conceives as valid for any kind of empirical science – there is in his writings another methodology: the *logic of situation*. This approach is specific to the social sciences and introduces important methodological variations in comparison with the general falsificationist framework, because it relies upon a basically stable *rationality principle* (rather than upon the re-examinability of a potentially falsifiable theory[10]) and it is grounded in a *specific* case of science (the economic analysis).

Situational logic and *situational analysis* are two expressions which Popper uses to reconstruct the problem situation in which the acting person finds himself or herself and also to show how and why his or her action constituted a solution of the problem as he or she saw it. The method of situational analysis is conceived as an objectivist method: it looks for the critical discussion of our tentative solutions (i.e., it seeks our attempts to reconstruct the situation). It assumes the principle of acting appropriately to the situation, a rationality principle understood as a *methodological postulate* instead of an empirical or psychological assertion that the man in most cases acts rationally. (Cf. Popper's 'Models, Instruments and Truth: The Status of the Rationality Principle in the Social Sciences', in his 1994. See especially p. 169.)

Noretta Koertge has given us a systematic restatement of Popper's method of situational analysis: (a) *description of situation*: agent A is in a situation of type C; (b) *analysis of situation*: in a situation like C, the appropriate thing to do is X; (c) *rationality principle*: agents always act appropriately to their situations; and (d) *explanandum*: therefore A did X. (Cf. Koertge 1975, p. 440; Caldwell 1994, p. 142.) In addition, Koertge offers us a more extensive version of situational logic as Popper's proper method to follow in the social sciences:

1 *Description of problem-situation:* A thought he was in a problem-situation of type C.

2 *Dispositional law:* For all such problem-situations A would use appraisal rule R.

3 *Analysis of situation:* The result of appraising C using R is X.

4 *Description of the agent's competence:* A did not make a mistake in applying R to C.

5 *Rationality appraisal principle:* All agents appraise their situations in a rational manner.

6 *Explanandum-1:* (Therefore) A concluded that X was the rational thing to do.

7 *Rationality principle:* People always act on the outcome of their rational appraisals.

8 *Explanandum-2:* (Therefore) A did X.

(Koertge 1975, p. 440. Cf. Caldwell 1994, p. 142)

Mark Blaug, who labels himself an 'unrepentant Popperian', has made a devastating criticism of the 'situational analysis', which leads him to the conclusion of incompatibility with the terms of the (general) methodology of falsificationism. (Blaug 1994, p. 113.) For him, what is surprising is that (1) Popper claimed situational analysis to be *one* legitimate mode of explanation in the social sciences; (2) he admitted that situational analysis was false as a *universal law* of economic behaviour, but nevertheless insisted that it should be maintained as an unexamined 'metaphysical' principle; and (3) he virtually implied that it should be retained because situational analysis had shown itself to be *fruitful* in the past, particularly in economics (i.e., it resembles the concept of 'rational choice' understood as the view that economic behaviour is simply individual maximising behaviour subject to constraints) (cf. Blaug 1994, p. 112).

According to Blaug, these three elements are not compatible with Popper's falsificationism:

(1) contradicts his 'unity of science' thesis, the doctrine that there is no difference in the structure of explanation in the natural and the social sciences and that all sciences must validate their theories in the same way. Likewise, (2) actually endorses one particular 'immunising stratagem' in the face of refutations of rationality, namely to retain the rationality principle and to place the blame for refutation on, say, the constraints, the limited information available to agents or any other feature of the test in question. Finally, and most damningly, (3) provides an inductive argument on behalf of rational choice models of behaviour – they have worked well in the past and so might work well in the future – which flies in the face of everything that Popper has ever written on induction.

(Blaug 1994, pp. 112–13)

This logic of situation and the topics of the methodology of social sciences are central in Popper's writings from 1944 to 1957, when he published *The Open Society and Its Enemies* (1992a [1945]) and *The Poverty of Historicism* (1991 [1957]). Both books belong to the period of predominance of the logico-methodological approach. Thus, when Popper deals with the problem of prediction in social sciences, his main focus of attention lies in the logical basis of prediction. More-over, this is the main reason which he gives to the refutation of 'historicism': '*I have shown that, for strictly logical reasons, it is impossible for us to predict the future course of history*' (Popper 1991 [1957], p. vi.). He insists (p. viii) upon the purely *logical* character of this methodological criticism:

> this argument, being purely logical, applies to scientific predictors of any complexity, including 'societies' of interacting predictors. But this means that no society can predict, scientifically, its future state of knowledge.

For Popper, the historicist doctrines of method are responsible for the unsatisfac-tory state of the theoretical social sciences (other than economic theory). He calls 'historicism'

> an approach to the social sciences which assumes that *historical prediction* is their principal aim, and which assumes that this aim is attainable by discovering the 'rhythms' or the 'patterns', the 'laws' or the 'trends' that underlie the evolution of history.
>
> (1991 [1957], p. 3)

Thus, he links historicism and prediction both in terms of social laws and in a softer sense of rhythms, patterns and trends. But he recognises that it is a con-structed position: 'I hope that . . . I have succeeded in building up a position really worth attacking' (ibid.).[11] In addition, sometimes he combines elements of 'historicism' and 'historism', which are two different views of social affairs. (Cf. Gonzalez 1984, especially pp. 131–2.)

Historicism is a technical term in Popper's writings. (On the terminological problems related to that methodological use, cf. Donagan 1974, especially pp. 905–9.) Moreover, among historians it has a quite different meaning (cf. Gonzalez 1996), closer to what Popper calls 'historism' (Popper 1992a [1945], vol. 2, pp. 208 and 214). He conceives historicism as a view of the social sciences in which *historical prediction* is the principal aim, and that aim is attainable by dis-covering what underlies the evolution of history (laws, rhythms, patterns or trends). (Cf. Popper 1991 [1957], p. 3.) Thus, it is a perspective based on predic-tion which can altogether affect the interpretation of social sciences. The main features of his conception of 'historicism' are: (i) its specific realm is the sphere of *necessity*, because the human being appears to be carrying on towards the future by irresistible forces (1991 [1957], p. 160); (ii) this view possesses a clear method-ological character, which highlights impersonal factors in social change, and it is connected with a *non-relativistic* orientation, which tends to dogmatism (what is true is the 'law of change'); and (iii) this position does not accept the epistemo-logical pluralism, because it assumes a *theoretical framework* to explain and to appraise the historical evolution of society (cf. Gonzalez 1984, p. 114).

Historism is, for Popper, the opposite conception to historicism. In fact, the features which he attributes to 'historism' are quite different from historicism: (a) historism rejects a static view of the social world and criticises the idea of 'human nature' or *ontical structure* of the person (the human being – in the extreme version – does not have freedom: he or she *is freedom*); (b) this approach denies the existence of truth as an absolute value, which leads it towards a methodological *relativism* in the main advocates; and (c) it offers a defence of a *pluralistic epistemological* framework, which impedes the existence of a stable conceptual framework to appraise the contents of social sciences and increases the insistence in the importance of each historical period. (Cf. Gonzalez 1984, p. 110. In economics, the importance of each historical period is emphasised by G. von Schmöller; cf. Gonzalez 1991.) Following this approach, it seems difficult to have scientific prediction in social sciences (among them, economics).

Although historicism and historism present quite different views on the role of prediction in social sciences, the two have common roots in the past: (1) they share an *intellectual humus* in the European context of the eighteenth century and acquire their characteristic profiles during the nineteenth century; (2) both approaches rely upon the idea of change in human affairs, emphasising the *historicity* of the human person as a social being; and (3) they are open to a methodological perspective of social sciences grounded in the history, but they show an important difference: historicism lacks the relativistic approach which is characteristic of historism, and in addition historicism exhibits a tendency towards dogmatism in the explanation of social events. (Cf. Gonzalez 1984, pp. 111–12.)

Concerning historicism – the thesis of *historical prediction* of social affairs as the main aim of social sciences – Popper distinguishes two methodological versions: dualistic ('anti-naturalistic') and monistic ('pro-naturalistic'). The point of separation between them is in the applicability of methods of physics in social sciences: for the dualists the methods of natural science cannot grasp the peculiarities of social sciences, whereas for the monists the methods of physics are applicable in the realm of social phenomena.[12]

This methodological divergence affects the role of prediction. On the one hand, the *dualistic historicism* defends the inexactness of social prediction, due to the complexity of social structure as well as to the interconnection between prediction and the predicted events (cf. Popper 1991 [1957], p. 13), and it accepts the methodological essentialism, which makes social prediction more difficult than natural prediction insofar as this position includes a criticism of the use of quantitative methods in social science (cf. p. 31). On the other hand, the *monistic historicism* insists on the causal analysis for social sciences, which is in tune with the dominant tradition in natural sciences, and it supports the methodological nominalism, where the task of science is only to describe how things behave (instead of penetrating the essence of things in order to explain them) (cf. pp. 28–9).

Both historicisms – dualist and monist – are rejected by Popper as poor methods:

he thinks that they do not bear any fruit. Afterwards, he presents a refutation of historicism in the Preface to *The Poverty of Historicism*, written more than a decade after the original publication of the book in *Economica*.[13] The argument may be summed up as follows: (i) the course of human history is strongly influenced by the growth of human knowledge; (ii) we cannot predict, by rational or scientific methods, the future growth of our scientific knowledge; and (iii) we cannot, therefore, predict the future course of human history (cf. Popper 1991 [1957], pp. vi–vii).

But Popper's strong claims about the predictability of future events in the history of the predictor raise problems about human rationality and the rationality of science itself.[14] According to Peter Clark (1995, p. 153),

> the arguments of the *Poverty of Historicism* to the effect that social trends and forces are unpredictable and that the growth of knowledge is inherently unanticipatable seem to fly in the face of ordinary human experience and apparently throw into doubt the rationality of activities which form the basis of social structures which are fundamental to modern society. Modern developed societies do behave in predictable fashion and we have good reasons for believing that to be so.

(For example, the insurance companies and the government departments spend huge quantities of resources in time and money in trying to anticipate the environment in which they will develop in the future.)

A careful interpretation of Popper's texts against historicism can show us that he does not exclude the *possibility* of prediction in social sciences as such or even that he does not deny its *legitimacy* as a test for the theory (including economic theory). What he clearly rejects is the 'historical prediction' understood as prediction of large-scale social phenomena,[15] such as the society without classes of Marxism or K. Mannheim's predictions for the society as a whole (cf. Gonzalez 1984, pp. 122–3). Furthermore, Popper also rejects the opposite extreme: the exactness of specific predictions in social realms, such as the financial predictions (e.g., the price of shares in the stock market). His main claim is the impossibility of anticipating today *what we shall know only tomorrow*, a position which he considers compatible with predicting that certain developments will happen under certain conditions (cf. his 1991 [1957], p. vii).

Again, this approach has serious problems, because it diminishes the *rationality* of scientific activity. Besides the theoretical reasons in favour of future advancement of science, there are also practical reasons: the major research councils in science appraise research projects and rate them worthy of support (or not if they think that it is impossible in principle to anticipate how that knowledge will grow).

> The rationality of the activities of the science research councils must, in part, hinge upon the correctness of the conception that it is possible to

predict to some extent at least which projects are likely to be successful,
and that fundamentally involves predicting how knowledge will evolve.
(Clark 1995, p. 153)

Therefore, Popper does not succeed in his attempt to refute the possibility of predicting historical developments which may be influenced by the growth of our
knowledge. However, both in terms of theoretical and practical reason, the
intrinsic difficulties of getting an *accurate* prediction of the growth of knowledge,
especially in the realm of social sciences, should be assumed.

4 Popper's methodological conception of prediction and economics

Regarding economics, Popper's methodological views have been influential for
some decades. This influence can be seen through relevant economists. The list
of economists whose methodological writings reveal a Popperian influence
includes well-known authors such as Chris Archibald, Jack Birner, Mark Blaug,
Lawrence Boland, Bruce J. Caldwell, D. Wade Hands, Friedrich Hayek, Terence
W. Hutchison, Joop Klant, Kurt Klappholz, Spiro Latsis and Stanley Wong.[16]
Among these, there are two names which are particularly influential: Mark Blaug,
a historian of economic thought who became especially interested in the
methodology of falsificationism, and Friedrich von Hayek, a winner of the Nobel
Prize in economics who has been influenced by Popper since the 1950s, if not earlier.[17] To some extent, these two authors represent two different perspectives
within the methodology of economics: the broad scope and the restricted scope.
(Cf. Gonzalez 2000, pp. 13–59 and especially pp. 43–56.) In effect, Blaug usually
tries to connect the methodology of economics with the problems of the general
methodology of science, whereas Hayek's primary interest is in the particular
problems of the methodology of economics.

Albeit that Popper has had a clear methodological influence on economists (cf.
de Marchi 1988 and 1992), economics was not a subject of special interest to
him. Nevertheless, his writings on the methodology of social sciences point out
some problems related to economic prediction, such as its *possibility* as scientific
knowledge and its *inexactitude* as social knowledge related to the future. Besides
his specific comments on economic predictions, we should take into account his
approach on the methodology of social sciences – the logic of situation – and his
position in general methodology of science, which is critical of instrumentalism
and keen on realism.

On the first problem of economic predictions – its possibility as scientific
knowledge – he stresses that the argument against historicism does not refute the
possibility of every kind of social prediction: 'it is perfectly compatible with the
possibility of testing social theories – for example, economic theories – by way of
predicting that certain developments will take place under certain conditions'
(Popper 1991 [1957], p. vii). For him, the argument only refutes the possibility of
predicting historical (or economical) developments to the extent to which they

may be influenced by the growth of our knowledge (and that this affects large-scale economic phenomena).

The second issue – the problem of *inexactitude* – arises from the connection between social predictions and the predicted events.[18] He exemplifies it in economics: 'suppose, for instance, it were predicted that the price of shares would rise for three days and then fall. Plainly, everyone connected with the market would sell on the third day, causing a fall of prices on that day and falsifying the prediction' (Popper 1991 [1957], p. 13). This means – for him – that an exact and detailed social scientific prediction (i.e., an accurate economic prediction) is impossible. Moreover, in the connection between social predictions and the predicted events he sees a threat to objectivity and valuation in social sciences. Thus, 'it may, in an extreme case, even *cause* the happening it predicts: the happening might not have occurred at all if it had not been predicted. At the other extreme the prediction of an impending event may lead to its *prevention* (so that, by deliberately or negligently abstaining from predicting it, the social scientist, it may be said, could bring it about, or could cause it to happen)' (p. 15).

Even though Popper tries to deny that the *connection* between social predictions and the predicted events has a real effect in distinguishing the social sciences from the natural sciences (cf. Popper 1992b [1976], pp. 121–2), his reflections on this issue show us – in my judgment – differences between social sciences (and, among them, economics) and natural sciences: on the one hand, in the social realm there is a clearer interplay between *predictions* (e.g., economic predictions based on a theory and previous empirical knowledge) and *expectations* (e.g., what the agents expect could happen after the prediction); and, on the other hand, there may be an additional *second level* about the previous level of predictions and expectations (it could be the case of a metaprediction about the effects of the previous prediction and it is possible that the agents could have expectations about other agents' expectations).

Following Popper's example of the prediction of the rise and decline of the price of a share, it seems clear that it is a more complex event than a natural phenomenon insofar as *different* levels intervene in it. Above all, there is, first, an interaction between the observer's prediction and the agents' response to it; and, second, the agents are interested not just in the economic prediction but also in what other agents make of it (cf. Hollis 1992, p. 41). In effect, in some economic areas, such as stock exchanges and financial markets, there are several levels due to a connection between economic factors and psychological components, which make economic prediction more complex than weather prediction. Thus, the problems of the possibility of economic prediction and the question of its inexactness should be analysed in connection with the issue of *complexity*, which goes beyond the level of natural science.

Taking into account his remarks on social prediction (i.e., his criticism of large-scale prediction of human history by scientific or any other rational means as well as his objections to exactness of prediction of social affairs), economic predictions are still *possible* in Popper's methodology but they are also *unreliable*. The consequence for economics of his criticism of historicism is the rejection of two extemes: on the one hand, the scientific prediction of large-scale economic phenomena (such the future triumph of the proletariat in Marxism), and, on the other hand, the exactness of the scientific prediction of concrete economic events (such as the shares in the stock market). In other words, what he accepts is a kind of 'generic prediction', that is, a prediction which is not specific in the details but which can be used as a test for economic theory. In this regard, it seems that he is not far from some economists who defend the creativity and innovation of economic affairs, a view different from the mainstream conception in economic methodology.

Explicitly, Popper recognises a difference between predicting a *singular event* (e.g., 'when will the next rise in the rate of unemployment in Western Ontario be?') and predicting a certain *kind or type of event* (e.g., 'why is there a seasonal increase and decrease of unemployment in the building industry?'). In the first case, natural science can succeed (e.g., 'when will the next lunar eclipse occur?'), whereas a social science, such as economics, is in a very difficult position: 'the Newtonian method of explaining and predicting singular events by universal laws and initial conditions is hardly applicable in the theoretical social sciences' (Popper 1994, pp. 165–6). But, in the second case, when the aim is to predict a kind or type of event, economics is in a much better position: it operates by the method of constructing *typical* situations or conditions (i.e., the method of constructing models).

This distinction shows a resemblance with theses of the Austrian school of economics, as Popper himself recognises (cf. Popper 1994, p. 166): the view is connected with Friedrich von Hayek's idea that in the social sciences there is less 'explanation in detail' and more 'explanation in principle' than in the natural sciences (cf. Hayek 1967a [1964]). In endorsing this similitude, it is clear that Popper is assuming a methodological similarity between explanation and prediction, which supposes a version of the thesis of symmetry between both methodological processes.

Usually, when Popper quotes an economist with approval, the name is F. A. von Hayek,[19] the leader of the Austrian school of economics who was awarded the Nobel Prize in 1974. The two share a methodological individualism in social sciences and show a distrust of the accuracy of economic prediction of singular events. In addition, they seem to adopt similar approaches on the rationality principle and in the issue of prediction of type of events. Moreover, there is a recognition by Popper (1994, p. 181, note 1) of the intellectual debt regarding the crucial notion of the *logic of situation*:

> I was particularly impressed by Hayek's formulation that economics is the 'logic of choice' [Popper here cites Hayek 1948, p. 35]. This led me to my formulation of the 'logic of situation'.[20] This seemed to me to embrace, for example, the logic of choice and the logic of historical problem situation. (The origin of this idea may explain why I rarely stressed the fact

that I did not look at the logic of situation as a deterministic theory: I had in mind the logic of situational choices.)

Throughout his work, Popper has made critical comments on instrumentalism, a methodological position which has been very influential in mainstream economic methodology, due to Milton Friedman's views (cf. Friedman 1969 [1953]).

> There is an important distinction which we can make between two kinds of scientific prediction, and which instrumentalism cannot make; a distinction which is connected with the problem of scientific discovery. I have in mind the distinction between the prediction of *events of a kind which is known*, such as eclipses or thunderstorms on the one hand and, on the other hand, the prediction of *new kinds of events* (which the physics call 'new effects') such as the prediction which led to the discovery of wireless waves, or of zero-point energy, or to the artificial building up of new elements not previously found in nature. It seems to me that instrumentalism can account only for the first kind of prediction: if theories are instruments for prediction, then we must assume that their purpose must be determined in advance, as with other instruments. Predictions of the second kind can be fully understood only as discoveries.
>
> (Popper 1989a [1963], pp. 117–18)

Anti-instrumentalism and defence of methodological realism are two sides of the same coin in Popper's approach. He accepts that a scientific theory may be applied to practical problems and, in this sense, they could be actual or potential instruments. But they are not *merely* instruments, because we may learn from science something about the structure of our world: they can include predictions which can lead us towards genuine discoveries. Moreover, 'science aims at truth, or getting nearer to the truth, however difficult it may be to approach truth, even with very moderate success' (Popper 1994, p. 174).

Methodologically, Popper accepts predictions (among them, economic ones) according to a realist approach: they can increase our knowledge and can be closer to the truth. In fact, he distinguishes *qualitative* predictions and *quantitative* predictions. The kind of test used can make the latter more reliable than the former:

> tests can be graded as being more or less severe. Qualitative tests, for example, are in general less severe than quantitative tests. And tests of more precise quantitative predictions are more severe than tests of less precise predictions.
>
> (Popper 1994, p. 94)

And it is clear that economics is, with social sciences as a whole, a discipline with a large number of quantitative predictions.

Another distinction in his writings, which also affects economics, is between *conditional* predictions and *unconditional* predictions. Both are scientific. In the conditional case, they assert that certain changes will be accompanied by other changes: 'we can learn from the economist that under certain social conditions, such as shortage of commodities, controlled prices, and, say, the absence of an effective punitive system, a black market will develop' (Popper 1959, p. 279).

But, in the unconditional case, there are two possibilities: (a) unconditional *scientific predictions*, which derives from conditional predictions together with historical statements which asseverate that the conditions are fulfilled (e.g., the evolution of a disease in a patient or the collapse of an economic sector given its evolution); and (b) unconditional historicial predictions or *prophecies*, when there is no justification in a theoretical science and these do not include conditional predictions. This last case – the historical prediction which he calls 'prophecy' – constitutes the core of the historicism, the social methodology which he rejects (ibid.).

To sum up, Karl Popper's methodological approach to prediction has been influential at three different levels: the general methodology of science, the methodology of social sciences, and the methodology of economics. However, each one of them has shown problems, such as the need for an initial *induction* for some predictions (corroboration could have predictive import); the differences in the *framework* for prediction in natural and social sciences (falsificationism is not the same methodology as the logic of situation); and the *complexity* of economic events (rather than the distinction between a singular event and a type of event) as real bedrock for the problem of accuracy of economic predictions. These deficiencies leave the door open to posterior methodological approaches and, among them, to Lakatos's methodology of scientific research programs, which was conceived to get round important problems facing Popper's approach.

Notes

1 'It is not our corroboration statements but our *theories* which allow us to make predictions (in the presence of observed 'initial conditions', of course), with the consequence that these predictions may be as hypothetical as the theories. *Thus our theories do have predictive import.* Our corroboration statements have no predictive import' (Popper 1974, p. 1029).
2 An analysis of Popper's relation with the economists of his own school is found in de Marchi 1988.
3 Imre Lakatos emphasised that 'falsificationism' can be understood in different ways, cf. his 1970.
4 'That only in this way can we explain and understand what happens in society: social events' (Popper 1985, p. 358, cf. Caldwell 1991, p. 14). In Popper's essay 'Models, Instruments, and Truth. The Status of the Rationality Principle in the Social Sciences' in his 1994, Popper writes: 'In my view, the idea of a social situation is the fundamental category of the methodology of the social sciences. I should even be inclined to say that almost every problem of explanation in the social sciences requires an analysis of a social situation' (p. 166.)
5 Cf. Popper 1992a [1945], vol. 2, p. 265. In his 1994, Popper writes: 'I regard the principle of adequacy of action (that is, the rationality principle) as an integral part of

every, or nearly every, testable social theory. Now if a theory is tested, and found faulty, then we have always to decide which of its various constituent parts we shall make accountable for its failure. My thesis is that it is *sound methodological policy* to decide not to make the rationality principle, but the rest of the theory – that is, the model – accountable' (p. 177).

6 'I suggest that it is the task of the logic of scientific discovery, or the logic of knowledge, to give a logical analysis of this procedure; that is, to analyse the method of the empirical sciences' (Popper 1968 [1959/1935], p. 27).

7 'Criticism of our conjectures is of decisive importance: by bringing out our mistakes it makes us understand the difficulties of the problem which we are trying to solve. This is how we become better acquainted with our problem, and able to propose more mature solutions: the very refutation of a theory – that is, of any serious tentative solution to our problem – is always a step forward that takes us nearer to the truth. And this is how we can learn from our mistakes.

'As we learn from our mistakes our knowledge grows, even though we may never know – that is, know for certain. Since our knowledge grows, there can be no reason here for despair of reason' (Popper 1989a [1963], p. vii).

8 His three worlds theory includes causal relations between them, and the world 3, which is the realm of science, has objective objects or entities, cf. Popper 1989b [1979], pp. 153–90, especially pp. 155–8.

9 Cf. Popper 1968 [1959/1935], p. 60. In addition, Popper points out: 'the term "prediction", as used here, comprises statements about the past ("retrodiction"), or even "given" statements which we wish to explain ("*explicanda*")' (p. 60, note 2).

10 In Popper, '(a) though potentially falsifiable, a theory may be currently untestable. (b) If a theory is potentially falsifiable, currently testable, and has been tested, then there are two possibilities: (i) If a test is positive, the theory is *corroborated*. . . . Corroboration does not mean *proven true*; Popper's *fallibilism* prohibits us from claiming that we have discovered the truth. (. . .) Nor should even consistently corroborated theory be viewed as *highly probable* or even *more probable*. This was the point of Popper's critique of inductive logic. It is a radical implication: Even perfect corroboration carries no evidential weight. (ii) If a test result is negative, the theory is *refuted* or *falsified*. Just as corroboration does not prove a theory true, refutation does not prove it false' (Caldwell 1991, pp. 3–4).

11 'I have tried to perfect a theory' (Popper 1991 [1957], p. 3).

12 There are some peculiar remarks in Popper's analysis, because he finds similarities among philosophers of quite different tendencies in social sciences: 'This historicist attitude was rather typical of the period [as] can be seen from the close similarity between the historicism of Marx and that of J. S. Mill. (It is analogous to the similarity between the historicist philosophies of their predecessors, Hegel and Comte)' (Popper 1992a [1945], vol. 2, p. 87).

13 The book was first published in three parts in *Economica*, vol. 11, no. 42 (1944), pp. 86–103; vol. 11, no. 43 (1944), pp. 119–37; and vol. 12, no. 46 (1945), pp. 69–89.

14 A strong criticism of his approach to historicism can be found in Urbach 1978, Urbach 1985 (especially pp. 137–9) and Urbach 1987 (especially pp. 30–2).

15 'Theoretical science on which to base those large-scale forecasts whose confirmation would mean the success of social theory' (Popper 1991 [1957], p. 41).

16 Cf. Caldwell 1991, p. 1. On the one hand, the list of economists whose general outlook has been influenced by Popper's work could be much longer, because there are also other well-known names such as Richard Lipsey and Neil de Marchi; and, on the other hand, the level of influence varies clearly from one author to another (e.g., Spiro Latsis is more Lakatosian than Popperian, and Bruce J. Caldwell and D. Wade Hands are clearly critical of central tenets of Popper's approach).

17 The relation between the two authors starts earlier than the 1950s. In fact Hayek

invited Popper to go to the London School of Economics from New Zealand, cf. Popper 1992b [1976], p. 120.

18   The influence of an item of information (historical or economical) upon the situation to which the information refers is what he calls the 'Oedipus effect', cf. Popper 1991 [1957], p. 13. However, in a previous paper he wrote that it also affects the natural sciences: 'One would expect the Oedipus effect to be a peculiarity of the social sciences and their subject matter, and that it is completely foreign to physics; but this is not the case' (Popper 1950, p. 189).

19   Popper dedicated to von Hayek *Conjectures and Refutations*.

20   Cf. Popper 1991 [1957], p. 149.

References

Albert, H. 1987. 'La posibilidad del conocimiento', in *Teorema*, vol. 14/1–2, pp. 127–44.

Blaug, M. 1994. 'Why I am not a Constructivist: Confessions of an Unrepentant Popperian', in R. E. Backhouse (ed.), *New Directions in Economic Methodology*. London: Routledge, pp. 109–36.

Caldwell, B. 1991. 'Clarifying Popper', in *Journal of Economic Literature*, vol. 30, pp. 1–33.

Caldwell, B. 1994. 'Two Proposals for the Recovery of Economic Practice', in R. E. Backhouse (ed.), *New Directions in Economic Methodology*, London: Routledge, pp. 137–53.

Chalmers, A. F. 1985. 'Methodological Individualism: An Incongruity in Popper's Philosophy', in Gregory Currie and Alan Musgrave (eds), *Popper and the Human Sciences*, Dordrecht: Martinus Nijhoff, pp. 73–87.

Clark, P. 1995. 'Popper on Determinism', in Anthony O'Hear (ed.), *Karl Popper: Philosophy and Problems*, Cambridge: Cambridge University Press, pp. 149–62.

Cohen, L. J. 1985. 'Third World Epistemology', in Gregory Currie and Alan Musgrave (eds), *Popper and the Human Sciences*, Dordrecht: Martinus Nijhoff, pp. 1–12.

Donagan, A. 1974. 'Popper's Examination of Historicism', in P. A. Schilpp (ed.), *The Philosophy of Karl Popper*, vol. 2, La Salle, IL: Open Court, pp. 905–24.

Flew, A. 1990. 'Popper and Historicist Necessities', in *Philosophy*, vol. 65, pp. 53–64.

Friedman, M. 1969 [1953]. 'The Methodology of Positive Economics', in M. Friedman, *Essays in Positive Economics*, 6th reprint, Chicago, IL: University of Chicago Press, pp. 3–43.

Gonzalez, W. J. 1984. 'La interpretación historicista de las Ciencias Sociales', in *Anales de Filosofía*, vol. 2, pp. 109–37.

Gonzalez, W. J. 1990. 'Ambito y características de la Filosofía y Metodología de la Ciencia', in W. J. Gonzalez (ed.), *Aspectos metodológicos de la investigación científica*, 2nd edition, Ediciones Universidad Autónoma de Madrid and Publicaciones Universidad de Murcia, Madrid – Murcia, pp. 49–78.

Gonzalez, W. J. 1991. 'Historismo y anti-historismo en la polémica metodológica entre G. Schmöller y C. Menger', in M. Valera and C. Lopez Fernandez (eds), *Actas del V Congreso de la Sociedad Española de Historia de las Ciencias y las Técnicas*, PPU-DM, Murcia, pp. 2027–41.

Gonzalez, W. J. (ed.). 1996. *Acción e Historia. El objeto de la Historia y la Teoría de la Acción*, Publicaciones Universidad de La Coruña, La Coruña.

Gonzalez, W. J. 2000. 'Marco teórico, trayectoria y situación actual de la Filosofía y Metodología de la Economía', in *Argumentos de Razón Técnica*, vol. 3, pp. 13–59.

Haack, S. 1977. 'Two Fallibilists in Search of the Truth', in *Proceedings of the Aristotelian Society*, sup. vol. 51, pp. 63–84.

Hands, D. Wade. 1985. 'Karl Popper and Economic Methodology. A New Look', in *Economics and Philosophy*, vol. 1, pp. 83–99.

Hands, D. Wade. 1993. 'Popper and Lakatos in Economic Methodology', in U. Mäki, B. Gustafsson and C. Knudsen (eds), *Rationality, Institutions and Economic Methodology*, London: Routledge, pp. 61–75.

Hayek, F. A. 1948. *Individualism and Economic Order*, London: Routledge and Kegan Paul, and Chicago, IL: University of Chicago Press.

Hayek, F. A. 1967a [1964]. 'Degrees of Explanation', in F. A. Hayek, *Studies in Philosophy, Politics and Economics*, Chicago, IL: University of Chicago Press, pp. 3–21.

Hayek, F. A. 1967b [1964]. 'The Theory of Complex Phenomena', in F. A. Hayek, *Studies in Philosophy, Politics and Economics*. Chicago: University of Chicago Press, pp. 22–42.

Hayek, F. A. 1994. *Hayek on Hayek* in S. Kresge and L. Wenar, (eds), Chicago, IL: University of Chicago Press.

Hollis, M. 1992. 'Historical Prediction', in W. H. Newton-Smith and J. Tianji (eds), *Popper in China*, London: Routledge, pp. 37–54.

Hutchison, T. W. 1960 [1938]. *The Significance and Basic Postulates of Economic Theory*, 2nd edition, New York: Kelley.

Koertge, N. 1975. 'Popper's Metaphysical Research Program for the Human Sciences', in *Inquiry*, vol. 18, pp. 437–62.

Koertge, N. 1979. 'The Methodological Status of Popper's Rationality Principle', in *Theory and Decision*, vol. 10, pp. 83–95.

Lakatos, I. 1970. 'Falsification and the Methodology of Scientific Research Programmes', in I. Lakatos and A. Musgrave (eds), *Criticism and the Growth of Knowledge*, Cambridge: Cambridge University Press, pp. 91–196.

Lakatos, I. and A. Musgrave (eds). 1970. *Criticism and the Growth of Knowledge*. Cambridge: Cambridge University Press.

Lipsey, R. G. 1963. *An Introduction to Positive Economics*, London: Weidenfeld.

de Marchi, N. 1988. 'Popper and the LSE economists', in N. de Marchi (ed.), *The Popperian Legacy in Economics*, Cambridge: Cambridge University Press, pp. 139–66.

de Marchi, N. (ed.). 1992. *Post-Popperian Methodology of Economics*. Boston: Kluwer.

Martin Santos, L. *et al*. 1970. *Simposio de Burgos. Ensayos de Filosofía de la Ciencia, en torno a la obra de Sir K. Popper*, Madrid: Tecnos.

Mirowski, Philip. 1989. *More Heat than Light, Economics as Social Physics. Physics as Nature's Economics*, Cambridge and New York: Cambridge University Press.

Niiniluoto, I. 1984. *Is Science Progressive?* Dordrecht: D. Reidel.

Nola, R. 1987. 'The Status of Popper's Theory of Method', in *British Journal for the Philosophy of Science*, vol. 38, pp. 441–80.

O'Hear, A. 1980. *Karl Popper*, London: Routledge and Kegan Paul.

O'Hear, A. (ed.). 1995. *Karl Popper: Philosophy and Problems*, Cambridge: Cambridge University Press.

Popper, K. R. 1950. 'Indeterminism in Quantum Physics and in Classical Physics', in *British Journal for the Philosophy of Science*, vol. 1, pp. 117–33 and pp. 173–95.

Popper, K. R. 1959. 'Prediction and Prophecy in the Social Sciences', in P. Gardiner (ed.), *Theories of History*, London: Macmillan, pp. 276–85.

Popper, K. R. 1968 [1959/1935]. *The Logic of Scientific Discovery*, revised edition, London: Hutchinson. English translation of *Logik der Forschung*. Vienna: Springer.

Popper, K. R. 1974. 'Replies to my Critics', in P. A. Schilpp (ed.), *The Philosophy of Karl Popper*, vol. 2, La Salle, IL: Open Court, pp. 961–1,197.

Popper, K. R. 1979 [1932–3]. *Die beiden Grundprobleme der Erkenntnistheorie*. Tubinga: Mohr.
Popper, K. R. 1982a. *The Open Universe: An Argument for Indeterminism*, London: Hutchinson.
Popper, K. R. 1982b. *Quantum Theory and the Schism in Physics*. Totawa, NJ: Rowman and Littlefield.
Popper, K. R. 1985. 'The Rationality Principle', in K. R. Popper, *Selections* (David Miller, ed.). Princeton, NJ: Princeton University Press, pp. 357–65.
Popper, K. R. 1989a [1963]. *Conjectures and Refutations* (fifth edition). London: Routledge.
Popper, K. R. 1989b [1979]. *Objective Knowledge*, revised edition, Oxford: Clarendon Press.
Popper, K. R. 1991 [1957]. *The Poverty of Historicism*, London: Routledge.
Popper, K. R. 1992a [1945]. *The Open Society and Its Enemies, vol. 1: Plato; vol. 2: Hegel and Marx*, fifth edition, London: Routledge.
Popper, K. R. 1992b [1976]. *Unended Quest*, enlarged version, London: Routledge.
Popper, K. R. 1992c [1983]. *Realism and the Aim of Science*, London: Routledge.
Popper, K. R. 1992d. *In Search of a Better World*, London: Routledge.
Popper, K. R. 1994. *The Myth of the Framework: in Defense of Science and Rationality* (M. Notturno, ed.), London: Routledge.
Popper, K. R. 1996. *The Lesson of this Century*, interviewed by G. Bosetti, London: Routledge.
Popper, K. R. 1999 [1994]. *All Life is Problem Solving*. London: Routledge, *Alles Leben ist Problemlössen*, Piper, Munich, 1994, translated by Patrick Camiller.
Putnam, H. 1974. 'The 'Corroboration' of Theories', in P. A. Schilpp (ed.), *The Philosophy of Karl Popper*, vol. 1, La Salle, IL: Open Court, pp. 221–40.
Rescher, N. 1998. *Predicting the Future: An Introduction to the Theory of Forecasting*, New York: State University of New York Press.
Ryan, A. 1985. 'Popper and Liberalism', in G. Currie and A. Musgrave (eds), *Popper and the Human Sciences*, Dordrecht: Martinus Nijhoff, pp. 89–104.
Salmon, W. 1988 [1981]. 'Rational Prediction', in A. Grünbaum and W. Salmon (eds), *The Limitations of Deductivism*, Berkeley, CA: University of California Press, pp. 47–60, reprinted from *British Journal for the Philosophy of Science*, vol. 32, pp. 115–25.
Schilpp, P. A. (ed.). 1974. *The Philosophy of Karl Popper*, 2 volumes, La Salle, IL: Open Court.
Schwartz, P., C. Rodriguez Braunand and F. Mendez Ibisate (eds). 1993. *Encuentro con Karl Popper*, Madrid: Alianza Ed.
Suchting, W. A. 1972. 'Marx, Popper, and 'Historicism'', in *Inquiry*, vol. 15, pp. 235–66.
Suchting, W. 1985. 'Popper's Critique of Marx's Method', in G. Currie and A. Musgrave (eds), *Popper and the Human Sciences*, Dordrecht: Martinus Nijhoff, pp. 147–62.
Urbach, P. 1978. 'Is Any of Popper's Arguments against Historicism Valid?', in *British Journal for the Philosophy of Science*, vol. 29, pp. 117–130.
Urbach, P. 1985. 'Good and Bad Arguments against Historicism', in G. Currie and A. Musgrave (eds), *Popper and the Human Sciences*, Dordrecht: Martinus Nijhoff, pp. 133–45.
Urbach, P. 1987. 'The Scientific Standing of Evolutionary Theories of Society', in *London School of Economics Quarterly*, vol. 1, pp. 23–42.
Watkins, J. 1978. 'The Popperian Approach to Scientific Knowledge', in G. Radnitzky and G. Andersson (eds), *Progress and Rationality in Science*, Dordrecht: D. Reidel, pp. 23–43.
Wilkins, B. T. 1978. *Has History Any Meaning?* Ithaca: Cornell University Press.
Worrall, J. 1978. 'The Ways in Which the Methodology of Scientific Research Improves on Popper's Methodology', in G. Radnitzky and G. Andersson (eds), *Progress and Rationality in Science*, Dordrecht: D. Reidel, pp. 45–70.

POPPER VERSUS ANALYTICAL
PHILOSOPHY?

Jeremy Shearmur[1]

While Popper could be seen as an analytical philosopher, his work has not – a few points aside – had the sort of role in the development of contemporary analytical philosophy that has, say, that of Carnap or of Quine. This chapter argues that there is, indeed, something distinctive about Popper's approach, something which may usefully be contrasted with ideas that are widely accepted within contemporary analytical philosophy. It discusses the assumption within analytical philosophy that underlying ordinary claims about knowledge there is some true logical form which represents the 'correct' way of representing and analysing things, Popper's view of the significance of scientific knowledge for epistemology, and Popper's arguments for the importance of attempting scientific reduction but against the assumption that naturalism must be correct. The latter are extended into an argument against the presumption of naturalism in ethics. More generally, the chapter argues for Popper's view that truth is more likely to emerge from the contention of substantive, competing viewpoints rather than from allegedly neutral 'analysis' – and that we would benefit from an engagement with Popper's distinctive perspective, even if in the end it should turn out to be incorrect.

1 Introduction

Early in 2001, the philosophy program in the School of Humanities at the Australian National University was discussing its teaching needs for 2002. We reached the issue of who could undertake teaching in a 'European Philosophy' course. Keen to be helpful, I asked: 'Is Popper a European Philosopher?' – and was firmly put in my place by a resounding 'No' from our (then) contemporary French philosophy specialist.

At the same time, I have become acutely aware – through participation in a reading group on themes in analytical philosophy for our staff and graduate students, as well as when hearing papers given by colleagues from the strongly analytical philosophy program in ANU's Research School of the Social Sciences – that there is a sense in which Popper is not an analytical philosopher either. Indeed, if one looks at standard works on epistemology, on metaphysics (including the philosophy of mind), and on philosophy of language, Popper either does not figure, or, in the case of the philosophy of mind, he is typically dismissed out of hand, by way of some critical comments on some bold but wild suggestions by Sir John Eccles (in their 1977), to which there is no particular reason to suppose that Popper himself subscribed.[2] This might be contrasted with the canonical status accorded to Quine and even, to a degree, to Carnap in the development of modern analytical philosophy.

The resulting situation seems interesting. For there are many respects in which Popper presents significant alternatives to what one finds in analytical philosophy; both in respect of substantive ideas, and as to the whole way in which one should be operating. At the same time, there are obviously many specific philosophical views that Popper shares with particular analytical philosophers.

In the rest of this chapter, I will offer an account of what seem to me to be some of these differences. In the short space available, I will miss out much, and I will not be in a position to argue that Popper is correct. Indeed, it is far from my view that everything that Popper suggested works. My book on his political philosophy (Shearmur, 1996) offered, in passing, what I take to be a telling critique of some aspects of his work; and I personally can't see how his approach copes with problems suggested by Nelson Goodman's New Riddle of Induction. But it none the less seems to me that Popper's views merit explication – and sometimes reconstruction – just because they do, when taken as a whole, offer a significant alternative to commonly taken approaches in contemporary analytical philosophy. Further, this task is necessary just because his views, when seen as offering a distinctive approach to philosophy, are not as well known as one might expect. While some of his work in the philosophy of science has been extensively debated, the kind of picture that I am offering here often seems to me only to be familiar to those who studied with Popper at the LSE.

This is all particularly important because of one feature of Popper's approach which does seem to me correct, and to which I will return at the end of this chapter, namely that the path to wisdom in philosophy and elsewhere, is by way of competing substantive approaches in dialogue (cf. Popper 1945, ch. 23, and also Popper's theory of the empirical basis in his 1959 [1935]), rather than through some kind of 'neutral' analysis (cf. Popper 1976, end of section 7). Objectivity, Popper has argued, is best achieved as a product of inter-subjective dialogue. And from this perspective, an interesting approach to philosophical problems different from our current ones is likely to be valuable, even if, in the end, it should turn out *not* to be correct.[3]

There are various different ways in which a chapter such as this might be written. One path would be to take a historical approach, and to discuss ways in which Popper's work developed, notably from the biological psychology of Otto Selz (cf. ter Hark 1993, pp. 585 ff., and also ter Hark 2002), and the distinctive traditional of naturalised Kantianism that stemmed from the work of Leonard Nelson and his revival of the approach of Jakob Fries (cf. Popper 1962, pp. 2–12).[4] Along these lines, Popper's substantive views might be understood as the product of an encounter between an unorthodox scholar who combined such a background with scientific realism,[5] and the Vienna Circle. But for me, personally, to attempt such an account would be premature; not least as the German-language scholarship on which I would have to call has not yet been translated.[6] Instead, I will address myself to some of Popper's substantive ideas.

I will, thus, discuss a few ideas, and will then turn – in a somewhat speculative mode – to a recent paper by Michael Smith, an able analytical philosopher whose work seems to me to well exemplify certain current ideas. I will use it to illustrate some of the differences to which, in my view, a Popperian approach might lead us.

2 Popper versus Platonism of Logical Form

The English translation of Popper's *Logik der Forschung, The Logic of Scientific Discovery*, included a 'Preface, 1959', which he had also given in 1958 at a conference in France on analytical philosophy. Popper there set out some of the differences between his approach to philosophy, and those kinds of analytical philosophy common at the time at which he was writing. In the first part of this, he offered some criticism of formalistic approaches to the language of science. He here comments (1959 [1935], p. 20):

> perhaps owing to the spiritual consolations offered by the hope for knowledge that is 'exact' or 'precise' or 'formalised', the chosen object of their linguistic analysis is 'the language of *science*' rather than ordinary language. Yet unfortunately there seems to be no such thing as 'the language of science'. It therefore becomes necessary for them to construct one.

And Popper then goes on to discuss some of the problems that such philosophers had in the construction of formalised languages adequate to the expression of physics. His own favoured approach, by contrast, is one which does not adopt any particular language or method, but uses anything that helps people to see their problems more clearly.[7]

Let me start by trying, somewhat speculatively, to offer an extension of Popper's comments here. It is a slightly daunting enterprise, both because there is much in Popper which is at odds with what I will advocate and also because I – a Popperian rather than an analytical philosopher by training – here feel that I am rushing in, where angels should fear to tread.

My concern is to take issue with an approach which seems widely shared among analytical philosophers, but which it is, perhaps, not too easy to articulate precisely. The idea is that logical analysis can reveal to us the real, underlying structure behind commonsense or scientific claims. A particular way of representing things, using logic (exactly which logic sometimes being a matter of dispute) is thought to tell us what claims actually amount to. I have also been struck by the way in which analytically trained philosophers are inclined to wish to represent even points made in discussion, in symbolic and general form – much as, it seems to me, their medieval forebears wished to put things into Hebrew; but at least they had the excuse that they thought that Hebrew was the language of God. By comparison, our more ordinary ways of proceeding are seen as being about on a par with the activities of people in Plato's cave. Indeed, once one has understood that the true logical structure of things is available to us, it would seem silly to operate other than by having recourse to it. My question, however, is as to whether we have reason to believe that such a thing exists.

In trying to make such an argument from the perspective of Popper's work, I have, however, a problem on my hands. For Popper himself has been taken as a proponent of just such an approach. One (extraordinary) discussion of Popper's contributions to metaphysics (Ackermann 1995) in a recent handbook even represented his main contribution as a thesis about what the correct Procrustean bed is, in terms of which scientific theories should be logically represented. Other things might be said for such a view of Popper. He was most interested in developments in mathematical logic in the early and mid-twentieth century, and might be argued to have sometimes made use of them in a somewhat uncritical manner. When Popper was in New Zealand, he corresponded with Carnap about the works on logic that Carnap was then producing, sending Carnap detailed comments on his books, as he received them. Popper's previous encounter with Tarski, in Vienna, had made a great impression on him. Not only, as Popper has often recounted, did this affect his ideas about truth, but he also made use of Tarski's ideas about consequence classes in his work on verisimilitude. In addition, Popper – from the late 1940s – embarked on a massive (if eventually unsuccessful) programme of work in logic, which has been argued to take as its starting-point some of Tarski's ideas about deduction.[8]

It would, however, I think be wrong to think of Popper as concerned with a search for a particular logical form, in which to correctly represent our claims to knowledge. There is, perhaps, a risk that in his work – as in that of so many others who were impressed with the development of symbolic logic in the twentieth century – the use of tools from this repertoire may sometimes have served to prejudge substantive issues.

Popper's view of logic, however, seems to me more a functional or an instrumentalist one than a Platonist one. In his 'A Realist View of Logic, Physics and History' (in his 1972, pp. 285–318), Popper explored what he called a 'realist' view of logic. This, however, was not a Platonist view; rather, it was an approach within which our aim was taken to be the attainment of truth, and, he suggested, logics were to be chosen to assist us in the achievement of that goal. This led him to advocate a weak logic when our aim was constructive proof, and a powerful logic when our aim was criticism.

However, it might be objected, what about Popper's view of science: was not this a resolutely logical one? For, surely, it is almost a cliché that Popper's views were exclusively logical, as compared, say, with Kuhn's more sociological approach. (For a *contrasting* view of Popper's work, see Jarvie 2001.)

There is something to be said for this. But it seems to me that it is not fully correct. For one of the crucial points in Popper's argument, in *The Logic of Scientific Discovery*, is that a purely logical approach is insufficient to guarantee the character of a body of knowledge as falsifiable. Clearly, there may be statements – as J. W. N. Watkins's discussion of 'all-and-some' statements in his 'Confirmable and Influential Metaphysics' makes clear (Watkins 1958) – which may be confirmed but not falsified, as a consequence of their logical form. But Popper's discussion, in *The Logic of Scientific Discovery*, is interesting because it explicitly recognises the insufficiency of logical form as an indicator of the scientific status of a theory. That is to say, Popper recognises that – as a consequence of the arguments that Duhem and other conventionalists had offered – it would be possible to protect any particular *prima facie* falsifiable statement against empirical falsification, as a consequence of people's choosing to divert responsibility for the empirical difficulties elsewhere. This might be done in *ad hoc* (content-decreasing) ways. Popper argued that we needed to adopt certain methodological rules to preclude our behaving in this way, if we wished to be able to learn effectively from experience. But it was also sometimes possible to direct away such responsibility in a manner that is methodologically acceptable – i.e. in cases in which a *prima facie* empirical problem is explained in terms of a change in background assumptions, in such a way that one's system of theories is rendered more testable. Such ideas subsequently played a major role in Imre Lakatos's *Proofs and Refutations* and his 'methodology of scientific research programmes' (cf. Lakatos 1976).

These ideas deserve more analysis than I am able to give them here. (There are, it seems to me, certain parallels to C. I. Lewis's notion, in his 1946, of the 'pragmatic a priori'.) However, the first idea – of the adoption of 'ad hoc conventionalist stratagems' – would seem to suggest that, if one understood the meaning of a claim in a non-holistic manner, it was in fact being changed, *ad hoc*, so as to drop content that proved problematic, as in a shift from 'All swans are white' to 'All non-antipodean swans are white'. Clearly, this would seem somewhat uninteresting if it were done explicitly. But the force of Popper's idea would seem to depend on the possibility of this being done inadvertently – e.g. so that those involved, or their interlocutors, are not conscious of the fact that there has been a change in the meaning of the claim that is being made. This, in turn, opens up two further issues. First, that meanings may well not be transparent to us, such that we would need to understand the *actual* use of language in order to be able to work out the content of what was being asserted: that introspection by native speakers, even that upon which there was consensus (for such behaviour may well be shared by a group of people), might well not be enough. Second, as I have argued elsewhere (cf. my 1980 and my 1985) what is involved in such behaviour may go beyond our linguistic practice, to explicitly sociological factors: that it is possible, for example, that unbeknown to the people involved, their institutions are functioning *as* methodological rules which protect certain of their ideas from contrary experience, or from having to encounter contradictions, because problems are diverted, or are not raised in ways that would serve to call the underlying ideas into question.

But if all this is the case, what are we to make of critical work in philosophy, of the development of logic, and so on? It is, I suggest, something that should be understood not as telling us the true nature of meaning, or the true underlying structure of the claims that we are making, but, rather, as something that we construct, as a way in which we can render our meanings and practices an object of critical reflection. Popper has often suggested in his later work, that there is a real difference between a subjective belief or disposition, and the content of this when it is articulated in language and, better still, written down. Consequently, I suggest that we should understand our activities in this field – something that, in my view, urgently requires complementation by the explication of and critical reflection on methodological rules and sociological practices – as a way in which we, artificially, are able to objectify, and thus to work critically together upon, our knowledge.

3 The significance of science for epistemology: basic statements

In the Preface 1959 to his *Logic of Scientific Discovery*, with which I started these reflections, Popper also indicated that he was at odds with the approach of 'ordinary language' philosophers. A key point of difference from the latter was Popper's view that, if one wished to study knowledge, one should take the growth of scientific knowledge, rather than commonsense knowledge, as one's model.

What is the upshot of this? I would like to suggest the *combination* of the following points:

(a) First, Popper has, obviously, stressed the fallibility of our knowledge, and its theoretical character. From his perspective – as in that of Kant and of Whewell, before him – our understanding of the world involves our bringing of conceptions and interpretations to it. Not only does what we impute to our experience and understanding of the world transcend anything that may be said to be given to us by those causal processes that impinge upon us. But there may be significant respects in which what we take to be the case in what we are experiencing, may be incorrect.

(b) Second, our experience of the world comes ready-interpreted, not only in terms of our explicit theories and linguistic categories, but also, in Popper's view, by way of theory-like expectations and presuppositions being built into our very sense organs and physiology. (If it is objected: but this involves mixing in substantive empirical claims with 'foundational' ideas, my response would be to say that Popper's epistemology is best understood as a coherence theory. Within this it would be claimed that some areas in our knowledge, and some procedures, are the way in which we can best learn about the world – i.e. observation, and basic statements. But about all this, I will say a little more, later.)

(c) Third, what Popper had to say about that against which our claims are to be tested is, in my view, best interpreted as an open-ended, inter-subjective consensus as to what is the case. Popper here wrote of psychological experiences as having a causal role in prompting us to make such statements, but not of them as having an epistemological role. Such a view is controversial, and a number of people who have been influenced by Popper – including my teachers Alan Musgrave (e.g. in his 1999), John Watkins (e.g. in his 1984) and Eli Zahar (e.g. in his 1995) – have, in various ways, suggested that such an approach should be revised, in the direction of different forms of psychologism (in which such basic statements are, in some sense or other, taken as justified by psychological experiences).

(d) My own view here – as elsewhere – is that it is worth seeing what can be done with what is *distinctive* about Popper's approach; accordingly, I'd favour exploring a non-psychologistic interpretation of this aspect of his work. At the same time, what Popper has written seems to me much too brief to constitute an adequate theory on its own, and thus as standing in need of elaboration. Such an elaboration would, clearly, involve more than just a re-affirmation of Popper's view, and would, itself, constitute a distinctive theory in its own right. I will not inflict such a thing on you here (not least, as I have started to do so in another paper – Shearmur 2002 – which offers a critique of the views of Watkins and, especially, of Zahar). But to put things very briefly, it seems to me that an interesting way to go, is to see Popper's view as leading us towards what one might call a layered coherence theory of knowledge (but not of truth). People can issue statements describing what they claim is there to be observed. These are then subject to evaluation, in terms of their inter-subjective acceptability. This, one would claim *within* a coherence theory of knowledge, is the place in our knowledge from which we can best learn what the world is like. An observation statement is, thus, a statement made, after making an observation, of what you claim is there. As with other claims subject to inter-subjective evaluation, we may come to be able to internalise the kinds of checks that others may make on such statements, so that we may eventually be able to handle them fairly adequately if we are on our own (much after the fashion of an actual Robinson Crusoe). But – like anyone left in isolation for a long period – we could well imagine that our basic statements might get increasingly idiosyncratic, if we were not subjected to *actual* checks by other people.

Popper's work in this field is at least known about, although it seems to me that it has not made the impact that it deserves as an alternative to current ideas. This is in part because the kind of empiricism with which Popper's ideas, so understood, contrasts, is often thought so obviously correct that alternatives are not taken seriously. It is in part because Popper's views, as I have indicated, are sometimes under-developed. It is also, I believe, because few of those few people interested in Popper's work have gone on to elaborate how it stands as an alternative to more widely accepted views, and to challenge those views from such a perspective. In my view, John Watkins, the early Paul Feyerabend, Alan Musgrave and Hans Albert were the only people to do this at all effectively; and two of them are, now, alas, dead. There is, I believe, much here to be done in terms of taking issue with more fashionable approaches in epistemology. But rather than elaborating on these issues, I would like to turn, instead, to Popper's treatment of reduction and of naturalism.

4 Popper on reduction and against naturalism

My third theme thus relates to reduction, and to the issue of naturalism. Popper's approach was at odds with the kind of naturalism that, today, seems to be very commonly taken for granted. This is interesting rather than just idiosyncratic because Popper was not only 'pro' science, but was also well informed about work in the natural sciences to the point where he was able not only to discuss the interpretation of, but also to attempt to make contributions to, work in several different scientific fields, right into his old age.

Popper's view here might be best described as a *prima facie* anti-naturalism, combined with an openness to scientific as opposed to philosophical reduction.

If we take our lead from the older Popper, it is also open to us, on similar grounds, to espouse a *prima facie moral* cognitivism and realism; one which, as I shall argue, may be understood as *prima facie non*-naturalistic.

Let me start with Popper's ideas about reduction. In his 'A Realist View of Logic, Physics and History', Popper set out a contrast between what he called a 'scientific' and a 'philosophical' reduction. The former he argued to be valuable, but difficult to achieve. By a scientific reduction, he meant the explanation of some sphere, without residue, in terms of another. What he meant here about its difficulty, may be seen from the first part of his 'Scientific Reduction and the Essential Incompleteness of All Science',[9] in which he surveyed some areas of science, and indicated the extent to which full scientific reductions had not, in fact, yet been accomplished. Popper's view, however, was that the *attempt* at reduction was methodologically fruitful, even if it is not fully successful.

I suggest that one might add to his argument the idea that, for a reduction to be complete, one would need not only the full explanation of the phenomena in one sphere in terms of another, but also the kind of relationship to hold between them, that Popper discussed in chapter 5 of his *Objective Knowledge*; namely, of a 'fact-correcting' kind:[10] i.e. that the reduction *replaces* the earlier description. If this is correct, then it was Paul Feyerabend who, in the philosophy of mind, when advocating a *scientifically* based eliminative materialism, was after the right *kind* of thing, *if* reduction is to be achieved.[11] (It is, I think, important because if one asserts identity without eliminative reduction, one ends up with a theory in which each of the two kinds of things comes to acquire the properties of the other, in addition to its own original ones. That is to say, in order to explain some property such as consciousness in ourselves and in animals, one ends up attributing something consciousness-like to things – such as ordinary physical objects –

which, *prima facie*, would not seem candidates for possessing them, at all, and for which there seems no possibility of testing.)

By way of contrast with scientific reduction, what Popper referred to as 'philosophical reduction' is a matter of giving an account of things without referring to what one wishes to eliminate. Popper elsewhere explained the same idea, by way of drawing a parallel with the way in which an infestation of lice was dealt with in Vienna, after the First World War: the problem was solved, by simply not *talking* about lice! In this material, Popper took issue with Quine, and with his use of Occam's razor. Popper's reason for doing so, is that, he argued, to proceed in such a way dissolves the problems in such a way that we don't learn anything about the world; something that we would learn in the light of, say, our undertaking the difficult task of advancing a real, but perhaps unsuccessful, attempt at scientific reduction. What, according to Popper, we should do, is to start by recognising the richness and plurality of what there is in the world, prior to then attempting scientific reductions.

Indeed, Popper, playing with a phrase of Quine's, made the claim that 'only if Plato's beard is sufficiently tough, and tangled by many entities, can it be worth our while to use Occam's razor'.[12] (The latter point should, surely, be interpreted in terms of attempted scientific reductions, rather than just talking about things while invoking as few entities as possible.)

This – the fluffing up of Plato's beard – seems to me the approach that underlies Popper's contributions to *The Self and Its Brain* (Popper and Eccles, 1977), and much of his discussion about 'worlds 2 and 3'. But what of naturalism? In this context, it is important that one distinguishes between two different ways in which we might interpret naturalism. The first takes science as it is, and asks: to what extent can we, in fact, currently explain everything in scientific terms. The second sense of naturalism is programmatic: it is concerned not with what we can explain now, but with what some future science might be able to explain. Popper typically discusses naturalism in the first sense. It is in this context that Popper argues (in his 1963, ch. 12, and in his and Eccles's 1977), for the inadequacy of non-dualist–interactionist theories of mind, and for what one might call *prima facie* interaction between properties that are not scientific, and scientific ones. Such interaction Popper discussed, further, in terms of his ideas about 'world 2' and 'world 3'. Some of this latter discussion, however, might seem to go beyond the fluffing of Plato's beard, to the development of arguments to the effect that we will never be able to explain everything naturalistically, even in terms of some future natural science.

The second – and programmatic – sense of naturalism would seem to me popular within analytical philosophy. The difficulty, however – and this goes also for the assessment of Popper's stronger arguments against reduction – is that it is not clear *how* we are to discuss them. For there would seem to be two alternatives. Either a completed science would be something much like our existing science. But in this case naturalism would appear to be false. Or – and this seems to me likely – we are dealing with a science of the future, the theoretical and empirical content of which we can't say anything much about, other than that we would expect some of our more successful science to turn out to be a limiting case of it (but where we can't, now, say how). The problem here, however, is that it is not clear how we can discuss the pros and cons of claims about such a naturalism, and whether or not those things which we can't currently explain could be explained in terms of it, just because we have no idea what it would actually look like.

But what, you may well ask, does this have to do with analytical philosophy? I will explain this in the next section, by way of a discussion of some claims made in a recent paper by my colleague at the ANU Research School of Social Sciences, Michael Smith. He, in ways that echo some well known arguments by J. L. Mackie,[13] sets out some ideas which seem to me widely accepted by analytical philosophers, but which are challenged by Popper's approach. To be sure – and this I must reiterate – it is one thing to state what Popper's views are, another to elaborate upon them where necessary, and, especially, a third to show that they can withstand hard-hitting critical argument. But, or so it seems to me, Popper's ideas, just because they are cogent and not obviously incorrect, deserve to be treated more seriously than they have been, to date, just because they do offer an informed alternative to approaches common within contemporary analytical philosophy. I will explore these differences by way of a view that Popper did not himself discuss, but which I think there is *some* evidence to attribute to him in his later work, on the basis both of his published writings (I have reviewed the case for this in 1996), and of scattered comments in unpublished writings; namely, a non-naturalistic ethical realism, although I do not wish to claim that Popper was consistent on this point. This is, accordingly, something for which I wish to break a lance, using arguments suggested by Popper's work, rather than a view that I am attributing to him.

5 Michael Smith's case against non-naturalistic ethical realism

Such a view is strongly criticised in the course of an article by Michael Smith (his 2000). Smith there writes (p. 23):

> If there is some feature of torturing babies that makes it true that torturing babies is wrong, then, in giving an account of the feature, we are constrained by our conception of the world in which we live. This means, in turn, that we are constrained by the truth of *naturalism*, the view that the world is amenable to study through empirical science. [In the light of what follows, this must be read as entirely amenable to such study. – J. S.] This is because, given the success of empirical sciences in providing explanations of various aspects of the world, it is extremely plausible to hold that the world is entirely amenable to study through the empirical sciences. Naturalism accordingly entails that the only features we have any reason to believe objects have are one and all naturalistic features, features that are themselves posits, or composites of posits, of

empirical science. The upshot is therefore that, if any form of moral real-ism is true at all, then it must be a form of Naturalistic Moral Realism.

This statement of faith is not all that he says, however; for Smith claims that non-naturalistic moral realism also faces two problems.

The first is that: 'it must explain how we come to a knowledge of these extra, spooky, non-natural properties' (p. 25); referring to G. E. Moore, Smith claims that Moore 'could hardly claim that we come by knowledge of them via observa-tion, for any property knowable in that way is, by definition, naturalistic' (ibid.). After exploring, and criticising, the idea that we might come to a knowledge of them by way of inference from naturalistic properties, Smith argues (p. 26) that all that we are left with

> is some non-empirical sort of observation, a sort of spooky sixth sense which allows us to detect the presence of spooky non-natural properties. But as soon as the idea is stated it is plain that it is, in reality, too absurd even to contemplate.

Smith then continues (still on p. 26) to discuss a second problem – that non-naturalistic moral realism

> must explain why there aren't possible worlds in which . . . non-natural properties which Moore supposes to be identical with moral properties float free of the natural properties with which they are coinstantiated in actuality . . . If non-natural properties are distinct from natural proper-ties then, it seems, we should be able to pull them apart modally. But, given that moral properties supervene on natural properties, it follows that we cannot pull them apart modally.

I will offer some remarks on all this, in the light of the points concerning Popper's work upon which I have commented earlier.

First, it seems to me that Smith is simply wrong in his comments about obser-vation. If I describe what I see, it will include that things are solid, red, green, beautiful, sexually attractive to a middle-aged heterosexual man, good and bad. That is to say, what we see – and the kinds of statements that we issue about them, and which are found acceptable by others – includes properties of many different kinds. They include properties that, currently, are not within the com-pass of natural science, and ones that are. Further, the natural sciences obviously include some properties that are, and some that are not, observable in this sense. The issue, however, runs deeper than this. For we need also here to consider Popper's arguments concerning the contribution that interpretation plays in observation, all the way down – i.e. including at the level of our sensory organs. If his view is here correct, it just does not work to equate what is observed with what is naturalistic. Accordingly, Smith's argument from observability, which goes back at least to J. L. Mackie, seems to me simply no good as an argument against non-naturalism in ethics.

But what of the other argument – which depends on ideas about supervenience? For what it is worth, I am happy enough with the idea that ethical properties are, primarily, properties of biological organisms and their products, and possibly also of bits of the purely natural world that they care a lot about. There may also be various kinds of necessary causal relationship here, too – e.g., to take a non-ethical example, if we have a certain kind of nervous system, then we may experience pain (as a conscious phenomenon) in distinct ways. Similarly, however, particular kinds of conscious experience may have distinctive effects upon our physical systems.

But what of supervenience – i.e. the idea, going back in this form to Davidson but with a considerable pre-history, that if two things are physically identical, they must be identical with respect to other properties, as well?

First, I am not so sure that we should accept it. An artifact and an oddly shaped naturally occurring piece of rock might well be physically identical; but it is not obvious that we have to say that they must have the same aesthetic properties. If one were to respond to this, as my colleague Brian Garrett suggested to me, by saying that the two would not be identical because they had different *prior* physical states, it is worth noting that the notion of physical being invoked would seem to be at odds with current *scientific* understandings, in which, as I understand it, the character of a physical system does not depend on its past history. (Clearly, something may have dispositional characteristics which were a product of its past history; but the idea is that if something else could be given these same characteristics by different means, it would be the same, physically, and would behave in the same way, in the future.)

Further, in the light of Popper's arguments about the falsity of naturalism in the first sense, supervenience *may* not be true. For it is at least possible that at least some of the defects of naturalism today might be permanent defects of any feature of naturalism: it may simply be the case that the world as described by a completed physical science would have to be understood as open to non-physical causal effects. And if this is the case, it is possible that those causes operate in such a way that supervenience is incorrect.

Should, however, supervenience nonetheless be correct, in the light of Popper's arguments it would not necessarily be something that matters. For supervenience would seem to have force – say, if invoked in the way that Smith does – only if we claim that the physical world is causally closed or self-contained. If, however, we see the physical world as open – and by this I mean causally open – to the influence of psychological states and, through them, to ideas including moral ideas, and to theories, then it is beside the point whether or not, if two things are physically identical, they are also identical in other respects. For what things are like, physically, if we understand this in terms of current scientific knowledge, *may* have itself to be explained by invoking not just natural laws, but other things, too. (After all, in the light of our *current* knowledge, we would, presumably, have to admit that to understand how, physically, these words got to be on the present sheet of paper, we would have to refer not just to natural laws, but also to the abstract logic of my argument. Accordingly, I may surely claim that there is a case for a kind of *prima facie* pluralism here, while we also have no way of knowing that this pluralism may not also represent the final truth about these matters, too.)

Smith can, if he so wishes, invoke his belief in naturalism in the second sense: in the idea that a completed science can explain everything, and that the physical world is causally closed. But there seems to me no reason to believe that this theory is true, just because we have all kinds of knowledge about things that science cannot currently explain. We *may* be able to explain these things in the future, scientifically. But we may not, and I don't see how we can tell, now, what it will be possible to explain in the light of some future science. In the meantime, it seems to me important to assert that naturalism in the *first* sense is false, and that there is every reason *now* to champion non-naturalistic ethical theories even if, in the fulness of time, we may be able to reduce them scientifically, and thus show that naturalism is, in fact, correct. At the very least, Popper's approach seems to me to suggest that there is no problem about someone – such as myself – currently favouring non-naturalistic ethical realism, if I so wish; not least, as there are, I think, other telling arguments in its favour (on which see, for example, McNaughton 1988), as well as Popper's more general case against scientific reduction, and for the fluffing up of Plato's beard. Of course, all that we can accord ethics is a *prima-facie* non-naturalistic status. But that, until we actually have to hand science that successfully reduces the ethical to things naturalistic, is surely enough.

6 Conclusion

Let me, in conclusion, remind you of what it is that I have been arguing. It is that analytical philosophy, as it currently exists, seems to me to have been oddly untouched by an engagement with Popper's views. To be sure, there has been much critical discussion of his ideas on induction, and there have been many, many papers about verisimilitude. Occasional themes from his work also receive critical treatment, but typically against assumptions of contemporary analytical philosophy similar to those with which I have here engaged. My belief is that Popper offers an interesting alternative to such views. In this chapter, I have set out some aspects of what a Popperian view might look like, and have tried to indicate the kinds of ways in which some ideas within analytical philosophy might be taken issue with, from such a perspective.

Clearly, however, it is one thing to give a quick sketch of such ideas, quite another to offer a reasonably explicated version of them; still another, to show that they can, themselves, withstand hard critical scrutiny. But such an effort seems to me worthwhile even if, in the end, it should turn out that these views of Popper's are simply incorrect. For there is another view of Popper's which seems to me both attractive and plausible; namely, that pluralistic competition between different theories not only plays a key role in the development of science but that, more generally, the path to objectivity is by way of inter-subjective criticism. This – as opposed to an analytical attitude which tries to judge everything on its merits, and which sees a passionate interest in a particular perspective as a dangerous source of prejudice – seems to me, in itself, good reason for putting some work into the development of a Popperian perspective, in critical dialogue with other views.

Accordingly, in my view, the task for those who find Popper's work at all interesting is not just to celebrate the 100 years since his birth, but to look forward to, say, whatever our own portion of the next 100 years might be, as involving the development of what is distinctive about Popper's perspective – even if, like a challenging scientific theory, it should, in the end, turn out to be incorrect.

Notes

1 I would like to thank David Miller and Ian Jarvie for criticism and suggestions, and also (appropriately critical) audiences at Christchurch and at the ANU.
2 Popper collaborated with Eccles in *The Self and Its Brain*. While they were in many respects in agreement, there were also some substantive differences between them. (In addition it is worth noting that each writer wrote his part of the book himself – and after the 'dialogue' had taken place – and to my knowledge (I was Popper's Assistant at the time) they were not involved in any substantial discussion about their respective contributions. Eccles was firmly in the Cartesian tradition, in the sense of denying animal consciousness; while Popper explicitly took the view that there were degrees of consciousness in different creatures. Also – as I have indicated in the text – Eccles made some striking empirical claims, but I know of no evidence that Popper subscribed to them.
3 The parallel here is, obviously, with J. S. Mill's *On Liberty*.
4 Note also the role of 'Fries' trilemma' in Popper (1959 [1935]), the discussion of Fries and of Nelson in Popper (1932), and the references to Nelson in Popper's discussion of leadership in Popper (1945), chapter 7.
5 Where Popper's involvement in the German translation of Lenin's *Materialism and Empirico-Criticism* is worth noting.
6 First, here, is Popper's 1932; next, much of Nelson's epistemological writing, and, in addition, Dahms, 2002 delivered at Popper 2002 Centenary Congress in Vienna and currently available only in German.
7 See Popper 1959 [1935], section 38 and Appendix *viii.
8 See Lejewski (1974) and Schroeder-Heisler (1984).
9 Popper 1974.
10 See Popper, 'The Aim of Science', in his *Objective Knowledge*. I would not wish to claim that the approach suggested in the text should also apply to reduction in mathematics and logic.
11 Compare his 1981.
12 See Popper, 'A Realist View of Logic, Physics and History', in his *Objective Knowledge*, p. 301.
13 See chapter 1 of his 1977.

References

Ackermann, Robert. 1995. 'Popper, Karl', in Jaegwon Kim and Ernest Sosa (eds) *A Companion to Metaphysics*, Oxford and Cambridge, MA: Blackwell, pp. 402–3.

Dahms, H.-J. 2002. 'Popper's First Steps in Philosophy: Leonard Nelson's Paradoxes of Sovereignty and Epistemology, and Popper's Attempted Solutions', paper delivered at Popper Centenary Congress in Vienna (currently available only in German).

Feyerabend, P. 1981. 'An Attempt at a Realistic Interpretation of Experience', in *idem, Realism, Rationalism and Scientific Method: Philosophical Papers I*, Cambridge: Cambridge University Press.

Jarvie, Ian. 2001. *The Republic of Science*, Amsterdam and Atlanta GA: Rodopi.

Lakatos, Imre. 1976. *Proofs and Refutations*. Cambridge: Cambridge University Press.

Lejewski, C. 1974. 'Popper's Theory of Formal or Deductive Logic', in P. A. Schilpp (ed.) *The Philosophy of Karl Popper*, La Salle, IL: Open Court, pp. 632–70.

Lewis, C. I. 1946. *Analysis of Knowledge and Valuation*, La Salle, IL: Open Court.

Mackie, J. L. 1977. *Inventing Right and Wrong*, London: Penguin Books.

McNaughton, David. 1988. *Moral Vision*, Oxford: Blackwell.

Musgrave, Alan. 1999. 'Critical Rationalism', in his *Essays on Realism and Rationalism*, Amsterdam and Atlanta, GA: Rodopi, pp. 314–50.

Popper, Karl R. 1945. *The Open Society and Its Enemies*, London: Routledge.

Popper, Karl R. 1959 [1935]. *The Logic of Scientific Discovery*, London: Hutchinson.

Popper, Karl R. 1962. 'Julius Kraft 1898–1960', in *Ratio*, vol. 4, pp. 2–12.

Popper, Karl R. 1963. *Conjectures and Refutations: The Growth of Scientific Knowledge*, London: Routledge Kegan Paul Ltd.

Popper, Karl R. 1972. *Objective Knowledge: an Evolutionary Approach*. Oxford: Oxford University Press.

Popper, Karl R. 1976. *Unended Quest: an Intellectual Autobiography*, Glasgow: Fontana/ Collins.

Popper, Karl R. 1979. *Die beiden Grundprobleme der Erkenntnistheorie*, Tubingen: Mohr.

Popper, Karl R. and John C. Eccles. 1977. *The Self and Its Brain*, Berlin and New York: Springer.

Schroeder-Heisler, P. 1984. 'Popper's Theory of Deductive Inference and the Concept of a Logical Constant', *History and Philosophy of Logic*, vol. 5, pp. 79–110.

Shearmur, Jeremy. 1980. 'The Religious Sect as a Cognitive System', in *Annual Review of the Social Sciences of Religion*, vol. 4.

Shearmur, Jeremy. 1985. 'Epistemology Socialized?', in *et Cetera*, Fall issue.

Shearmur, Jeremy. 1996. *The Political Thought of Karl Popper*, London and New York: Routledge.

Shearmur, Jeremy. 2002. 'Karl Popper and The Empirical Basis', delivered at Popper 2002 Centenary Congress, Vienna 2002.

Smith, Michael. 2000. 'Ethical Realism', in Hugh LaFollette (ed.), *The Blackwell Guide to Ethical Theory*. Malden, MA: Blackwell.

ter Hark, Michel. 1993. 'Problems and Psychologism: Popper as Heir to Otto Selz', in *Studies in History and Philosophy of Science*, vol. 24, pp. 585–609.

ter Hark, Michel. 2002. 'The Historical Roots of Popper's Searchlight Theory of Mind and Knowledge: A Tribute to Otto Selz', delivered at the Popper 2002 Centenary Congress in Vienna.

Watkins, J. W. N. 1958. 'Confirmable and Influential Metaphysics', *Mind*, vol. 67, pp. 344–65.

Watkins, J. W. N. 1984. *Science and Scepticism*, London: Hutchinson, and Princeton, NJ: Princeton University Press.

Zahar, Eli. 1995. 'The Problem of the Empirical Basis', in A. O'Hear (ed.), *Karl Popper: Philosophy and Problems*. Cambridge: Cambridge University Press, pp. 45–74.

6

MY ADVENTURE WITH POPPER AND WITTGENSTEIN

Peter Munz

Contrary to the conventional view that Popper and Wittgenstein were opposed to each other, the later Wittgenstein and Popper must be seen to be complementing one another. To start with, both Popper and the later Wittgenstein were agreed that the philosophical tradition in which both knowledge and meaning were taken to be derived from observations and ought to be reducible to them, was wrong. However, there was a gap in Popper's philosophy because he believed that when truth is discovered, meaning will take care of itself. But since, in Popper's view, general propositions can never be verified, their truth remains uncertain and, therefore, there must be a way of understanding what they mean which does not depend on their truth. This way was provided by the later Wittgenstein's demonstration that meanings do not come from what is being observed, but from the habits of speech communities. But Wittgenstein's thought about meaning was deficient in that it failed to distinguish between speech communities able to generate propositions which had meaning and those able to generate propositions which were true as well as meaningful. Popper made up for this deficiency by showing that propositions which are true as well as meaningful can only be generated in socio-political orders which are free and open enough to allow unlimited criticism.

* * *

When I studied philosophy first under Popper and later under Wittgenstein, I embarked on what was to become the greatest philosophical adventure of my life. I have always seen it as an adventure because I had not intended to study philosophy at all under anybody and my links to Popper and to Wittgenstein were entirely accidental. This accident proved truly adventurous because the conjunction of these two men led me eventually to a totally unexpected insight. What is more, since I am the only person in the world who studied under both men, the adventure proved a lonely one and, not having been embarked upon by anybody else, it yielded an original insight which has not been had by anybody.

But let me begin at the beginning. I had intended to be a historian because in my teens, in Italy, I was a fervent Marxist and wanted to study history to understand why the proletarian revolution would be as inevitable as Marx had predicted. I began my studies at Canterbury College in Christchurch, New

114

Zealand. In my first year I was told that a certain Karl Popper, a lecturer in philosophy, had been blaming Plato for the advent of fascism in the twentieth century. Having been brought up in the Germanic, idealist, humanistic tradition, I was convinced that Plato could not be wrong because he represented the highest aspirations of justice and intelligence. In my youthful enthusiasm I published a paper in a student journal to this effect, under the title 'Don't Blame Plato'. A few days later a very short man beckoned to me in the library. He introduced himself as Karl Popper and told me that I was wrong in defending Plato and asked me whether I was interested in learning why I was wrong. I was eager to learn and Popper invited me to his study and at that moment there began a life-long friendship. Popper's way of explaining was exemplary and convincing. He told me that Plato's idea of justice was based on the illusion that one could know for certain what everybody deserved. Plato, in other words, pretended to a knowledge which nobody could possibly possess. I was so fascinated by Popper's modest clarity and the logic of his reasoning that I began to attend all his lectures in philosophy and became an avid pupil. Popper explained that not even the best of knowledge is as certain as many people believed, because it could never be the conclusion of inductively collected observations. The inference from a limited number of observations to a general law was logically as illicit as Hume had argued. But Popper went further. He explained that in spite of this fact, there was no need to share Hume's despairing scepticism: for knowledge *was* possible. It consisted of hypotheses which had failed to be falsified. There is no need to enlarge here on this view of knowledge because it has by now become widely known. It completely undermined the old positivism which rested on the view that knowledge resulted from induction and was valid because of its derivation from induction. We, in Christchurch, were completely ignorant of the state of philosophical discussion in the rest of the world at that time, and Popper only mentioned *en passant* that there were people, especially in Vienna, who held a very different view which they called Logical Positivism – a view according to which knowledge was valid only if it could be reduced exhaustively to verifiable sense observations. Popper's logic that positivism cannot work because the truth of a conclusion does not guarantee the truth of the premises while the *falsity* of a conclusion demonstrates the falsity of the premises, was totally impeccable and we all thought that the Viennese Circle people who could not see this must be strange fuddy-duddies.

When I finished my historical studies and obtained a first class honours degree, I won a scholarship which would take me to an overseas university. By that time I had been appointed to be the assistant to Freddy Wood, the professor of history at Victoria College in Wellington. When I was wondering where to continue my studies, Freddy Wood offered to write to Jim Davidson, one of his former pupils who was a fellow of St John's College in Cambridge. Through Davidson I gained admission to St John's College in spite of the heavy demand for places after the war, and planned to do research in medieval history for a Ph.D. degree. After settling in, I discovered that Wittgenstein was holding seminars in philosophy and I could not resist the temptation to ask for permission to attend. Wittgenstein received me sitting in a deck chair in an otherwise unfurnished room in Whewell's Court of Trinity College. He grunted permission, provided I would not be what he called a 'tourist'. I promised to attend regularly, twice a week. He then asked where I came from and where I had studied philosophy. I mentioned Popper in the innocent belief that since both he and Popper were from Vienna, they would have been acquainted. But Wittgenstein grunted again: 'never heard of him'. I recalled then in my own mind that Popper had admitted to knowing of Wittgenstein, but had done so in unfriendly terms. He had in fact told me that the *Tractatus* read as if it had been written in a coffee house. Popper's wife overheard this remark and corrected him: 'No, Karl,' she said, 'it was actually written in the trenches of the First War!' Popper replied with a dismissive wave of his right arm: 'maybe, but Wittgenstein is the sort of man who cannot tell the difference between the trenches and a Viennese coffee house'. I came to know later that Popper was very unjust because Wittgenstein took life even more seriously than Popper did – which is saying a lot.

I joined Wittgenstein's seminar and before long came to be very disappointed. True to my promise I kept attending, but could not understand why that man had acquired such a reputation in Cambridge. Wittgenstein sat in his deck chair and the students crouched on the floor. Wittgenstein buried his head in his hand and shook his head and mumbled things and from time to time he uncovered his head and looked at us and said: 'thinking about thinking' or 'when you mean what you mean, you mean what the usage of your language-game commands' or 'whatever you mean, you cannot define it by pointing at it'. He always broke off in the middle of such sentences and glowered at us on the understanding that we would know what he meant. He also came, again and again, back to such sentences as 'when you have a philosophical problem, you must understand that you are misusing language. If you spoke correctly, there would be no philosophical problems'. Behind this remark I took there to be the assumption expressed in the *Tractatus*, that every word ought to be a picture of what one can observe, no less and no more – an assumption which was clearly out of keeping with the thought that in speaking we are following the rules of a game rather than portraying or reporting observations. Much later I understood that Wittgenstein had changed his mind; but at the time he never commented on this fact and, tantalisingly, evaded all questions to this effect.

Compared to the precise clarity of Popper's lectures on the deficiencies of induction, I found Wittgenstein's musings disappointing. It also occurred to me that it is really impossible to follow Wittgenstein's advice and correct one's language in terms of one's language. There ought to be, I reasoned to myself, at least a meta-language to correct the first language. I had read the *Tractatus* and it struck me that Wittgenstein's meanderings about language were often incompatible with what he had written in the *Tractatus*. I also told myself that there was an inconsistency in Wittgenstein's musings about meaning. He always countered a question or an objection by saying: 'What do you mean?', thus putting the ball back into the critic's court. But had he been consistent, he ought to have said, not 'what do you mean?', but 'which language-game's rules are you following in what you are saying?'. In short, I was puzzled and discontented. I also was not prepared to accept Wittgenstein's contention that there were no philosophical problems, but only self-inflicted linguistic puzzles. Bearing the *Tractatus* in mind, I kept asking myself whether 'all souls are immortal', if it was taken to be a puzzle rather than a problem, would have to be solved by showing that it failed to be reducible to elementary propositions which were pictures of reality; or whether it should be solved by showing that it employed words in ignorance or in defiance of the rules of a certain language-game. If the latter was the right way of solving such puzzles, I smelt here the underlying beginnings of an absolute relativism.

During my first term in Cambridge in October 1946 there took place that famous meeting at King's College where Popper had been invited to address the Moral Sciences Club of which Wittgenstein was the President. The meeting was crowded and no less a person than Bertrand Russell sat in an armchair, smoking his pipe and facing the open fire, with Popper on his left and Wittgenstein on his right. Popper began by saying that he had been invited to mention a puzzle and try to solve it. He added, provocatively, that in his view puzzles were trivial and that he would prefer to speak about a genuine philosophical problem. Wittgenstein got very agitated and, glowering, demanded to know what Popper meant by 'problem'. Popper replied that induction was such a problem. When Wittgenstein heard this he reached for the red hot poker from the fire and waved it in the air. Russell took the pipe out of his mouth and said: 'Wittgenstein, put down this poker at once'. Wittgenstein obeyed, but soon after got up, walked out and slammed the door. My heart and mind was entirely on Popper's side and there is no point in rehearsing what happened next, when Popper was left in control in a meeting which, apart from me, consisted of Wittgenstein devotees. For many years after this meeting, I took that clash to be symbolic of two diametrically opposed ways of thinking about knowledge. I must mention, though, that there was a historical accident in my understanding of this opposition. Wittgenstein's *Philosophical Investigations* had not yet been published and there was no way, at that time, in which I could inspect a coherent argument behind his performance in the weekly seminars. For that matter, Popper did not even know of the views expressed in the seminars and took Wittgenstein to be the Wittgenstein of the *Tractatus*.

As I then saw it, there was Popper on one side, explaining how one can gain rational knowledge about the world we are living in, even though it is not gained by the traditional method of induction. On the other side there was Wittgenstein who did not care for knowledge but maintained that people form speech communities, each with its own rules and that truth and falsity, sense and nonsense had to be defined in terms of one's obedience to whatever rules were obtaining in one's community and that those rules would differ from community to community. A blunder, he often remarked, is only a blunder in one's language-game. There is no blunder as such. By Popperian standards there was very *much* such a thing as an absolute blunder!

I began to see the opposition of the two men in a historical context. Both were reacting against the conventional philosophies which had stood behind the scientific revolution and the Enlightenment. These conventional philosophies had seen knowledge as resulting from observations and had made their way and gained popularity by rejecting the mediaeval view that true knowledge came from consulting authorities such as Aristotle or the Bible. They had taken for granted that, provided there was initial and prior observation, the results could be formulated in language: one observation, one word. This conventional view survived right down to the early twentieth century and found its formula in the doctrine of the Vienna Circle that 'the meaning of words is the method of their verification' or in propositions 5 and 4.01 of Wittgenstein's *Tractatus* which stated that propositions are truth-functions of elementary propositions understood (2.1ff.; 4.01f.) as pictures of reality. Both Popper and Wittgenstein had recognised the flaw in this conventional philosophy: observations and words, they had come to see, do not automatically match. Popper put this clearly in the second paragraph of section 30 of his *Logic of Scientific Discovery* of 1934 where he said that it is impossible to build knowledge on what one has observed or is able to look at. Similarly, Wittgenstein, at almost exactly the same time and ten years after the publication of the *Tractatus*, on 1 July 1932, told Waismann: 'In the *Tractatus* I was unclear about logical analysis and ostensive definition. I thought at that time that there was a "connection between language and reality"'.

Popper had recognised that we cannot put our observations into words, because the observations are too diffuse to allow a simple verbal assignation. We need a word, he was saying, so that we can know where to look and what to look for. Wittgenstein had put it the other way round. He had recognised that when we are uttering a word, we cannot convey or explain its meaning by pointing at what we intend it to mean. Having both recognised the flaw in conventional positivism, they wheeled off in opposite directions. Popper amended the flaw by showing that, contrary to the conventional view (e.g. Newton's claim that *hypothesis non fingo*), knowledge results from making a hypothesis and observing what the hypothesis dictates. If the observation falsified the hypothesis, the hypothesis had to be dropped and replaced by a different one. This way he retained the initial rationalism and avoided the facile assumption that observations come first and can be described in so many matching words. Wittgenstein headed into the opposite direction. He threw out the baby with the bath water and lost all interest in knowledge and sought to explain how words come to have meaning and can be understood by people other than the original speaker. As long as words have meaning, it does not matter whether they refer to something beyond them, i.e. whether the sentences they form are true or false.

Many years later when I came across the philosophical irrationalities of postmodernism in the shape of the unphilosophical rhetoric of Foucault and Derrida, I began to realise that Wittgenstein had issued a generous invitation to their postmodern pseudo-thinking. When he had argued that one cannot define what one means by looking or pointing but only by checking whether one is conforming to the rules of the language-game one is playing, he had opened the door to Derrida's pompous pretension that when we are speaking, there is nothing present we are referring to, but that we are merely constructing a text which we can interpret with the help of another text which can be interpreted with the help of yet another text and so forth, indefinitely. I then set up a symbolic picture of philosophy in the second half of the twentieth century. There was Popper on one side, determined to *amend* some flaws in the Enlightenment by explaining that while induction is no road to knowledge, we can still have rational knowledge by making hypotheses which are falsifiable. If they remain unfalsified, they are taken to be provisionally true. But we must always bear in mind that they might be falsified in the future and replaced by better ones. On the other side, there was Wittgenstein and postmodernism who turned *against* the Enlightenment with the contention that all knowledge is simply a text which some people agree on and interpret by providing more texts. All these texts are relative to a language-game. Change the rules of the game and the texts will cease to make sense. The question of their truth or falsity cannot even arise.

Eventually, in 1985, I published a book under the title *Our Knowledge of the Growth of Knowledge* which was based on the opposition between Popper and Wittgenstein. I put Popper's philosophy of knowledge on one side and described how Wittgenstein's philosophy that all meanings are relative to a language-game is not only self-contradictory, but incompatible with what we know about evolution, that is, about the way we have come to be what we are. Evolution by natural selection, I argued, guarantees that we can and must have knowledge about our environment, otherwise we could not have emerged; and that Popper's explanation of how we come to have knowledge is compatible with Darwinian evolution, while Wittgenstein's resignation that all we can do is to play language-games and observe the rules, is incompatible with it. I formulated all this in an epigram: 'According to Popper, all knowledge is relatively absolute; and according to Wittgenstein, all knowledge is absolutely relative.' I meant to say that for Popper there is genuine knowledge, but it can never be final, that is, absolute; it can only be 'verisimilitudinous'. But for Wittgenstein whatever knowledge there is, is never real knowledge about the world because it is relative to the rules of the language-game according to which it is formulated linguistically. When I told Popper about this epigram, he dismissed it as too facile. All the same, when he asked me what the book was about, he had smiled contentedly at my reply that it showed that he was right and that Wittgenstein was wrong. But later he remarked somewhat petulantly: 'How can you compare me to Wittgenstein? He was an ideologue; but I discovered a truth!' – meaning: I discovered that in spite of the fact that induction does not work, we can have genuine knowledge.

I cannot recall at what precise point the adventure began to deepen in the sense that I began to see beyond this stark opposition. Whenever it was, I was led to a complete revision of my view of the relation between Popper and Wittgenstein. Instead of seeing the way they represented diametrically opposed ways of

dealing with their discovery of the flaws in conventional Enlightenment philosophy, I came to see that they were complementary to each other and that it
was only their very unphilosophical temperaments which prevented them from
recognising it. Popper could have improved his understanding of the role of
language in the formulation of hypotheses prior to observation, by using Wittgenstein's *Philosophical Investigations*; and Wittgenstein could have improved his
understanding of the roles of speech communities, language-games and of what
he called 'forms of life', had he paid attention to Popper's social and political
thought and its relevance to the growth of knowledge. In short, I began to understand that that meeting in Cambridge in 1946, famous for the poker incident
which underlined the hostility between these two men, ought to have run a different course and ended in a confession of friendship and mutual support.

In Popper's thought, language occupies a central place. It is because of the evolution of language, he explained especially in his *Objective Knowledge* of 1972,
that humans can formulate hypotheses and theories. Such hypotheses are like
disembodied organisms and are subject to the same evolutionary pressures as biological organisms, which one could consider to be embodied theories. Surviving
organisms embody a great deal of knowledge about their environment. If the
environment changes or if they change, that knowledge ceases to be adaptive and
becomes obsolete, but it takes generations for it to be discarded by the gradual
extinction of the species. Human knowledge, on the other hand, in the shape of
theories which are being falsified, can, since it is no more than a linguistic proposition, be abandoned at the drop of a hat. As Popper put it: where human
knowledge is concerned, our theories can die in our stead. We can abandon theories and do not have to wait for the human species which holds them to die out.
Language, in this view of the evolution of knowledge, makes a crucial difference.
But Popper left it at that. He never went on to ask himself how it is that we can
understand such language when it clearly does not just report observations, but
advances theories *before* observations are made and, indeed, directs us to the
observations we *ought* to be making. It is of the essence of a Popperian hypothesis
not only that it must be falsifiable but also that it goes beyond the information
given. In going beyond the information given it states something which one
cannot point at, that is, it states something which cannot be defined ostensively –
for the very simple reason that what it states has not yet been observed. It refers
to something which is not there, in front of our eyes. As a typical example I
would mention Darwin's hypothesis that species are unstable. All he had ever
observed and had received ample information from farmers about, is that one can
make changes inside a species by artificial breeding. The hypothesis that by natural selection one species can change into another species was a bold hypothesis
which went beyond the information he had collected. So, how is it that we
can understand propositions which cannot be defined ostensively? For a Popperian account of the acquisition of knowledge to work, we need not only language –
as he himself emphasised – but a language which conveys meanings even
though what is being meant cannot be pointed at. It must be a language which is

semantically viable even though there is nothing audible or visible to which it appears to be referring. The semantics of this kind of language must not depend on ostension. If they do not depend on ostension, what *do* they depend on? It is here that Wittgenstein would have proved helpful.

Wittgenstein himself, simply looking at human language, explained that its meanings cannot be defined ostensively. If one utters a word like 'rabbit' and points at a rabbit, he reasoned, there is a multiplicity of possible meanings. One could mean 'mammal', or 'rabbithood', or 'running fast', and so on. This proves that pointing (i.e. ostension) does not help and that, to convey meaning, one cannot go behind language or, as Peirce put it more wittily long before Wittgenstein, one cannot exit from the dictionary: one can explain a word by another word, but one cannot leave language and substitute a physical gesture. It follows that when people understand the uttered word, they must have a source *other* than ostension for their understanding. This argument gains depth if one does something Wittgenstein never did and considers the *evolution* of human language. One will then find that in *pre*-human languages, meanings can be and are indeed defined ostensively. Languages in the form of communication systems are widely prevalent among pre-human species. Bird songs communicate messages; vervet monkeys have explicit signals which warn against leopards as distinct from warnings against eagles. Bees communicate the direction in which honey is to be found to their fellows; and ants take the scent of oleic acid to be a signal of death and react by dragging whatever smells of oleic acid out of the nest, even if the smelling ant is alive. I call all such communication systems two-dimensional. They report and signal facts, that is, they communicate what is and what exists. Ants and vervet monkeys and birds and bees make unequivocal responses to such two-dimensional language, that is, by their behaviour. The responses triggered by their shrieks are the unequivocally ostensively defined *meanings* of their shrieks or their songs or their gestures. Human language is very different. It is three-dimensional in that it can also communicate messages and meanings about events which have not taken place, about events which cannot possibly take place or which might or might not happen in the future, or which one wishes to have or not to have happened. The meanings of a two-dimensional language – what the shrieks, gestures, songs refer to – are defined automatically by the responses they trigger. They are, so to speak, defined ostensively. Such ostensive definitions are not always available in a three-dimensional language, for the very obvious reason that whatever one is intending one's sentences to be referring to, may not be present or has not yet happened. Because of this gap between two-dimensional and three-dimensional language, many linguists maintain that human language is so different from pre-human communication systems that it is unique and that pre-human systems of communication do not deserve to be called languages. This widely held separation of two-dimensional language from three-dimensional language obscures an important point and ought, therefore, to be abandoned, no matter what so many linguists are saying. Our human three-dimensional systems are descended from two-dimensional systems and have evolved, through modification, from the former. The Popperian theory of knowledge, it must be clear, requires a three-dimensional language. The question is, what were the pressures which made these modifications emerge and be selected for retention?

The chief pressure was the large human brain. I know this sounds paradoxical because we intuitively connect a large brain with great intelligence and in English we take 'brainy' and 'intelligent' to be synonymous. Why should a large brain be a pressure to modify two-dimensional language into three-dimensional language? Indeed according to many contemporary theories, the large brain, far from being a pressure making for language, is itself the *result* of the pressures presented by social living. According to this theory, when one is living in a society, it will be advantageous to deceive one's fellows and to simulate intentions or actions in order to deceive and gain an advantage. Hence when one is living socially, the larger the brain the more adaptive it will be because a large brain enables its bearer to be clever enough to trick, take advantage of and exploit his or her fellow citizens – all faculties which are believed to be essential for social intercourse. I believe this theory which is temporarily very fashionable, to be profoundly wrong because it fails to consider neuroscientific findings. The truth of the matter is that the brain is not a unitary organ like the pancreas or the kidneys, designed to fulfil a special task. It consists, on the contrary, of billions of neurons and more billions of different connections between them. As a result, neurological research has found that the brain does not act like a single organ but that there is endless division of labour. When one sees a chair in front of one's eyes, there will be an impact on one's retina. From the retina neurons lead to neurons in the brain and it is here that the divisions occur. The height of the chair will be registered in one region, the colour in another, and the time and the place of the chair in yet other regions. What is more, it would appear that colour is registered faster than shape, so that there is also asynchronicity. There has never as yet been an explanation of how it is that that same brain comes up in the end with a unitary word such as 'chair'. Neuroscientists have called this the binding problem. How are the different registrations bound together?

If there is as yet no simple explanation, one can see that knowledge of a three-dimensional language which can utter words meaningfully *before* there is a corresponding sensation to which they refer, is a strong candidate for a solution. It may well not be the only explanation, but it will go a long way to a solution of the binding problem if one is in command of such a three-dimensional language. With a large brain, a two-dimensional language is of no help, because it can only produce sounds or gestures which refer either to one or to another of the many registrations into which the large brain breaks up the sight of a chair. But given the brain's division of labour it cannot assemble all the different registrations because they do not present themselves as a single whole. Hence the large brain, instead of being an asset, is a liability which has to be compensated for. And one of the compensations which tends to control the damage the large size causes, is the modification of two-dimensional language, the meanings of which *can* be defined ostensively, into three-dimensional language, the meanings of which

122

need *not* be defined ostensively. But how is the modification achieved? What has to happen for two-dimensionality to be modified into three-dimensionality?

If the meaning of sentences formed cannot be defined ostensively, there is only one conceivable alternative to generate meanings. People have to get together and form a community in which certain types of linguistic expressions are understood by habit and by mutual consent. People get used to their body language as well as to their sentences because of the over-arching consensus. The members of such a community obey certain conventions and all know what those conventions are and understand what is being conveyed by them. There is reigning linguistic usage and, in short, such a community is what Wittgenstein called a form of life. The members are following rules and in this way, they are playing a language-game. Thinking in terms of evolution, we must envisage that when people were beginning to suffer from the deficiencies of the two-dimensional language they were using, because their large brains required more than a single response to a certain shriek or song, those people who were able to form speech communities, were able to survive. Those who did not, did not survive, at least not for long. The advent of speech communities controlled the damage caused by the oversized brain. Wittgenstein never thought in terms of evolution and was, indeed, sceptical of it. But he did explain how three-dimensional languages function and why the way they do, differs from the way two-dimensional languages function. The latter get to function by simple ostensive definition of the shrieks and songs they consist of. We can extend Wittgenstein's insight by showing how the two-dimensionality of language came to be modified via the emergence of forms of life or cultures. I suggest that Wittgenstein provided the much-needed support for the Popperian theory that we gain knowledge by inventing hypotheses *before* we make observations. Such Popperian hypotheses have to be formulated in three-dimensional language and the requirements of three-dimensional language can best be explained in terms of Wittgenstein's understanding that the meanings of such a language derive from the rules of a language-game which obtains in any one speech community. In this way, Popperianism is supported and enriched by Wittgensteinianism!

However, the debt is also on the other side. Let me explain. Wittgenstein was famously careless as to the constitution of these forms of life. In his view, anything at all would do. You can have a group of religious fanatics, you can have a traditional tribal community, you can have a largish family, you can have a democratically run community or a fascist dictatorship. Every one of these communities would be able to harbour the rules for forming meaningful sentences. The rules would differ from group to group. What was legitimate in one community might not be legitimate in another. But he had nothing whatever to say about the politico-social form such groups had to take. If I have argued above that Popper was enriched by Wittgenstein, I am now saying that Wittgenstein has to be enriched by Popper. Popper carefully distinguished between the constitutions of these communities. Groups which were closed and ruled either by dictators or by iron tradition were able to form three-dimensionally meaningful sentences – but were unable to form sentences which could claim to be genuine knowledge. For hypotheses to be true they not only had to be part of a three-dimensional language. They also had to be put forward in a community in which there was enough freedom for them to be examined and, if found wanting, to be discarded and replaced. By Popperian standards, the Wittgensteinian view that any community will do, is stultifying. One has to take care to lay down minimum conditions of social structure for three-dimensional languages to be used for genuine hypotheses.

In this way I began to understand that there was a deficiency in Wittgenstein as well as in Popper and that the deficiencies in the one could be made up by the thought of the other. In 1946 and for many years after, I had taken it that when Wittgenstein appeared to have threatened Popper with a poker, this clash was symbolic of the two diverging trends in modern philosophy: Popper's revision of the Enlightenment Project on one side; and Wittgenstein's total rejection of the Enlightenment, on the other. But once I had seen that the deficiencies of the one could be remedied by the other as well as the other way round, I began to understand that these two philosophers were complementary and needed one another. I no longer saw the poker incident as symbolising deep and fundamental divergences, but came to see it as nothing more than a farce. How much of a farce is best appreciated when one recalls that at that time Wittgenstein's careful argument about the impossibility of ostensive definition in a three-dimensional language was not widely known and certainly not known to Popper. The *Philosophical Investigations* had not yet been published. At most, the argument was known to the small number of the members of Wittgenstein's seminar in Cambridge to whom he had communicated it verbally and not always in the most coherent way. Popper at that time knew only of the *Tractatus*. He fundamentally disagreed with the *Tractatus* and took its proposition 5 as the quintessential flaw in the positivism which had been upheld ever since the so-called scientific revolution and throughout the Enlightenment. He could not possibly have known that by that time Wittgenstein had himself seen the error of his way and, as he had put it to Waismann in 1932, rejected propositions 5 and 4.01 and all they implied, as decisively as did Popper himself. But for these historical accidents, the road was open to a full understanding that Popper and Wittgenstein were barking up the same tree, albeit from different sides. It became clear that they could have learnt from each other. Popper could have come to a better understanding of the way three-dimensional language operates; and Wittgenstein could have come to a better appreciation of how stultifying it was to consider all language-games to be of equal and comparable value.

In this way, my philosophical adventure had a fruitful outcome because it led me to write a book which was published in 1999. It is entitled, somewhat cheekily, *Critique of Impure Reason*. In that book I availed myself fully of the way Popper was complemented by Wittgenstein and Wittgenstein by Popper. The book is about psychological knowledge. Psychological knowledge is a marginal kind of knowledge. It is knowledge of what we loosely call our states of mind. There is endless controversy as to what we mean by mind, whether it is so subjective that only the person who is having the mind can say what the state is, or whether there are ways in which outsiders too can tell. During the past ten years there has been a real breakthrough in the shape of two books by Antonio Damasio – *Descartes' Error* of 1994 and *The Feeling of what Happens* of 1999. Damasio has shown that in between our neurons and what we call our fully conscious mind, there are somatic markers. As far as I know, nobody has ever before recognised that there is something *in between* the silent chemistry plus physics of the neurons and articulated conscious mind. People have either been 'eliminative materialists' who see nothing but neurons; or mentalists who see the mind as separate from or at best incomprehensively influenced by neurons. Materialists like Paul Churchland, to cite a gross example, claim that we have no psychological knowledge because such as it is, it cannot be reduced to neuronal events. And people like Colin McGinn, on the other side, give up in despair, because they see no way in which one could explain how 'the water of neurons is being changed into the wine of consciousness' or, to speak with Gerald Edelman, how 'matter can become imagination'. Damasio's discovery of the in-between state has made it for the first time possible to understand the true relation between neurons and so-called mental events (i.e., the states we are conscious of). McGinn's water can indeed be transformed into the wine of consciousness and Edelman's matter can be seen to become imagination *via* the in-between state, the somatic markers, though neither Edelman nor McGinn has as yet seen it this way. Psychological knowledge is knowledge of those somatic markers which are the subjective feels we are aware of. They are generated by neuronal, that is physical and chemical events in our body. The neuronal events themselves are not felt or sensed. The somatic makers are *felt or sensed*, but they do not contain enough information for us to say what they are. At most, they are indescribable moods we are aware of. Being indescribable but virulently noticeable, they are crying out for a label. Psychological knowledge consists of knowledge of these markers. And this is where Popper and Wittgenstein come in. Popper argued, and there is no reason why we should disagree with him, that we can only claim to have knowledge if what we think we know is falsifiable. Clearly, there is nothing in those markers which would enable us to say that anything we say about them is falsifiable. They simply do not contain the kind of information which would conceivably falsify any statement made about them. As a result, Popper had a very insouciant way of dismissing all psychological knowledge as nothing better than alchemy or astrology – that is, as superstition. Coming from a different perspective, Wittgenstein concurred. If we wanted to speak about those somatic markers, i.e. our feels, we would have to use a purely *private* language. But he showed convincingly that there can be no such thing as a private language, for it is impossible to make a private reference to one's sensations. True, one could simply name a sensation, but one would never be able to say whether such naming is correct. To be sure that one knows what would count as a correct name, there would have to be an *independent* criterion. Next time one has what one thinks is the same sensation, one can try the same name, but there can be no telling whether the sensation so named really is the same sensation or whether it ought to be labelled differently. As I said, Wittgenstein and Popper, though coming from different perspectives, are in complete agreement on this point that such subjective sensations cannot be known, that is, cannot be named. But the Popperian purely negative conclusion is unsatisfying, because these markers are noticeable and cannot be ignored. This is where Wittgenstein will help. According to Wittgenstein, we can make meaningful statements as long as they conform to the rules of a language-game. We do not have to dismiss a statement simply because there is no information which might falsify it. If we now take it that a statement about those somatic markers is a statement formed according to the rules of a language-game, we can proceed to psychological knowledge about those markers – a knowledge which, if we follow nothing but Popper, would have to be dismissed as superstition. But if we have recourse to Wittgenstein, we can understand that such knowledge comes from the language-game we have decided to play rather than from the somatic markers themselves. Such knowledge cannot be defined ostensively, for we cannot point to the markers themselves and say: 'this is what I mean'. The markers are subjective, ineffable feels and no amount of pointing would explain or define the meaning of what we are saying about them. But if we take it that the language-game we are engaged in *interprets* these somatic markers, we can arrive at psychological knowledge of these somatic markers. The problem of psychological knowledge can be solved at least partially, when we understand that the somatic markers we feel are being got at from two different sides. They are *caused* by neuronal events; and *interpreted* in terms of the language-game or form of life we choose to be participating in. When applied to Damasio's identification of somatic markers, Popper and Wittgenstein between them, are shedding a lot of light on the old intractable mind/body problem and certainly more light than Popper and Eccles, adhering as they did to a conventional dualism, had been able to shed in their *The Self and Its Brain*.

It is hardly necessary for me to explain that in bringing Popper and Wittgenstein together in this way, I am going beyond anything the two men themselves would necessarily subscribe to. What is more, I am also expanding Damasio's finding that there are somatic markers. Damasio is a neuroscientist and not given to philosophical analysis. He himself believed, very unphilosophically, that we have no difficulty in describing the content and feels of these markers in so many words. Words, he believes, attach themselves automatically to all the many feels our neurons generate. In this assumption he is clearly wrong. Damasio is not alone in making such a wrong assumption. On the contrary, in my *Critique of Impure Reason*, I have a long list of people who also take it for granted that words come automatically with our sensation of those feels. But Popper is right. Insisting on falsifiability as the sole criterion of knowledge, he would conclude that we can have no proper knowledge of these somatic markers. But Wittgenstein too is right. He would say that that falsifiability is not the sole or, perhaps any, criterion of knowledge. As long as a description of those markers is performed according to the rules of a language-game, the description is meaningful, not absolutely so, but at least in terms of a given language-game. The choice of the game is open to us. It can be Christian or Freudian, Stoic or Buddhist, or whatever. Whichever game we engage in, the markers can be interpreted meaningfully.

I cannot resist the temptation to end by telling you how Popper and Wittgenstein would have responded to my suggestion that they complement each other. Popper would have said: 'your trouble is that you have not read what I have written'. And Wittgenstein would have shaken his head and muttered uncomprehendingly: 'What on earth do you *mean*?' And so the last conclusion must be that, in spite of my argument, both philosophers had enough unphilosophical temperament to resist philosophy. Philosophy, it has to be reluctantly conceded, does not necessarily make philosophers philosophical.

7

AN EPISTEMIC FREE-RIDING
PROBLEM?

Christian List and Philip Pettit[1]

Karl Popper noted that, when social scientists are members of the society they study, they may affect that society. If the individuals to whom a theory initially applies come to understand that theory, then this understanding may affect their behaviour in such a way that the theory ceases to be applicable. This may be called the problem of reflexivity. In this chapter, we identify such a problem in an apparently unlikely area: in the area of Condorcet's famous jury theorem. Suppose that each individual member of some decision-making body has an equal chance greater than 0.5 of making a correct judgment, and suppose further that all individuals' judgments are independent from each other. Then the jury theorem states that the majority will make a correct judgment with a probability approaching 1 as the number of individuals increases. We argue that, if the individuals come to understand the jury theorem, then they may cease to make independent judgments, thereby undermining one of the conditions for the application of the theorem. Specifically, we suggest that the individuals may be faced with a temptation to free-ride on the epistemic efforts of others. We first develop the problem in some detail and then ask whether there are any escape routes that can protect the jury theorem against the effect of reflexivity.

1 Introduction

One of the hallmark themes of Karl Popper's approach to the social sciences was the insistence that when social scientists are members of the society they study, then they are liable to affect that society. In particular, they are liable to affect it in such a way that the claims they make lose their validity. Cf. Popper 1963, p. 16:

> The interaction between the scientist's pronouncements and social life almost invariably creates situations in which we have not only to consider the truth of such pronouncements, but also their actual influence on future developments. The social scientist may be striving to find the truth; but, at the same time, he must always be exerting a definite influence upon society. The very fact that his pronouncements do exert an influence destroys their objectivity.

Suppose that someone propounds a novel theory of social behaviour, and that the theory is well confirmed by how people actually behave. Imagine that the success of the theory leads to its coming to be widely understood and accepted. And now suppose that the very fact of such popularisation has an effect on how people behave, leading some or all of them to act contrary to the theory's predictions. Where this happens, the theory is undermined in the general manner that Popper describes. The people to whom it is supposed to apply become reflectively aware of it, and this reflection causes a reaction that impacts negatively on the applicability of the theory. Our chapter is concerned with this sort of influence, one that we describe as reflexivity.[2]

We focus, more particularly, on how reflexivity may operate in a rather unlikely area. The theory we take as our target, if indeed it can be called a theory, is the jury theorem that was first identified by the eighteenth-century French thinker, the Marquis de Condorcet, and that has recently attracted renewed attention (Grofman, Owen and Feld 1983, Lahda 1992, Estlund 1994, Austen-Smith and Banks 1996, Feddersen and Pesendorfer 1998, List and Goodin 2001, List 2004). We argue that Condorcet's result is subject to a reflexivity effect of broadly the kind that Popper had in mind. If people come to be aware of the theorem, and to accept it, then in some circumstances they may act in a way that undermines some of the preconditions for the application of the theorem, so that the theorem ceases to apply to them. More specifically, they may do this as a result of a temptation to free-ride on the epistemic efforts of others.

The material in this chapter is divided into three sections. We introduce the jury theorem in the first section. We look at the core problem in the second. And we consider in the third section whether there are any escape routes that can protect the jury theorem against the effect of reflexivity. We present the arguments of the opening two sections, first in an informal way, and then in a more formal, technically exact manner. Although the technical presentation is essential for formulating the arguments properly, readers who wish to skip it can get a sense of our argument from the informal presentation.

2 The Condorcetian background

2.1 An informal presentation

Suppose that there is an issue of fact on which a number of individuals are each to judge. Let the issue be whether something is the case or not the case – assuming that it must be one or the other. The fact that it is the case will be represented as '$X = 1$', the fact that it is not the case as '$X = 0$'. The issue may be observational: say, whether the car in an accident drove through the lights on the red or not. Or it may be empirical but more speculative: say, whether the population size of the United States is greater than 300 million or not. Or it may be adjudicative, as in whether a defendant is guilty or not guilty. Or it may be theoretical, as with the issue of whether or not quarks can exist separately from one another. Or whatever: there is no limit on the possibilities in play.

Suppose that the members of the relevant group each have a better-than-random, i.e. better than 0.5, chance of making a correct judgment. Suppose, more demandingly, that they each have the same chance of making a correct judgment; say, a chance of 0.6. Suppose, further, that their individual judgments are independent, given the relevant fact of the matter. This means, roughly, that any individual's chance of making a correct judgment is not increased or decreased by any facts about how any of the other individuals have judged the issue. It is not the case, for example, that anyone defers to another, always copying the judgment of the other.[3] And suppose, finally, that they each reveal their own judgment truthfully when the group takes a vote on the issue in question. These independent judgments we describe as the *private judgments* of the individuals.

What does it mean to say that each individual has a chance, or *competence level*, of 0.6 of making a correct judgment? It means that if $X = 1$, then the individual has a 0.6 probability of judging that $X = 1$; and that if $X = 0$, the individual has a 0.6 probability of judging that $X = 0$. The individual has that competence level in tracking the fact that the proposition under judgment is true, if it is true; and has the same competence level in tracking the fact that the proposition is false, if it is false (Nozick 1981).

Condorcet showed that if these conditions are met, and every group member casts a vote on the issue, then two remarkable consequences follow. The first is that the probability of the majority making a correct judgment on the issue (assuming there is no tie) will be greater than that of any one individual's making a correct judgment; in our example, it will be greater than 0.6. And the second is that as the group size increases, the probability of the majority making a correct judgment approaches 1. The lesson is that under the conditions outlined, there is epistemic safety in numbers. No one individual has a better chance of making a correct judgment than the majority, and going along with the majority looks like a better and better epistemic strategy as the group size increases.

We do not present the formal argument for the jury theorem here but it is not difficult to get a sense of why it holds. Consider a biased coin that has a 0.6 probability of coming up heads and a 0.4 probability of coming up tails. Now think about the chance of the coin coming up heads on a single throw; this is 0.6. And then ask yourself whether there is a greater chance of its coming up heads more often than not, as you keep throwing it. Intuitively, there is a greater chance of this happening than there is of the coin coming up heads on a single throw. Let each coin toss represent the judgment of an individual, and let heads represent a correct judgment, and tails an incorrect one. Then our reasoning about the coin should make it plausible that there is a better chance of the majority making a correct judgment than there is of any single individual making a correct judgment.

So much for the first part of Condorcet's result. The second – that the probability of the majority making a correct judgment approaches 1 as the group size increases – can also be made plausible by analogy with the coin case. Again imagine a coin that has a 0.6 probability of coming up heads and a 0.4 probability of coming up tails. Think about how often you expect the coin to come up heads and how often tails when it is thrown repeatedly. Statistically, you expect it to come up heads 60 per cent of the time and tails 40 per cent of the time. First consider the case of ten throws. The expected heads–tails pattern is 6–4. But the actual pattern may still deviate from this expected one: it might be 7–3, or 5–5, or occasionally even 4–6. But now consider the case of a hundred throws. Here the expected heads–tails pattern is 60–40. Again, the actual pattern may deviate from this; it might be 58–42, or 63–37, or 55–45. But intuitively it will be less likely than in the case of ten throws that we get heads less than 50 per cent of the time. Finally, consider the case of a thousand, ten thousand, or a million throws. Given the expected frequency of 60 per cent, it will be less and less likely that the coin comes up heads less than 50 per cent of the time. By the law of large numbers, the actual frequency of heads will approximate the expected one increasingly closely as the number of throws increases. This implies that the probability of getting a majority on the 'heads' side rather than the 'tails' side approaches 1 as the number of throws increases.

Condorcet described the result as a jury theorem and it is easy to see why it might apply to multi-member juries making a judgment on whether or not a defendant is guilty. The use of simple majority voting in that case is somewhat problematic, though, if we are primarily concerned, not with the chance of the jury getting the right answer, but rather with the chance of the jury not convicting an innocent person. But we leave aside that complication here. There are many different cases where that complication does not arise.

Some of those cases, like the jury example, involve a collective body of people who act together with a view to making a judgment that is definitive in some way. They may involve a committee deciding on who should get a prize, raising the question with every candidate of whether he or she has made the best contribution or not. Or they may involve an appointments or promotions or examinations committee of a parallel kind. Or any of a variety of similar bodies: say, the commission that is required to judge on whether a certain proposal should be accepted or not, or the board of an organisation that has to judge on what course of action should be recommended to members, and so on.

But Condorcet's issue arises even in cases where there is no collective body making a joint decision. Take as an example the community of scientists in a given subject-area. While these scientists will collaborate and compete with one another, thereby establishing a community, they will not constitute a collective body that has a task to discharge that parallels the task of a jury or committee. But the jury theorem still has a lesson for such a community. If we suppose, perhaps fancifully, that each member has the same greater than 0.5 chance of making a correct judgment on a given issue, then the majority has a greater chance still of making a correct judgment and this chance approaches 1 as the size of the community increases. Here too there is safety in numbers.[4]

2.2 A formal presentation

We assume that there are two possible states of the world:

X = 1 (e.g. 'guilty');
X = 0 (e.g. 'not guilty').

For simplicity, we assume that each of these two states has an equal prior probability of 0.5, but this assumption plays only a minor role for most of our argument. Consider a jury with n members, labelled 1, 2, . . . , n, where $n > 1$. Each juror i makes a *private judgment* J_i about the state of the world. The private judgment J_i takes the value 0 or 1. The judgment J_i is said to be *correct* if and only if it coincides with the state of the world X. Following Condorcet's original framework, we assume:

Competence. For each x (0 or 1), each juror i has a probability $p > 0.5$ of making the private judgment $J_i = x$, given that the state of the world is $X = x$.

The parameter p is interpreted as the *individual competence level* of juror i. By our competence assumption, all jurors have the same individual competence level.

Independence of private judgments. The private judgments of the n jurors, $J_1, . . . , J_n$, are independent from each other, given the state of the world.
Private judgment voting. Each juror i submits the private judgment J_i as his or her vote, denoted V_i, i.e. $V_i = J_i$.

The last two conditions jointly entail that the votes of the n jurors, $V_1, . . . , V_n$, like the private judgments, are independent from each other, given the state of the world.

Suppose the votes $V_1, . . . , V_n$ are aggregated by simple majority voting. Specifically, let $V = V_1 + . . . + V_n$ be the total number of votes for '$X = 1$'. Then $V > n/2$ means that there is a majority of votes for '$X = 1$' (e.g. for 'guilty'), and $V < n/2$ means that there is a majority of votes for '$X = 0$' (e.g. for 'not guilty'). Let P_n be the probability that there will be a majority of votes for '$X = 1$' among the n jurors, given that the state of the world is $X = 1$. Then P_n is also equal to the probability that there will be a majority of votes for '$X = 0$' among the n jurors, given that the state of the world is $X = 0$. The parameter P_n can be interpreted as the *collective competence level* of the n-member jury. We can now state the jury theorem formally:

Condorcet jury theorem
- If n is odd (ruling out majority ties), the n-member jury is collectively more competent than each individual juror, i.e. $P_n > p$.

132

- The jury's collective competence level P_n converges to 1 as the number of jurors n tends to infinity.

3 The core problem

3.1 An informal treatment

The jury theorem is good epistemic news, identifying a prospect whereby a group of individuals might be collectively better at tracking the truth on a given issue than any of the group members. But the theorem will apply only if every group member does his or her bit. All members must form a judgment independently of the judgments of others, letting that judgment reflect their individual competence level. They must be willing to go with their own private judgment when they cast their vote. They may have deliberated together and listened to the evidence and argument produced by others but, in the end, they must go their own epistemic way.

To put this otherwise, the good results predicted by the jury theorem are an aggregate effect of individual efforts to be epistemically independent. When the group members are independent in this way, then they will each individually have a 0.6 chance of making a correct judgment, even when the votes of the other group members are given. That is, the conditional probability of each making a correct judgment, given how others vote, will still be 0.6. This is analogous to our coin example. No matter how the other coin throws turn out, the chance of the coin coming up heads on any one throw will always be 0.6. Even if, against the odds, the coin has come up tails ten times in a row, the chance of its coming up tails on the next throw will still be only 0.4. Similarly, regardless of how others vote, the probability, conditional or unconditional, of any one individual's making a correct judgment on the issue under consideration will remain fixed at 0.6.

We can express these points more formally by referring to the degree of support that the votes of the individuals and the group give to the hypothesis that things are, or are not, how the individuals or the group judge them to be. Call this hypothesis H. The unconditional degree of support that an individual vote gives to H can be interpreted as the warrant that that individual's voting in a given way provides for believing in H. Likewise, the unconditional degree of support that the group's vote gives to H can be interpreted as the warrant that a given voting pattern across that group as a whole provides for believing in H.

Like the concept of probability, the concept of degree of support comes in an unconditional and a conditional form. We can consider not only the unconditional degree of support that an individual's vote gives to H, but also the conditional degree of support that the vote gives to H, given the votes of the other individuals. The conditional degree of support can be interpreted as the additional warrant that the individual's vote provides for believing in H, given that we have already observed the votes of the other individuals.

When the votes of different individuals are independent from each other, the conditional and unconditional degrees of support take the same value: the conditional degree of support associated with each individual's vote, given the votes of the others, is equal to the unconditional degree of support that the vote provides. This implies that, when the group members' judgments are independent from each other, then the unconditional degree of support that the group's vote as a whole gives to H is simply the sum of the unconditional degrees of support that the individual votes each give to H. So the degree of support provided by each individual vote contributes in full measure to the degree of support given to H by how the group as a whole votes. And the degree of support given to H by the voting pattern across the group is an increasing function of the number of individuals voting in support of H. But, as we will see, when independence is violated, the conditional and unconditional degrees of support can come apart.

Now we are in a position to see how popularisation of the Condorcet jury theorem may undermine the theorem's conditions and in some cases put the result in jeopardy.[5] Suppose that the group members become aware of the theorem, recognising that the chance of the majority making a correct judgment is greater than the chance of any one individual making a correct judgment. There are several kinds of conditions under which this awareness can feed back onto the individuals' behaviour, impacting negatively on the conditions of the Condorcet jury theorem. We focus on three such sets of conditions, addressing the most benign one first and turning to the less benign ones next.

3.1.1 Updating in truthful deliberation

Suppose that prior to taking a vote on the issue in question, the group engages in collective deliberation and the individuals all reveal their private judgments to each other. As before, we assume that each individual has a greater than 0.5 chance of making a correct private judgment, and that the private judgments of different individuals are independent from each other, given the relevant fact of the matter. For the moment, we also assume that the individuals all reveal their private judgments truthfully. This is a crucial assumption; below we discuss the case where it is relaxed.[6]

In the scenario presented the individuals can each observe the pattern of private judgments across the group as a whole, and they each have the opportunity to revise their own judgment when a vote is subsequently taken. So there are two stages. At the first (deliberation) stage, the individuals reveal their private judgments to each other; at the second (voting) stage, they each submit a vote. We further assume that, at the voting stage, each individual cares about submitting a correct judgment as his or her vote, even if this may involve a change from his or her original private judgment.

Suppose I am one of the individuals and have observed the pattern of private judgments across the group. I believe that these judgments satisfy the conditions of the Condorcet jury theorem, as assumed above. Should I stick to my own private judgment when submitting my vote, or should I do something else?

If the majority of private judgments coincides with my own private judgment, this should reinforce my belief that I have made a correct judgment, and so I should stick to it. But if the majority of private judgments is different from my own one, then my understanding of the Condorcet jury theorem should lead me to reason as follows. There is a much better chance that the majority will have made a correct judgment than that I will have made a correct judgment. In terms of degree of support: if the majority judges that H is true while I privately judge that H is false, then the majority gives a much greater degree of support to H than my own private judgment gives to the negation of H. So I should update my judgment, following the majority opinion. So in either case – whether or not the majority opinion coincides with my own private judgment – I should vote in accordance with the majority opinion. My own private judgment disappears from the scene at this point. Notice, however, that in the present scenario my own private judgment will have made its epistemic contribution, as it will have made a contribution to the majority opinion at the stage of group deliberation.

This reasoning is symmetrical across the group. Under the conditions outlined, all individuals will engage in the same reasoning and, at the voting stage, they will each submit a vote according to the majority opinion that was established at the deliberation stage. The effect of this is unanimity at the voting stage. Whichever opinion commands a majority at the deliberation stage will become the unanimity opinion at the voting stage.[7]

Although the votes, unlike the private judgments, do not satisfy the independence requirement of the jury theorem, the theorem's main prediction is not undermined here. The probability that the group unanimously makes a correct judgment at the voting stage will simply equal the probability that the majority makes a correct judgment at the deliberation stage. By the Condorcet jury theorem, the latter probability is greater than the probability that any one individual makes a correct private judgment, and converges to one as the group size increases. So, likewise, the former probability – that the group unanimously makes a correct judgment at the voting stage – will have these properties.

Here reflexivity will undermine Condorcet's assumptions that individuals vote their private judgments and that different individuals' votes, as opposed to private judgments, are independent from each other. But, interestingly, it will not undermine Condorcet's conclusion: the group's collective competence will still be greater than the competence of each individual member, and will still approach 1 as the group size increases. This is because the individuals will each have applied the majority calculus in their own reasoning, making their voting decision by identifying the majority opinion among all individuals' private judgments, including, crucially, their own one.

Reflexivity will, however, undermine another prediction of Condorcet's framework. In Condorcet's original case, where all individuals vote their own private judgments, the degree of support given to the hypothesis that things are as the majority says they are is an increasing function of the majority size. This means that information about the majority size also gives us information about the degree of support this majority gives to the hypothesis in question. But in the present case, where the majority opinion at the deliberation stage is turned into a unanimous opinion at the voting stage, this fine-grained information gets lost. Regardless of whether the original majority supporting the hypothesis was narrow or broad, we will always obtain a unanimous vote across the group (see also Goodin 2002).[8]

3.1.2 Epistemic free-riding

The case of reflexivity we have just identified is a relatively benign one. While reflexivity undermines some of Condorcet's assumptions, it does not undermine Condorcet's main conclusion. We will now see that, if the conditions of the previous case are subtly modified, reflexivity can have much less benign consequences.

As before, each individual has a greater than 0.5 chance of making a correct private judgment, and the private judgments of different individuals are independent, given the relevant truth of the matter. Again, prior to taking a vote, the individuals can observe the judgments expressed by (some of) the other individuals. In the previous case, we described this as a deliberation stage. But the assumption can be met in this case without requiring a distinct stage of that sort. The individuals may for example observe some of the others' judgments if voting takes the form of an open ballot. The judgments are expressed by a show of hands, and an individual can take a moment to observe how many others raise their hands before deciding whether or not to raise his or her own hand too. The most important difference from the previous case is that we do not assume that the individuals will always reveal their private judgments truthfully. They may of course do so, but we will not take this for granted.

Suppose that one or more individuals satisfy the following conditions:

- however much they care for the group's making a correct judgment, they each have a motive for wanting to be correct in the judgments they individually express;
- they each believe that others express their private judgments truthfully.[9]

Imagine that these conditions are fulfilled in my case. I have observed the judgments expressed by the others and have to decide what judgment to express myself. As I assume that the others' judgments are all independent as required by the jury theorem, I come to believe that there is a better chance that the majority will have made a correct judgment on the issue in hand than that I will have individually made a correct judgment. Thus I stand a better chance of expressing a correct judgment by expressing the same judgment as the majority does than by expressing my own private judgment. So I should withhold my private judgment and go along with the majority; and when I submit my vote I should vote as I expect the majority to vote, rather than as my private judgment would lead me to vote.

Can conditions like these be fulfilled? Given the idealising assumption that the members of a group have an equal, greater than 0.5 chance of making a correct private judgment on a particular issue, we think they can. There are many possible reasons why I might want to express a correct judgment myself, ranging from the case where I want for selfish reasons not to appear to be wrong on some issue – say, the case where my reputation or perhaps even my remuneration as a group member depends on my track record at making correct judgments – to the case where I have commendable motives for wanting to get the issue right: say, the case where as a member of a scientific community I want to communicate the truth to my students or colleagues, or I want to organise my research around sound assumptions. In many such cases I may have good reason to believe that others are unlikely to think as I do, even if they are aware of Condorcet's result; and that they are likely to come down in majority support – a majority that forms independently of my own private judgment – for one or another position.

So the popularisation of the Condorcet theorem may have the consequence that one or more group members will be led to free-ride on the efforts of others. When only one individual free-rides like this, always withholding their own private judgment and expressing the judgment of the majority, then they will raise their individual chance of expressing a correct judgment on the issue, by Condorcet's result. Thus the *unconditional* degree of support that their revised judgment provides for the hypothesis that things are as their judgment suggests will equal the degree of support provided by the majority – which is strictly greater than the unconditional degree of support that their independent private judgment would have provided. But the *conditional* degree of support their updated judgment gives to that hypothesis, given the judgments of the other individuals – i.e. the contribution their revised judgment makes to the overall degree of support provided for that hypothesis by the group's set of judgments – will fall to zero. That marks the free-riding character of their behaviour. Their 'judging' as they do will contribute nothing to the warrant that the majority judgment provides for the hypothesis. Moreover, their 'judging' as they do might mislead the group into thinking that the warrant is greater than it actually is. If their free-riding is not transparent – that is, if the group assumes that all individuals expressed independent judgments when in fact some were free-riding – then their judgment will suggest, mistakenly, that the warrant is that corresponding to a majority of k out of n individuals, when really it is that corresponding to a majority of $k-1$ out of $n-1$ individuals.

But again the reasoning is – at least potentially – symmetrical across the group. If more than one individual free-rides in the manner described, withholding their own private judgment and deferring to the judgment of whatever majority they expect to form, then the consequences can be quite dramatic. Suppose, for example, that votes are taken sequentially; that is, the individuals submit their votes one by one in a particular sequence, and each individual can observe the votes submitted earlier in the sequence. Then the first individual will vote his or her private judgment, since there will not be any majority for this individual to defer to. The second individual will presumably still vote his or her private judgment, since there is no reason to think that the first individual was more likely to have made a correct judgment. But now, beginning with either the third or the fourth individual in the sequence, the temptation to free-ride may arise. After the first three votes have been cast – or, in case the first two individuals agree, after the first two votes have been cast – there will typically be a majority in one or the other direction.[10] Thus any individual whose vote is taken subsequently will be led to think that the preceding majority is more likely to have made a correct judgment than they are. To be precise, any individual will be led to think this if they believe that the individuals earlier in the sequence expressed their private judgments truthfully.[11] So the individual who cares about expressing a correct judgment will withhold their own private judgment and go with the majority of individuals preceding them in the sequence.

In this fashion, any majority that accidentally emerges among the first two or three jurors may grow further and further, suggesting, mistakenly, an increasing degree of support for the hypothesis that things are as this growing majority says they are. But in fact the degree of support for that hypothesis will not increase at all beyond the first two or three individuals. All subsequent votes will simply be the result of epistemic free-riding and not the result of the expression of independent private judgments, and therefore the conditional degree of support these subsequent votes give to the hypothesis in question is zero. It is easy to see that, depending on the particular sequence in which the votes are taken, any voting outcome could in principle emerge like this, and the good news of the jury theorem is undermined quite dramatically. The phenomenon we have described is sometimes referred to as an informational cascade (Bikhchandani, Hirshleifer and Welch 1992).

3.1.3 A classical free-riding problem?

Under the conditions given, free-riding may occur, but there is none the less a disanalogy with the classical free-riding problem of the n-person prisoners' dilemma. A central condition in our case was that each individual acts on the assumption that others express their private judgments truthfully. By contrast, a classical free-riding problem requires that it is in an individual's interest to free-ride not only under one specific assumption about how others behave, but under every such assumption – or at least under most of them (Pettit 1986). In short, a classical such problem requires that free-riding is the dominant strategy. But in the present case, while individuals may be tempted to free-ride if they believe that others express independent private judgments, that temptation may decline if they believe that others are free-riding too.[12] Were I to think that everyone in the group was simply expressing the judgment they expected the majority to express – for instance, were I to think that the majority is the result of an informational cascade rather than the result of the agreement among independent private judgments – then I would have no reason to think that going along with the majority would increase the chance of being correct. And so I would cease to free-ride – I would begin to express my independent private judgment – under that assumption.

There is a further, slightly different set of conditions, however, under which something closer to a classical free-riding problem might arise. The individuals each value the group's making a correct judgment on the issue in question, but they do not care too much about making a correct private judgment themselves. None the less, each individual has the capacity to make an independent private judgment satisfying Condorcet's assumptions. If an individual chooses to exercise this capacity, then he or she will have a greater than 0.5 chance of making a correct private judgment, and the private judgments of different individuals will be independent in the relevant manner. However, exercising that capacity – making an independent private judgment – is costly; it requires time and effort.

So, instead of the previous conditions, the following is true of the individuals. Apart from the case where their own vote is pivotal for the group vote, they each have a preference ranking as in a prisoners' dilemma. They each prefer that they should all vote independently than that no one should do so, since they value the group's being right about the issue; and for the same reason they prefer that more others, rather than fewer others, vote independently. But, as they find it burdensome to vote independently themselves, each most wants to be a lone defector – a lone non-independent voter – and least wants to be a lone conformer – that is, the only person to vote independently.

Under these conditions, and absent the prospect of being pivotal, we can see how the members of the group, having learned about Condorcet's result, might each be tempted to free-ride. Each will think that to the extent that others vote independently, there is lesser reason for them to bother doing so: except for the case where they are pivotal, the contribution that their independent voting would make is not going to be large enough to compensate for the effort. And each will think equally that to the extent that others do not vote independently, the same is true: except for the case where they are pivotal, the contribution that their independent voting would make is going to represent an effort wasted.

While this set of conditions would give rise to something closer to a classical free-riding problem, it is probably less likely to be fulfilled than the previous set. Less likely, but still possible. Consider the case where a fairly large committee has to make some collective judgment, for instance on the merit of different candidates for a job or different submissions for a prize. Voting independently in such a case might be burdensome, involving a lot of research and consideration, and yet everyone on the committee might prefer that it get the result right. If everyone puts aside the chance of being the pivotal voter – the larger the group the lower that chance – then each will be tempted to think that if others vote independently, the effort of ensuring independence will not be required; and that if others do not vote independently, the effort of ensuring independence will be wasted. The present free-riding problem is similar to the rational ignorance problems discussed in the literature: it may sometimes be rational to remain ignorant rather

139

than to engage in the costly acquisition of information (Brennan and Lomasky 1993, ch. 7).

3.2 A formal treatment

We begin by introducing the concept of degree of support in general terms, namely in terms of the support some item of evidence gives to some hypothesis. We then apply that concept to Condorcet's framework. First, we discuss the unconditional degree of support an individual juror's vote – for or against '$X = 1$' – gives to the hypothesis that $X = 1$. Second, we discuss the unconditional degree of support the vote of the entire jury gives to that hypothesis. Third, we discuss the conditional degree of support an individual juror's vote gives to the hypothesis, given the votes of the other jurors. Finally, we sketch the reflexivity problem.

3.2.1 The concept of degree of support

Let H be some hypothesis and E some item of evidence. We use the notation $Pr(A)$ to denote the unconditional probability of A, and $Pr(A \mid B)$ to denote the conditional probability of A, given B. For any item of evidence E, the *unconditional degree of support* E gives to H is defined as

$$l(H, E) := \log\left(\frac{Pr(E \mid H)}{Pr(E \mid \neg H)} \right)$$

(Fitelson 2001). Note some properties of this measure of the degree of support:

- The [degree of support E gives to H] is related to the [probability that H is true, given E] as follows. Let $r = Pr(H)$ be the prior probability that H is true. Then

$$Pr(H \mid E) = \frac{r}{r + (1-r) \, exp(-l(H, E))}.$$

- The measure also has the following property:

$$l(H, E) \begin{cases} > 0 & \text{if } Pr(H \mid E) > Pr(H) \\ = 0 & \text{if } Pr(H \mid E) = Pr(H) \\ < 0 & \text{if } Pr(H \mid E) < Pr(H). \end{cases}$$

This means: If the measure is positive (respectively negative), then observing the evidence E increases (respectively decreases) our degree of belief in H.

The degree of support can also be defined conditionally. For any two items of evidence E_1 and E_2, the *conditional degree of support E_2 gives to H conditional on E_1* is defined as

$$l(H, E_2 \mid E_1) := \log\left(\frac{Pr(E_2 \mid H \wedge E_1)}{Pr(E_2 \mid \neg H \wedge E_1)} \right).$$

The *conditional* degree of support can be interpreted as the additional warrant E_2 gives to H, given that we have already observed E_1.

It can easily be seen that, for any two items of evidence E_1 and E_2, the degree of support the *conjunction* of E_1 and E_2 gives to H is

$$l(H, E_1 \wedge E_2) = l(H, E_1) + l(H, E_2 \mid E_1).$$

Now consider the special case where E_1 and E_2 are independent from each other conditional on H (and on $\neg H$). Such independence implies $Pr(E_2 \mid H \wedge E_1)$ $= Pr(E_2 \mid H)$ and $Pr(E_2 \mid \neg H \wedge E_1) = Pr(E_2 \mid \neg H)$. Therefore we have

$$l(H, E_2 \mid E_1) = l(H, E_2),$$

i.e. [the conditional degree of support E_2 gives to H, given E_1] equals [the unconditional degree of support E_2 gives to H]. Therefore

$$l(H, E_1 \wedge E_2) = l(H, E_1) + l(H, E_2),$$

i.e. the degree of support is additive. The distinction between unconditional and conditional degree of support is crucial for the discussion below.

3.2.2 The unconditional degree of support an individual juror's vote gives to H

Let us restate Condorcet's framework in terms of hypothesis testing (List 2004). We make Condorcet's original assumptions of competence, independence of private judgments, and private judgment voting. Let H denote the hypothesis that $X = 1$ (e.g. that the defendant is guilty). Suppose we want to test H. Each juror's vote V_i is a potential item of evidence relevant to H. What degree of support does each such vote give to H?

Suppose our evidence is that juror i has voted for '$X = 1$'. We have

$$l(X = 1, V_i = 1) = \log(p / (1-p)). \qquad (*)$$

Thus $l(X = 1, V_i = 1)$ is greater than 0, so long as $p > 0.5$. This makes sense from an intuitive perspective: observing that a juror with competence $p > 0.5$ has voted for '$X = 1$' makes $X = 1$ more likely to be true. Moreover, by our assumption that the prior probability of each state of the world is 0.5 (i.e. $r = 0.5$), the posterior probability that $X = 1$, given an individual juror's vote for '$X = 1$' is p.[13]

Next, suppose our evidence is that juror i has voted for '$X = 0$'. We have

$$l(X = 1, V_i = 0) = \log((1-p)/p). \qquad (**)$$

Then $l(X = 1, V_i = 0)$ is less than 0, so long as $p > 0.5$. Again, this makes intuitive sense: observing that a juror with competence $p > 0.5$ has voted for '$X = 0$' makes $X = 1$ less likely to be true. Here, by our assumption that the prior probability of each state of the world is 0.5, the posterior probability that $X = 0$, given an individual juror's vote for '$X = 0$' is p.[14]

3.2.3 The degree of support the vote of the jury collectively gives to H

What about the degree of support that the voting pattern across all jurors gives to H? Again consider the situation where all of Condorcet's original conditions are satisfied. Suppose our evidence E is that precisely h out of n jurors have voted for '$X = 1$'. For simplicity, suppose the first h jurors have voted for '$X = 1$', while the remaining n–h jurors have voted for '$X = 0$'; that is, we consider the evidence

$$E = (V_1 = 1 \wedge V_2 = 1 \wedge \ldots \wedge V_h = 1) \wedge (V_{h+1} = 0 \wedge V_{h+2} = 0 \wedge \ldots \wedge V_n = 0).$$

By Condorcet's conditions of independence of private judgments and private judgment voting, the votes of different jurors are independent from each other conditional on the state of the world X. Thus the degree of support is additive, and we have:

$$l(X = 1, E) = m \log(p/(1-p)),\text{[15]}$$

where $m = h$–$(n$–$h)$ is the absolute margin between the number of votes for '$X = 1$' and the number of votes against '$X = 0$'.[16] The same result holds for any other set of h out of n jurors; the assumption that precisely the first h jurors voted for '$X = 1$' is no loss of generality here. Note the following:

- If there are more votes for '$X = 1$' than for '$X = 0$', then the jury's voting pattern supports $X = 1$.
- If there are more votes for '$X = 0$' than for '$X = 1$', then the jury's voting pattern supports $X = 0$.
- In both cases, the greater the difference between the number of 'guilty' and 'not guilty' votes, the greater the relevant degree of support.

By our assumption that the two possible states of the world have the same prior probability, the posterior probability that $X = 1$ (respectively, that $X = 0$), given the evidence that precisely h out of n jurors have voted for '$X = 1$' (respectively, for '$X = 0$'), is $p^m/(p^m+(1-p)^m)$, where m is as defined above. If the given evidence is only that a majority among the n jurors has voted for '$X = 1$' (respectively for '$X = 0$'), but the evidence does not include any information about the precise size of that majority, then the posterior probability that $X = 1$ (respectively, that $X = 0$) is P_n, i.e. equal to the collective competence level (List 2004).

3.2.4 The conditional degree of support an individual juror's vote gives to H, given the votes of the other jurors

Suppose that some, but not all, of the jurors – up to $n-1$ of them – have cast their votes. Let E denote the evidence constituted by the particular voting pattern across these jurors. Suppose juror i is not among those jurors who have already cast their votes. What is the *conditional* degree of support juror i's vote gives to H, given E? Suppose juror i votes for '$X = 1$'. Then the conditional degree of support juror i's vote gives to H, given E, is $l(X = 1, V_i = 1 \mid E)$. If Condorcet's conditions of independence of private judgments and private judgment voting are met, we have:

$$l(X = 1, V_i = 1 \mid E) = l(X = 1, V_i = 1) = \log(p / (1-p)).$$

An analogous result holds when juror i votes for '$X = 0$'.

$$l(X = 1, V_i = 0 \mid E) = l(X = 1, V_i = 0) = \log((1-p) / p).$$

In short, under independence of private judgments and private judgment voting, [the conditional degree of support juror i's vote gives to H, given the other jurors' votes] is equal to [the unconditional degree of support that juror's vote gives to H].

This fact is responsible for the power of the original jury theorem: under independence of private judgments and private judgment voting, the support different jurors' votes give to H is additive. There are no diminishing marginal returns on adding further jurors. Supposing that the competence condition is also satisfied, adding more and more jurors typically increases the degree of support the jury's voting pattern gives to the hypothesis that things are as the majority says they are, and there is in principle no upper bound to this increase.

3.2.5 Updating in truthful deliberation

As before, suppose the n jurors satisfy the conditions of competence and independence of private judgments. But, unlike before, we now suppose that there are two stages. In the first (deliberation) stage, the jurors reveal their private judgments to each other. We assume that they all reveal these judgments truthfully.[17] In the second (voting) stage they each submit a vote. A juror's vote may be either his or her own private judgment or a revised judgment, where the revision might be based on the juror's observation of the pattern of private judgments across the jury in the first stage. We assume that each juror cares about submitting a correct judgment as his or her vote, even if this requires deviating from his or her own private judgment.

Suppose juror i observes the private judgments across the entire jury, as revealed in the first stage, including juror i's own private judgment. This allows juror i to determine whether or not a majority of private judgments supports H, i.e. whether or not $J > n/2$, where $J = J_1 + \ldots + J_n$. For simplicity, assume that n is odd; so there is never a majority tie.

If juror i understands the Condorcet jury theorem, he or she will realise that the probability that the majority of private judgments across the jurors coincides with the state of the world, P_n, exceeds his or her own individual competence, p. The degree of support the majority judgment gives to H (or $\neg H$, depending on how the majority goes) exceeds the degree of support juror i's private judgment individually gives to H (or $\neg H$).

As we have assumed, at the second stage, juror i cares about submitting a correct judgment as his or her vote. Consider the following two voting strategies:

The private judgment strategy. Vote for '$X = 1$' (i.e. $V_i := 1$) *if and only if* $J_i = 1$.

The updating strategy. Vote for '$X = 1$' (i.e. $V_i := 1$) *if and only if* $J > n/2$.

The private judgment strategy is the one assumed in Condorcet's original result. What are the differences between the two strategies?

- On the private judgment strategy, juror i's probability of submitting a correct judgment as a vote is

$$Pr(V_i = 1 \mid X = 1) = Pr(V_i = 0 \mid X = 0) = p,$$

as in Condorcet's original framework.

- On the updating strategy, juror i's probability of submitting a correct judgment as a vote is

$$Pr(V_i = 1 \mid X = 1) = Pr(V_i = 0 \mid X = 0) = P_n,$$

which, by the jury theorem, is greater than p and can be arbitrarily close to 1 when the jury size n is large.

If juror i wants to submit a correct judgment as a vote with a high probability, he or she will adopt the updating strategy. Moreover, a rational juror should be moved by the epistemic force of the majority judgment. While a single private judgment in support of H (respectively $\neg H$) warrants only a degree of belief of p in H (respectively $\neg H$), a majority judgment in support of H (respectively $\neg H$) warrants a degree of belief of P_n in H (respectively $\neg H$),[18] which by the jury theorem is greater than p.

This reasoning is symmetrical across the n jurors, and they will therefore all adopt the updating strategy. We obtain the following result:

- Whenever a majority of private judgments supports the hypothesis that $X = 1$ at the first stage, all jurors will unanimously vote for '$X = 1$' at the second stage, i.e. if $J > n/2$ then $V = n$.
- Whenever a majority of private judgments supports the hypothesis that $X = 0$ at the first stage, all jurors will unanimously vote for '$X = 0$' at the second stage, i.e. if $J < n/2$ then $V = 0$.

So the original jury theorem, as stated above, continues to hold. This is because the majoritarian aggregation has been performed in the individual reasoning of every juror. Any single vote that results from a juror's application of the updating strategy will carry the same epistemic weight that the pattern of private judgments collectively carried at the first stage. The jurors will all speak with the same voice at the second stage. The unconditional degree of support a single juror's vote gives to H (or $\neg H$) at the second stage equals the degree of support the jurors' private judgments collectively give to that hypothesis at the first stage, i.e. for each juror i,

$$l(X = 1, V_i = 1) = l(X = 1, J > n/2) = \log(P_n/(1-P_n))$$
$$= l(X = 0, V_i = 0) = l(X = 0, J < n/2) = \log(P_n/(1-P_n)),$$

where $P_n = Pr(J > n/2 \mid X = 1) = Pr(J < n/2 \mid X = 0)$, as in Condorcet's original framework. So additional votes are redundant once all jurors have updated their judgments. As soon as the vote of a single juror is given, the conditional degree of support given to H (or $\neg H$) by every additional vote is zero. Formally, for any i and j (where $i \neq j$), we have

$$l(X = 1, V_j = 1 \mid V_i = 1) = l(X = 0, V_j = 0 \mid V_i = 0) = 0,$$

since, after every juror's updating of their judgment, $Pr(V_j = 1 \mid V_i = 1) = Pr(V_j = 0 \mid V_i = 0) = 1$.

In the present scenario, while Condorcet's conditions of competence and independence of private judgments are satisfied, the condition of private judgment voting is undermined by reflexivity, as is Condorcet's condition that the votes themselves, and not only the private judgments, are independent, given the state of the world. However, the effect of reflexivity is benign here, in that the central conclusion of the jury theorem continues to hold, as we have seen, albeit via a somewhat different mechanism.

However, what is lost at the second stage, after the updating, is the fine-grained information about the size of the majority for $X = 1$ (or for $X = 0$, as the case may be) among the private judgments. In Condorcet's original framework this information allows us to determine that the degree of support given to H by a majority of h out of n votes is precisely $m\log(p/(1-p))$, where $m = h-(n-h)$. In the present case, on the other hand, we can only determine, in a more coarse-grained way, that the degree of support given to H by a unanimous vote for H is $\log(P_n/(1-P_n))$.

3.2.6 The free-riding problem

We now subtly modify the conditions of the previous case. We still suppose that the jurors satisfy competence and independence of private judgments. But we change our assumption on what information each juror has about the other jurors' judgments. We now suppose that, prior to taking a vote, the jurors may observe the judgments expressed by some, but not necessarily all, of the other jurors. A case of particular interest here is the one of sequential voting: the jurors cast their votes by a show of hands one by one in a sequence, and each juror can observe the votes cast by the jurors preceding him or her in that sequence. Unlike before, however, we do not assume that the jurors will always express their private judgments truthfully; they might do so, but we do not presuppose this. But we continue to assume that each juror cares about submitting a correct judgment as his or her vote.

Our question is whether or not jurors will have an incentive to express their private judgments truthfully. Consider the sequential case just described. The jurors reveal their judgments – cast their votes – in a sequence, say 1, 2, 3 up to n. Suppose that jurors 1 up to $i-1$ have cast their votes, $V_1, \ldots, V_{i-1}$, and suppose, for the moment, that they have each voted their private judgments truthfully, i.e. $V_1 = J_1$, $\ldots, V_{i-1} = J_{i-1}$. Suppose it is now juror i's turn to cast a vote, V_i, and juror i acts on the assumption that the votes cast by jurors 1 up to $i-1$ are these jurors' truthful private judgments. To make things simple, we assume that i is an odd number.

So juror i knows the judgments (by assumption, the true private judgments) of jurors 1 up to $i-1$; and, moreover, juror i knows his or her own private judgment. This allows juror i to determine whether or not a majority among the judgments of jurors 1 up to i (including his or her own private judgment) supports $X = 1$, i.e. whether or not $V_1 + \ldots + V_{i-1} + J_i > i/2$.

Unless juror i is the first or second juror in the sequence, the understanding of the Condorcet jury theorem will lead him or her to reason as follows. Assuming that the other jurors have revealed their private judgments truthfully, the probability, P_i, that the majority among the i private judgments up to juror i coincides with the state of the world exceeds juror i's own individual competence, p. In degree of support terms, the degree of support the majority judgment among jurors 1 up to i gives to H (or $\neg H$, depending on how that majority goes) exceeds the degree of support juror i's private judgment individually gives to H (or $\neg H$).

So, as before, juror i may be tempted to adopt an updating strategy:

The updating strategy. Vote for '$X = 1$' (i.e. $V_i := 1$) *if and only if* $V_1 + \ldots + V_{i-1} + J_i > i/2$.

Again, contrast this with the private judgment strategy, introduced above:

The private judgment strategy. Vote for '$X = 1$' (i.e. $V_i := 1$) *if and only if* $J_i = 1$.

What are the differences between the two strategies in the present context? Note that the assumption that jurors 1 up to $i-1$ have revealed their private judgments truthfully is crucial here.

A   The implications for juror i's probability of submitting a correct judgment as a vote
- On the private judgment strategy, juror i's probability of submitting a correct judgment as a vote is

$$Pr(V_i = 1 \mid X = 1) = Pr(V_i = 0 \mid X = 0) = p,$$

as in Condorcet's original framework.
- On the updating strategy, juror i's probability of submitting a correct judgment as a vote is

$$Pr(V_i = 1 \mid X = 1) = Pr(V_i = 0 \mid X = 0)$$
$$= Pr(V_1 + \ldots + V_{i-1} + J_i > i/2 \mid X = 1)$$
$$= Pr(V_1 + \ldots + V_{i-1} + J_i < i/2 \mid X = 0) = P_i,$$

which, by the jury theorem, is greater than p and can be arbitrarily close to 1 when i is large.

So, if juror i gets certain private benefits for exhibiting (what appears to be) a high competence level in his or her voting pattern (e.g. a reward for his or her track record at voting correctly), then the juror has an incentive to adopt the updating strategy rather than the private judgment strategy. Moreover, as before, if juror i is rational, he or she should be moved by the epistemic force of the majority judgment among jurors 1 up to i: while juror i's private judgment in support of H (respectively $\neg H$) warrants only a degree of belief of p in H (respectively $\neg H$), the majority judgment among jurors 1 up to i in support of H (respectively $\neg H$) warrants a degree of belief of P_i in H (respectively $\neg H$),[19] which by the jury theorem is greater than p – assuming that jurors 1 up to $i-1$ have indeed truthfully revealed their independent private judgments.

B   The implications for the unconditional degree of support juror i's vote gives to H
- On the private judgment strategy, as shown in section 3.2.2, the unconditional degree of support juror i's vote gives to H or $\neg H$ is

$$l(X = 1, V_i = 1) = l(X = 0, V_i = 0) = \log(p / (1-p)).$$

- On the updating strategy, the unconditional degree of support juror i's vote gives to H or $\neg H$ is

$$l(X = 1, V_i = 1) = l(X = 0, V_i = 0) = \log(P_i/(1-P_i)),$$

which, by the jury theorem, is greater than $\log(p/(1-p))$ because $P_i > p$.

C **The implications for the conditional degree of support juror i's vote gives to H, given the votes of jurors 1 up to $i-1$**

- On the private judgment strategy, as shown in section 3.2.4, the conditional degree of support juror i's vote gives to H or $\neg H$, given the votes of jurors 1 up to $i-1$, is

$$l(X = 1, V_i = 1 \mid E) = l(X = 0, V_i = 0 \mid E) = l(X = 1, V_i = 1) = l(X = 0, V_i = 0) = \log(p / (1-p)),$$

where E refers to the voting pattern across jurors 1 up to $i-1$.

- On the updating strategy, the conditional degree of support juror i's vote gives to H or $\neg H$, given the votes of jurors 1 up to $i-1$, is

$$l(X = 1, V_i = 1 \mid E) = l(X = 0, V_i = 0 \mid E) = 0,$$

supposing that juror i is not pivotal for the majority among jurors 1 up to i, i.e. supposing that jurors 1 up to $i-1$ are not tied between '$X = 1$' and '$X = 0$'. This result is presented in more detail in the appendix on pp. 154–5.

Table 7.1 summarises implications B and C.

Note that, for any odd number i greater than 1, the value in box (3) is greater than the one in box (1), while the value in box (4) is smaller than the one in box (2). This means that, under the updating strategy, juror i's individual (unconditional) epistemic performance will be better than under the private judgment strategy, but his or her epistemic contribution to the collectivity will drop down to 0 (supposing that juror i is not pivotal for the majority judgment). Crucially, all of this depends on the assumption that jurors 1 up to $i-1$ reveal their private judgments truthfully.[20]

This means that, if all jurors act on the assumptions described in this section, jurors beyond the first few will typically not make an additional epistemic contribution. We can imagine a case where there are 10 jurors, each of whom has a competence level of 0.6. Let us suppose the state of the world is $X = 1$ and the pattern of private judgments across these jurors is as shown in Table 7.2.

Under the idealised behavioural assumptions of this section – which, as we

Table 7.1

Juror *i*'s strategy	The *unconditional* degree of support juror *i*'s vote for '$X = 1$' gives to the hypothesis that $X = 1$.	The *conditional* degree of support juror *i*'s vote for '$X = 1$' gives to the hypothesis that $X = 1$, given the votes of jurors $1, \ldots, i{-}1$
The private judgment strategy	$\log(p / (1{-}p))$ (1)	$\log(p / (1{-}p))$ (2)
The updating strategy	$\log(P_i/(1{-}P_i))$ (3)	0 (supposing that juror *i* is not pivotal)(4)

Table 7.2

$i =$	1	2	3	4	5	6	7	8	9	10
$J_i =$	1	0	0	1	1	0	1	1	1	0

have noted, may not hold in equilibrium – the order in which the jurors reveal their judgments – cast their votes – may crucially affect the outcome.

If the order in which votes are taken is 1, 4, 5, 2, 7, 3, 8, 9, 10, 6, then a majority for '$X = 1$' will form after the first few jurors and be supported by further jurors acting on the updating strategy. If the order is 2, 3, 6, 1, 4, 5, 7, 8, 9, 10, then a majority for '$X = 0$' will form after the first few jurors and be supported by further jurors acting on the updating strategy.

So the dilemma is that the updating strategy, while apparently individually rational under certain conditions once Condorcet's assumptions are understood and accepted, will undermine Condorcet's happy result at the collective level.

4 Beyond the problem

How serious are the reflexivity problems discussed here? We have seen that the effect of updating in truthful deliberation is relatively benign, especially when it is transparent that such updating takes place only at the voting stage, after the individuals have truthfully expressed their private judgments at the deliberation stage. The problems of free-riding, by contrast, are potentially more serious; and, as the differences between conditions leading to updating in truthful deliberation and ones leading to free-riding are only subtle, there may be a slippery slope between the more benign cases and the more serious ones.

Are there any escape routes from the reflexivity problems? We consider two possible such routes. The first is what we think of as a happy flaw in our character as reasoners, the second a particular institutional design.

4.1 A happy flaw

The problems characterised will arise only if one or more group members are indeed disposed to update their own judgments on learning the judgments of the others. The individuals will be so disposed only if they believe that all group members have a competence level that is sufficiently high to sustain Condorcet's result, so that the majority is more likely to make a correct judgment than any one individual. If they each think that others have the same competence level as they have, and that that competence level is greater than 0.5, then Condorcet's result will certainly apply. This is the condition under which the individuals, if they know about the jury theorem, may be inclined to update their judgments on learning the judgments of the others, and under which a reflexivity effect – either of the benign kind or of the more serious kind, depending on the scenario in question – may arise.

But here is where the happy flaw may cut in. Although, at first, the individuals each ascribe the same competence level to all others on a given issue, they may none the less find it difficult to give up their own view on that issue when the majority judgment conflicts with their own private judgment. Specifically, they may find it easier to revise the belief that others have the same competence level as they do than to give up their own view on the issue in question. If this is so, then they may be disposed, in cases of conflict between majority opinion and their own one, not to revise their own judgment but rather to revise their belief that others have the same competence level as they do.

This phenomenon would be a rational flaw. If I assign the same competence level to others as to myself on a certain issue, then I do so, not conditional on a majority of others agreeing with me, but rather unconditionally. Thus I should not revise the competence assignment to others in the event of finding that I am in the minority on a given question. We hypothesise, however, that in the practice of responding to being in the minority, I may find it difficult to follow Condorcet's theorem – a difficulty I may not have fully anticipated.

It is one thing to acknowledge that others are as likely as I am to make a correct judgment, in ignorance as to what their judgments are; here I may just look at our respective information, training, talent, track record, and the like. It is another to stick with this belief on finding that most others disagree with me, in a situation where Condorcet's logic would require me to change my own judgment on a given issue. I will naturally assess those others in the light of my own judgment on the issue in question and, given my natural disposition to stick with my own judgment – that represents, after all, how things seem to me to be – it will be tempting to decide that actually not all of those in the majority have as high a level of competence as I do.[21]

Thomas Hobbes (1991) supports this hypothesis about the difficulty of thinking that others are just as likely as we are to be right on some question, at least when their views differ from ours. He stresses that, while each of us will be conscious in such a case of what moves us, and why, we will not have that same intimate access to the reasoning of others:

such is the nature of men, that howsoever they may acknowledge many others to be more witty, or more eloquent, or more learned; Yet they will hardly believe there be many so wise as themselves: For they see their own wit to hand, and other men's at a distance.

(Hobbes 1991, p. 87)

If this line of thought is right, then the reflexivity problems discussed may be less troublesome than they might appear at first. At the point where I am considering whether to update my judgment, I may find that I am unable to make the kind of competence assignment required by the jury theorem, unable to think therefore that the majority has a chance of making a correct judgment that is greater than mine, and so unable to be relaxed about not voting independently.

In our first scenario – the one in which individuals engage in truthful deliberation prior to voting – the happy flaw may prevent unanimity from arising at the voting stage, even when a clear majority forms at the deliberation stage.[22] It is of course debatable whether updating in truthful deliberation is a desirable effect or not. But if updating is regarded as a desirable effect, as on many accounts, then what we described as a happy flaw may actually turn into an unhappy obstacle. In our second scenario – the one in which individuals care about being individually correct – the happy flaw may lead individuals to stick to their own private judgment, as they would have greater confidence in their own private judgment than in the judgment of the majority. In the third scenario – the one in which individuals care primarily about the group being collectively correct – it might mean, among other effects, that individuals do not necessarily prefer the case where all of the others judge independently to the case where none of them does so. If I am one of the individuals, I might wish not only to stick to my own private judgment, but perhaps even to persuade the others to update their judgments according to mine. In that scenario, of course, there may be a different motive for free-riding, associated with the group size and the small chance that my vote will make a difference, but there will not be a free-riding problem of a kind that stems specifically from people's awareness of Condorcet's result.

4.2 An institutional design strategy

Is there any way of guarding against the problems mentioned, short of relying on this facet of human nature to block their appearance? One way around the problems might be to ensure that no group member knows the judgments of the others. This would require voting to occur all at once, or to be veiled by secrecy procedures, without prior revelation of any private judgments among the group members. Would it mean eliminating all group deliberation, in so far as individuals might reveal their judgments by how they reason? It would certainly require eliminating the sort of deliberation that reveals private judgments but it might tolerate the sort that doesn't. This might consist, for example, in each person putting on the table considerations that they think may have been ignored by others, whether or not they themselves assign a high weight to those considerations.

It is important to notice, though, that this institutional strategy will not always be desirable. To the extent that our first scenario – updating in truthful deliberation – might be seen as an attractive one, the institutional strategy would block not only reflexivity of the worrisome kind – the one that undermines the main prediction of the Condorcet jury theorem – but also reflexivity of the more benign, deliberative kind. Deliberative democrats might therefore argue that the institutional strategy requires us to pay an unacceptably high price for the avoidance of free-riding.

The second point to notice is that the institutional strategy will not always be feasible with the problem in our second scenario – the one in which individuals care about being individually correct – or not at least in the version of that scenario that we illustrated by reference to a community of scientists. The reason is that in this sort of case, people do not make their judgments all at once, as they might do in a collective body like a committee, and, once made, their judgments are not readily capable of being shrouded from others. The example of a scientific community is perhaps closest to our case of sequential voting, where the individuals express their judgments one by one in a sequence, and where each individual can observe the judgments expressed by those individuals who come earlier in the sequence. Thus, after a certain point, the individuals will be in a good position to tell what the majority is likely to think and they will therefore be exposed to the temptation to go with the majority view.

But institutional veiling might work in the third scenario – the one in which individuals care primarily about the group being collectively correct. Since that scenario involves taking a vote at a fixed point in time, veiling of the vote would be feasible and it would deny all group members a knowledge of where the majority vote is likely to lead. For committees of a certain size it might be a very useful check. But again, it will not come without a price. In requiring the absence of the sort of interpersonal deliberation that reveals private judgments, it may remove the check provided by the individuals' interrogating and testing one another's judgments. And in doing this, particularly with relatively large committees, it may give rise to the distinct free-riding problem associated with members coming to think of their votes as insignificant. No one's vote will be likely to make a difference in a large committee and, absent the need to deliberate publicly about their voting intentions, no one will find it significant in social terms either. Thus individuals may be inclined to vote without serious thought or reflection. Again, this is a situation of rational ignorance (Brennan and Lomasky 1993, ch. 7).

However, while veiling the vote may block those reflexivity problems that arise from individuals' updating their judgments based on what they learn about the judgments of others, it will not always block a related, but somewhat different kind of reflexivity problem that has received attention in the literature, namely one that arises from particular strategic considerations. The problem can be illus-

152

trated by the case where a jury is required to be unanimous about a guilty verdict, as analysed by Feddersen and Pesendorfer.

Under their analysis, Condorcet's finding may lead each juror to reason as follows. Suppose I am one of the jurors and I believe that Condorcet's conditions – competence, independence of private judgments and private judgment voting – are fulfilled by the other jurors. If these others disagree among themselves about the guilt of the defendant, or if they all judge the defendant innocent, then I need not worry about how I vote; my vote will not make any difference, as unanimity is required for a guilty verdict. The only case where my vote will make a difference is the one where all of the others favour a guilty finding. But if all the others favour a guilty verdict, and if the conditions of the jury theorem are satisfied – as by hypothesis they are – then the chance of their being right is much higher than the chance of my being right, whatever my private judgment; moreover, if the competence level of each juror is sufficiently high, then, depending on my threshold of reasonable doubt, I should believe that guilt has been established beyond reasonable doubt. And so I should vote as the others do: that is, guilty. Thus, no matter what others do, voting guilty seems to make sense – at least under the assumption that others vote independently. It will make no difference to the outcome in the cases where others are divided or they think the defendant is innocent. And it will represent the judgment that is likely to be correct beyond reasonable doubt in the case where the others all vote for guilty.

Veiling the votes or blocking deliberation will have no useful effect in this case, since the reasoning just rehearsed – in essence a kind of dominance reasoning – does not require a knowledge of how the majority is likely to go. To reduce the threat of the problem, Feddersen and Pesendorfer advocate the use of special majority voting rather than unanimity rule. However, while the unanimity rule sharpens the strategic structure of the case, even the use of simple majority voting will not in general remove all incentives for misrepresentation of private judgments, as Austen-Smith and Banks (1996) have shown.

Notice that, like our cases of reflexivity, the cases analysed by Feddersen and Pesendorfer and by Austen-Smith and Banks arise on the assumption that Condorcet's conditions are fulfilled, but they arise for somewhat different reasons.

5 Conclusion

The problem of reflexivity, as described by Popper and others, is that a theory may cease to apply to a given population when it is popularised among members of that population. Those who proclaim the danger of reflexivity haven't often considered it in the context of the sort of theory illustrated by Condorcet's jury theorem. We hope that this chapter may show that the problem has a particular resonance in this case.

Consider how the jury theorem might work with a population, not of human agents, but of diagnostic machines. Let these machines operate independently of one another and let them each have the same, greater than 0.5 chance of being right on a certain issue; let them each have a competence level of 0.6. There is no doubt that the Condorcet jury theorem yields a useful and exploitable result in relation to such machines. It provides us with the remarkable assurance that the chance of a majority of the machines being correct in any judgment on that sort of issue is higher than the chance of any individual machine's being correct and that it approaches one as the number of machines in the population increases.

What our chapter has shown, we hope, is that no such reassuring result will be as straightforwardly available with a population of human beings, if they come to be aware of the result itself; not, at least, in conditions where the happy flaw fails to operate and where there is no suitable institutional design in place. Let such awareness materialise and the application of the theorem may be put in jeopardy. Human beings are liable to be tempted to take an epistemic free ride on the efforts of others, thereby violating the condition of mutual independence that the theorem presupposes. And to the extent that they succumb to that temptation they will undermine the application of the theorem in their own case; they will cook the goose that might have laid a golden egg. Their capacity to reflect on the theorem – the very capacity that marks them off from mere machines – is in this respect a disadvantage. Oscar Wilde once quipped that nothing succeeds like excess. Not in this case, alas; not when the excess is an excess of reflection.

Appendix

Suppose juror i adopts the updating strategy, i.e. $V_i = 1$ *if and only if* $V_1 + \dots + V_{i-1} + J_i > i/2$, where juror i has observed the votes of jurors 1 up to $i-1$.

Let E denote the voting pattern across jurors 1 up to $i-1$. The conditional degree of support juror i's vote, say $V_i = 1$, gives to H conditional on E is:

$$l(H, V_i = 1 \mid E) = \log\left(\frac{Pr(V_i = 1 \mid H \wedge E)}{Pr(V_i = 1 \mid \neg H \wedge E)}\right).$$

By the updating strategy, we have $V_i = 1$ if and only if $V_1 + \dots + V_{i-1} + J_i > i/2$. Suppose E is the evidence that *precisely* h among jurors 1 up to $i-1$ have voted for '$X = 1$'. Then juror i's private judgment is *pivotal* if and only if $h = (i-1)/2$, i.e. if and only if jurors 1 up to $i-1$ are tied between '$X = 1$' and '$X = 0$'.

If juror i's private judgment is pivotal (i.e. $h = (i-1)/2$), then $V_i = 1$ if and only if $J_i = 1$, i.e.

$$Pr(V_i = 1 \mid H \wedge E) = P(J_i = 1 \mid H) = p$$

$$\text{and } Pr(V_i = 1 \mid \neg H \wedge E) = P(J_i = 1 \mid \neg H) = 1-p.$$

If juror i's private judgment is not pivotal (i.e. $h \neq (i-1)/2$), then $V_i = 1$ if and only if $h > i/2$, i.e. $V_i = 1$ depends on H (or $\neg H$) only *through* E, and hence

$$Pr(V_i = 1 \mid H \wedge E) = Pr(V_i = 1 \mid E)$$
$$\text{and } Pr(V_i = 1 \mid \neg H \wedge E) = Pr(V_i = 1 \mid E).$$

Let π be the probability that juror i's private judgment is pivotal. Then

$$Pr(V_i = 1 \mid H \wedge E) = \pi p + (1-\pi) Pr(V_i = 1 \mid E)$$
$$\text{and } Pr(V_i = 1 \mid \neg H \wedge E) = \pi(1-p) + (1-\pi) Pr(V_i = 1 \mid E).$$

Therefore

$$l(H, V_i = 1 \mid E) := \log\left(\frac{\pi p + (1-\pi) Pr(V_i = 1 \mid E)}{\pi(1-p) + (1-\pi) Pr(V_i = 1 \mid E)} \right).$$

If juror i is always pivotal ($\pi = 1$), then $l(H, V_i = 1 \mid E) = l(H, V_i = 1) = \log(p / (1-p))$. If juror i is never pivotal ($\pi = 0$), then $l(H, V_i = 1 \mid E) = 0$.

The lower the probability π that juror i is pivotal, the lower is the value of $l(H, V_i = 1 \mid E)$, i.e. the lower is the conditional degree of support juror i's updated vote gives to H, given the other jurors' votes.

Notes

1 Christian List, Department of Government, London School of Economics; c.list@lse.ac.uk. Philip Pettit, Departments of Politics and Philosophy, Princeton University; ppettit@princeton.edu. We are grateful to Campbell Brown and Brett Calcott for comments and discussion.

2 Reflexivity need not be a bad thing. Consider a theory which shows that present social behaviour leads to certain undesirable consequences. The understanding of such a theory may lead the members of a given society to adjust their behaviour in such a way as to avoid the occurrence of conditions under which the theory applies. The theory will then have been undermined by reflexivity, but with an outcome that is more desirable than the one that would have occurred if the predictions of the theory had become true. Harsanyi (1976, p. 83) made a suggestion along these lines: 'Keynesian economics has enabled us to make much better predictions about the effects of various economic policies in conditions of mass unemployment. By this means, it has also enabled us to eliminate these very conditions, and to create a completely novel economic situation of continuing high employment, in which Keynesian predictions may no longer work.'

3 Whether or not the independence assumption is undermined by jury deliberation – and, if so, how exactly the jury theorem is affected – is a debated issue. See, for example, Estlund (1994) and Dietrich and List (2004).

4 The Condorcet jury theorem is robust to certain relaxations of the assumptions. A version of it still holds in certain cases where different jurors have different competence levels, but where the average competence is greater than 0.5 (e.g. Grofman, Owen and Feld 1983; Borland 1989), and in cases where there are certain dependencies between different jurors' votes (ibid.; Ladha 1992; Estlund 1994; but see Dietrich

and List 2004). Since the concern of this paper is not technical, however, we will here stick to the jury theorem in its simplest, classical form.

5   What do we mean by saying that the Condorcet jury theorem is undermined by reflexivity? The jury theorem can be stated as the following conditional: If conditions C hold, then prediction P follows; in short, C → P. Conditions C are the assumptions of the theorem: competence, independence of private judgments, and private judgment voting. Prediction P is the proposition that the probability of a correct majority judgment converges to 1 as the jury size increases. Since the conditional C → P is a mathematical truth, reflexivity clearly cannot undermine the truth of that conditional. We say that the jury theorem is undermined by reflexivity in the following case: (i) Initially, conditions C hold, and so prediction P is also true. (ii) The individuals in question learn that C → P. (iii) The understanding that C → P leads the individuals to change their behaviour in such a way that conditions C cease to hold.

6   Note that we are here considering an idealised limiting case. We do not claim that rational individuals will always reveal their private judgments truthfully in equilibrium. Recent game-theoretic work suggests that rational individuals may not in general do so. See Austen-Smith and Feddersen (2002) for a detailed investigation of the incentives on whether or not to reveal private judgments truthfully in group deliberation prior to voting.

7   Note that this simple reasoning depends on the assumption that all individuals assign an equal prior probability of 0.5 to both possible states of the world. In the absence of this assumption, the picture is much more complicated. If we relax the assumption, two individuals may still disagree even after having observed the same pattern of private judgments across the group as a whole. An individual who assigns a prior probability of 0.5 to $X = 1$ will be convinced, after observing a majority for $X = 1$, that the posterior probability of $X = 1$ is above 0.5. By contrast, an individual who assigns an extremely low prior probability to $X = 1$ may still think, even after observing a substantial majority for $X = 1$, that the posterior probability of $X = 1$ is below 0.5.

8   Goodin notes that this effect is a fairly robust prediction of a Bayesian framework. In a reasonably sized group, the epistemic force of the majority should convince the individuals in the minority to change their beliefs. However, he also notes that, in practice, the effect typically does not occur as predicted, and we are thus faced with a 'paradox of persisting opposition'. The reasons he discusses as to why opposition persists perhaps also suggest that the phenomenon of reflexivity discussed here is less severe than a purely Condorcetian perspective might lead us to think.

9   This is clearly an idealised assumption. We do not claim that rational individuals, who are aware of the incentive structure of the problem, will always believe that others express their private judgments truthfully. Indeed, once an individual is tempted not to express his or her private judgment truthfully, he or she should see that others may feel the force of the same temptation. See Austen-Smith and Feddersen (2002).

10 We here leave aside such unlikely cases as the one where all odd-numbered individuals privately judge that $X = 1$ while all even-numbered individuals privately judge that not $X = 0$.

11 Again, note the idealising character of this assumption. The belief that no others are free-riding may not be rationally sustainable in equilibrium.

12 And, as we have noted, the belief that no others are free-riding may be rationally unsustainable in equilibrium.

13 This result does not hold if the prior probability r takes a value different from 0.5.

14 Again, the result ceases to hold if $r \neq 0.5$.

15 Proof:

$$l(H, E) \quad = l(H, V_1 = 1) + l(H, V_2 = 1) + \ldots + l(H, V_h = 1)$$
$$+ l(H, V_{h+1} = 0) + l(H, V_{h+2} = 0) + \ldots + l(H, V_n = 0)$$

156

$$= h \log(p / (1{-}p)) + (n{-}h) \log((1{-}p) / p) \quad (\text{by (*) and (**)})$$
$$= (h - (n{-}h)) \log(p / (1{-}p))$$
$$= m \log(p / (1{-}p)), \quad \text{where } m = h - (n{-}h).$$

16 What is the implication of this result for the probability that H is true given the evidence E that h out of n jurors have voted for '$X = 1$'? By the formula stated above, we have

$$Pr(H \mid E) = \frac{r}{r + (1{-}r) \exp(-l(H, E))}$$

$$= \frac{r}{r + (1{-}r) \exp(-m \log(p / (1{-}p)))},$$

$$= \frac{r}{r + (1{-}r) \left((1{-}p)/p\right)^m},$$

which is exactly Condorcet's formula (see List 2004).

17 Compare our previous note on the idealising character of this assumption.
18 Again our simple result requires the assumption that the two possible states of the world have the same prior probability 0.5. Assuming a different prior probability or heterogeneous prior probability assignments across different jurors would make the picture much more complicated.
19 As before, note the assumption that the two possible states of the world have the same prior probability 0.5.
20 Again note the idealising character of this assumption. If our argument here is correct, then it also shows that this assumption will not generally hold in equilibrium. Suppose that it holds for jurors 1 up to $i{-}1$. Then, as we have seen, juror i may have an incentive not to reveal his or her private judgment truthfully. So the fact that the assumption holds for jurors. 1 up to $i{-}1$ will here prevent it from holding for juror i too.
21 There is an analogy with the phenomenon of confirmatory bias here, our 'tendency to attach more credence to evidence confirming rather than disconfirming our existing beliefs' (Goodin 2002, p. 128).
22 Compare our remarks above on Goodin's 'paradox of persisting opposition'.

References

Austen-Smith, D. and J. S. Banks. 1996. 'Information Aggregation, Rationality and the Condorcet Jury Theorem', in *American Political Science Review*, vol. 90, pp. 34–45.

Austen-Smith, D. and T. Feddersen. 2002. 'Deliberation and Voting Rules', working paper, Kellogg Graduate School of Management, Northwestern University.

Bikhchandani, S., D. Hirshleifer and I. Welch. 1992. 'A Theory of Fads, Fashion, Custom, and Cultural Change as Informational Cascades', in *Journal of Political Economy*, vol. 100, pp. 992–1026.

Borland, P. J. 1989. 'Majority Systems and the Condorcet Jury Theorem', in *Statistician*, vol. 38, pp. 181–9.

Brennan, G. and L. Lomasky. 1993. *Democracy and Decision: the Pure Theory of Electoral Preference*, Oxford: Oxford University Press.

Brennan, G. and P. Pettit. 1990. 'Unveiling the Vote', in *British Journal of Political Science*, vol. 20, pp. 311–33.

CHRISTIAN LIST AND PHILIP PETTIT

de Condorcet, M. 1976. *Condorcet: Selected Writings*, Indianapolis: Bobbs-Merrill.

Dietrich, F. and C. List. 2004. 'A Model of Jury Decisions where All Jurors have the Same Evidence', in *Synthese*, forthcoming.

Estlund, D. 1994. 'Opinion Leaders, Independence and Condorcet's Jury Theorem', in *Theory and Decision*, vol. 36, pp. 131–62.

Feddersen, T. and W. Pesendorfer. 1998. 'Convicting the Innocent: The Inferiority of Unanimous Jury Verdicts under Strategic Voting', in *American Political Science Review*, vol. 92, pp. 23–35.

Fitelson, B. 2001. 'A Bayesian Account of Independent Evidence with Applications', in *Philosophy of Science*, vol. 68 (Proceedings), pp. S123–S140.

Goodin, R. E. 2002. 'The Paradox of Persisting Opposition', in *Politics, Philosophy and Economics*, vol. 1, pp. 109–146.

Grofman, B. G. Owen and S. L. Feld. 1983. 'Thirteen Theorems in Search of the Truth', in *Theory and Decision*, vol. 15, pp. 261–78.

Harsanyi, J. C. 1976. *Essays on Ethics, Social Behavior, and Scientific Explanation*, Dordrecht: D. Reidel.

Hobbes, T. 1991 [1651]. *Leviathan*, Cambridge: Cambridge University Press.

Ladha, K. 1992. 'The Condorcet Jury Theorem, Free Speech and Correlated Votes', in *American Journal of Political Science*, vol. 36, pp. 617–34.

List, C. 2004. 'On the Significance of the Absolute Margin', in *British Journal for the Philosophy of Science*, vol. 55, forthcoming.

List, C. and R. E. Goodin. 2001. 'Epistemic Democracy: Generalizing the Condorcet Jury Theorem', in *The Journal of Political Philosophy*, vol. 9, pp. 277–306.

Nozick, R. 1981. *Philosophical Explanations*, Oxford: Oxford University Press.

Pettit, P. 1986. 'Free Riding and Foul Dealing', in *Journal of Philosophy*, vol. 83, pp. 361–79.

Popper, K. R. 1963. *The Poverty of Historicism*, London: Routledge and Kegan Paul.

8

THE ROLE OF EXPERIENCE IN POPPER'S PHILOSOPHY OF SCIENCE AND POLITICAL PHILOSOPHY

Graham Macdonald

The main task of the theory of knowledge is to understand it as continuous with animal knowledge; and to understand also its discontinuity – if any – from animal knowledge.

(Popper 1974, p. 1061)

In The Logic of Scientific Discovery *Karl Popper rejected any epistemological role for experience, allowing it only the role of motivating, or causing, our beliefs. This invites the criticism that falsification is only relative, and ultimately unjustified. In his political and ethical philosophy he was more charitable to experience; our suffering is a reason for acting so as to minimise that suffering. It is argued here that his evolutionary epistemology also leads to a position that must afford experience an epistemological role. It need not be sentences all the way down.*

1 Basic thoughts

In all his major work on the philosophy of science, Popper always, sometimes vehemently, differentiated himself from the positivists of the Vienna Circle. The main areas of disagreement with the positivists were over the importance of meaning, the possibility of inductive reasoning, and (as a consequence) over the manner in which science was to be demarcated from non-science.[1] Popper held that the issue of the meaningfulness (or otherwise) of sentences was relatively unimportant, it being reasonably obvious that both metaphysical claims and ethical judgments could be meaningful. Inductive inferences were invalid, so should be used neither in science nor as part of any criterion demarcating science from anything else. This led to the formulation of falsifiability as the demarcation criterion. To be brutally brief, a theory or hypothesis was scientific only if it was falsifiable. In what follows I wish to expand on how this was meant to work in

159

Popper's philosophy of science, and then proceed to discuss a crucial difference between his earlier methodological writing and his later political philosophy in his attitude to the reason-giving role of experience.

If scientific status is to be assured by the method of attempted falsifications, one has to say more about what is doing the falsifying, and Popper does not disappoint. In saying that any scientific theoretical system must satisfy the demarcation criterion, he says that it 'must represent a world of possible *experience . . . our* world of experience' (Popper 1959, p. 39. Italics in original). And he goes on to say (ibid.) that we distinguish our world of experience

> by the fact that it has been submitted to tests, and has stood up to tests . . . The theory of knowledge . . . may accordingly be described as a theory of empirical method – *a theory of what is usually called experience. . . . [I]t must be possible for an empirical scientific system to be refuted by experience.*

The qualification 'usually called' attached to 'experience' hints at the trouble to come; it is *singular statements* that turn out to play the role of potential falsifiers, and that do the falsifying when a theory fails a test. The major reason for this move to the linguistic is something shared by Popper with most of the positivists, the claim that '*statements can be logically justified only by statements*' (Popper 1959, p. 43). For Popper this meant that *criticism* was an inter-sentential affair. Subjective 'feelings of conviction' were irrelevant as guides to the merits of a scientific statement; such statements had to be objective, hence inter-subjectively testable. And this requirement (of inter-subjective testability) led to the denial of any 'ultimate' statements in science; every potential falsifier was itself potentially falsifiable, and so on, ad infinitum. The regress could be stopped only by scientists agreeing on which basic statements were to be appealed to in the testing process. And a consequence of this was accepted by Popper: 'what is to be called a "science" and who is to be called a "scientist" must always remain a matter of convention or decision' (Popper 1959, p. 53). Falsifiability was now made more precise, with the reference to experience excised: 'a theory is falsified only if the scientists have accepted basic statements which contradict it' (Popper 1959, p. 86).

This linguistic turn, and with it the rejection of any normative, justificatory role for experience, is a familiar feature of positivist and post-positivist analytic epistemology. As Popper characterised the position, it afforded a way out of an epistemological trilemma, one forged by the choice of dogmatism, infinite regress and psychologism. Refusing to budge from an arbitrary stopping point in the justificatory chain is a feature of dogmatism, refusing to stop anywhere produces the infinite regress, and psychologism supports the view that the regress can be nonarbitrarily stopped because our perceptual experience justifies our acceptance of basic statements.

[T]he decision to accept a basic statement, and to be satisfied with it, is causally connected with our experiences – especially with our *perceptual experiences*. But we do not attempt to *justify* basic statements by these experiences. Experiences can *motivate a decision*, and hence an acceptance or rejection of a statement, but a basic statement cannot be *justified* by them – no more than by thumping the table.

(Popper 1959, p. 105)

Psychologism, Popper held, foundered on the problem of universals and induction. All statements employ 'universal names' which go far beyond our experience, so no statement can be completely justified by any experience. In his attempt to avoid the trilemma Popper suggested formal and material requirements that basic statements must meet: they have to be singular existential statements (formal requirement) and (material requirement) the event so described must be

an '*observable*' event; that is to say, basic statements must be testable, inter-subjectively, by 'observation'. . . . I am using ['observation'] in such a sense that it might as well be replaced by 'an event involving position and movement of macroscopic physical bodies'.

(Popper 1959, pp. 102–3)

There is an enormous amount that can be said about this position, but what I wish to focus on now is the tension between the claims that (a) perceptual experience has no *epistemic* relation to our decision to adopt certain statements as basic, and (b) basic statements must be inter-subjectively testable by observation. The scare-quotes around 'observation' in the quote above indicate the nature of the tension, and the paraphrasing of 'observation' to 'an event involving position and movement of macroscopic physical bodies' doesn't help, given that an object is macroscopic only if it is observable. The question is: why must a basic statement meet this requirement, if observation plays no epistemic role in our acceptance of a statement as basic? Given that perceptual experience has only a causal role, why does not just *any* causation of our acceptance of basic statements do? On Popper's account, wouldn't it be just as rational to accept only those statements as basic that are accredited as such by our grandmothers? Or to accept as basic only those statements that begin with 'B'? (For this suggestion, see Ayer's acute discussion of the problem in his 1959.)

The non-sceptical answer to these questions has to be one that acknowledges the epistemic role of perceptual experience. The problem is that this is an extremely difficult task, as shown by the recent history of disputes about perceptual experience. The basic problem is one that Popper was well aware of: if our methods of hypothesis elimination are to be rational, they must be based on *reason*. We must have a reason to reject a hypothesis. But, to put it in fashionable terminology, the 'space of reasons' is conceptual space, so our reasons must come conceptualised. (See McDowell 1994 for a defence of this view.) Reasons must be capable of being grounds from which we can move to a conclusion, they must be available for evaluation, for weighing in the balance, for combining with other reasons, contradicting yet further reasons, and so on. Only conceptual items can meet these requirements, or so it is claimed. Now the Popperian claim, that statements can be logically justified (falsified) only by other statements, can be seen as simply a linguistic formulation of the conceptualists' thesis that reasons must be conceptually shaped. And the challenge to those who believe that experience has epistemically significant non-conceptual content is to show how it is possible for such non-conceptual content to function as a reason. (For recent defences of non-conceptual content see Heck 2000, Peacocke 2001 and Campbell 2002.)

It may be thought that the problem as posed is only serious because its formulation is individualistic. Popper insisted on inter-subjectively testable (falsifiable) basic statements chosen by the (relevant) group of scientists; such a set of basic statements were the 'foundation' for attempted falsifications, albeit only a temporary foundation. It is always open to the scientists concerned to change the set of basic statements thus relied upon. This 'fallibility' is not the problem, though. Imagine a group of people, claiming to be scientists (parapsychologists, say), deciding to accept a (bizarre, to us) set of basic statements for the purposes of testing their hypotheses. In what way could their procedures be criticised? For not having the same set of basic statements as other scientists? This would institute a form of mob rule; the set of basic statements accepted by the majority of those who call themselves scientists would prevail.

There is also a suggestion of circularity in the manner in which the 'relevant' group of scientists were to achieve their inter-subjective agreement. How is this to be done? This is what Popper says:

> [S]cientists try to avoid speaking at cross purposes . . . They try very seriously to speak one and the same language, even if they use different mother tongues. In the natural sciences this is achieved by recognising experience as the impartial arbiter of their controversies. When speaking of 'experience' I have in mind experience of a 'public' character, like observations, and experiments . . . and an experience is 'public' if everybody who takes the trouble can repeat it. In order to avoid speaking at cross-purposes, scientists try to express their theories in such a form that they can be tested, i.e. refuted (or else corroborated) by such experience.
> (Popper 1971, p. 218)

On this account it is the general repeatability of the experience that makes it public, and it is the publicity of experience that enables scientists using different languages to agree on the 'same' language for the purposes of – what? Describing their common experience? But then it had better be the case that the experience is common, the same, otherwise the agreed description will be fraudulent. The agreement will be to use the same syntactic expression, but unless this expression describes, or purports to describe, the same experience, the agreement will not do the work it is intended to do. Popper doesn't make this mistake; he rightly sees the agreement on language-use as a semantic issue. The scientists can speak different languages so long as the 'propositional content' of their accepted sentences is the same, and one guarantee of the sameness of propositional content is sameness of experience. For Popper's purposes here it has to be the common experience that both explains *and justifies* agreement among the scientists; it cannot be that the agreement on language is the basic datum.[2]

As it happens, Popper was not entirely consistent in his attitude to experience. There are numerous passages in his later work (after *The Logic of Scientific Discovery*) where experience is ascribed an important role. One example will suffice:

> [T]he mechanical engineer can [plan] because he has sufficient experience at his disposal, i.e. theories developed by trial and error. . . . [H]e relies on experience which he has gained by applying piecemeal methods. . . . The wholesale or large-scale method works only where the piecemeal method has furnished us first with a great number of experiences, and even then only within the realm of these experiences.
>
> (Popper 1971, vol. I, pp. 163–4)

Now it is not implausible to claim that this reference to experience, and others like it, can be paraphrased away, to make the epistemology of Popper's political philosophy more consistent with that of his philosophy of science. Not implausible, but the difficulty should not be underestimated. The piecemeal method of the mechanical engineer, as described, is piecemeal partly because there is a dynamic process of trial and error involved, one which it is difficult to see as testing by comparison of accepted basic statements to descriptions of the results of trials. In this case there does not seem to be a 'settled' set of basic statements upon which the mechanical engineer can depend. The piecemeal method seems to be piecemeal partly because of the novelty of the trials and errors, their unpredictability. If basic statements are those accepted by the community of scientists at any one time, it looks as though the mechanical engineer will have to call a committee meeting every time a trial gives rise to a novel situation.

Let's assume, for the sake of argument, that one could rephrase what it is that the mechanical engineer has that facilitates planning in terms friendly to a basic statement formulation, even if any such rephrasing is bound to appear clumsy. More interestingly, and less easily dispensed with, are two other areas in which Popper seems to make ineliminable use of the notion of experience, and it is to these that I now turn.

2 Utilitarian thoughts

The first illustration of experience playing an essential role in Popper's philosophy is taken from his thoughts on ethical policy-making, particularly his defence of negative utilitarianism. Popper thought that the proper task of government was to eliminate, or decrease, misery, rather than to promote happiness. Take the following:

> I believe that there is, from the ethical point of view, no symmetry between suffering and happiness, or between pain and pleasure. . . . [H]uman suffering makes a direct appeal, namely the appeal for help, while there is no similar call to increase the happiness of a man who is doing well anyway. . . . Instead of the greatest happiness of the greatest number, one should demand, more modestly, the least amount of avoidable suffering for all. . . . There is some kind of analogy between this view of ethics and the view of scientific methodology which I have advocated in my *The Logic of Scientific Discovery*. It adds to clarity in the field of ethics if we formulate our demands negatively, i.e. if we demand the elimination of suffering rather than the promotion of happiness. Similarly, it is helpful to formulate the task of scientific method as the elimination of false theories (from the various theories tentatively proffered) rather than the attainment of established truths.
>
> (Popper 1971, vol. I, p. 285)

Here it is simply impossible to see anything other than the experiences of pain and pleasure as having the significance assigned to them by Popper. It is, as one might say, the 'paininess' of pain that makes it an experience that we have reason to avoid. It is *that kind of experience* that we want less of, not just fewer descriptions of the experience. Now it may be objected that this is cheating. My earlier complaint was that Popper gave experience no *epistemic* role in his account of our acceptance of basic statements, and although there is a foundational role that the notion of experience plays in Popper's ethical thought, this has nothing to do with epistemology.

Strictly speaking this criticism is warranted; there is nothing in the above asserting that experiences of pain and pleasure are justificatory. It is, however, difficult to see how they could escape from being so. Popper is urging on us a view of ethics that would inform our actions, and in particular impressing on us the advantages of being a negative utilitarian in ethical matters. The most plausible interpretation of Popper's negative utilitarianism is that he is urging us, in considering how we should act, to adopt a policy of trying to minimise pain rather than maximise happiness. That is, he is saying we have *a reason* against acting in a certain way if so acting would cause a person or people to experience needless pain. In this picture what functions as the reason for not acting is the needless suffering inflicted, the experience of pain.

Could Popper avoid attributing to the experience the role of providing reasons for and against actions? A thought here may be that we can make him out to be some sort of second-order utilitarian, one who allows us our usual (first-order) reasons for action, those having to do with considerations stemming from love, friendship, kindness, fairness, and so on, insisting only that these reasons for acting are prone to produce actions that would maximise happiness (or minimise pain). This is not convincing as an interpretation of Popper, partly because this philosophical position had not been invented at the time Popper was writing, but more because there is nothing in Popper's writing to suggest he held this view himself. Even if he did, though, such a position still leaves experience as providing us with reasons to adopt certain first-order attitudes – those that incline us towards acting in such a way that will lead to the minimisation of pain. The painful experiences still function as reasons.

It may be objected that what I consider in choosing to act is the probability that the action will produce misery, and it is my *estimate* of that probability that is the reason for not acting. If I judge that it is probable that the action will cause suffering, then that is a reason not to act in that way. This makes the probability-judgment the reason, not the suffering itself, and so re-establishes the original position, one in which experience could play no rational part. But this is surely not right. Let's take a case in which my judgment is that my acting F-ly will do no harm, and it does do harm. I am mistaken. What am I mistaken about? It is certainly true that my judgment was wrong, but the natural way of putting this is to say I was wrong about there being a reason for not acting F-ly. I thought there was no such reason, and there was, namely the harm caused by acting F-ly. What Popper is saying in support of his negative utilitarianism is that what we must take into account in our deliberations as to what to do is the possibility that a projected action could cause pain. It is impossible to escape the conclusion that it is the ensuing experience of pain that is the reason against my acting in that way. My thought that I may cause pain is an intermediary here; it lets me know what will ensue. My reason against acting in that way is not that I have a thought that the action will cause pain, nor is it that the victim will have a thought that she is experiencing pain. The reason against so acting is that the resultant state of affairs will be one in which the victim experiences (needless) pain. *This* is the fundamental fact that I must take account of in my deliberations.

Again it may be objected that this is cheating. Of course, it may be said, our experiences of pain and pleasure are important in determining how we should act. Only a fool would deny this. But what, it may be asked, does this practical matter have to do with theoretical reason? After all, Popper doesn't deny that we do have experiences, nor that the experiences inflicted on us can be nasty. This is the whole point of his telling us to act in ways that minimise the nastiness. But, it will be said, this is exactly why practical and theoretical reason are disanalogous. The former has to do with the (experienced) consequences of actions, the latter has to do only with truth (or verisimilitude). The difference in subject matter makes for the difference in the role that reason gives to experience. Moreover, it may be said, the reasons of *practical* reason are meant to play a guiding role, nudging us towards this action and away from that, and it is this motivational feature that gives experience the importance it has. Theoretical reason does not have to motivate our actions, so we are not justified in transferring the role experience plays in practical reason to one that it plays in theoretical reason. We still have no grounds for thinking that experience must have this reason-giving property in theoretical matters.

One germane response to this is to remind ourselves that our predicament was brought about by noting a powerful trend in modern epistemology, one that denied to experience any justificatory role. This denial was justified on the grounds that experience was not the right kind of thing to be inference-worthy, and only inference-worthy states have the capacity to figure in arguments supporting conclusions. Reasons have to be able to support conclusions, so experience cannot be a reason. This is a very *general* claim about the disability of experience to play any reason-giving role; it is a claim about reason, regardless of subject-matter. If what has been said about the relation of experience to reason in practical matters is right, then this very general claim must be false.

If this *is* right then Popper would have to allow that experiences *can be* more intimately related to rationality than he allows for in his philosophy of science. A blanket prohibition on experience providing us with reasons does not seem credible. But this concession may seem to yield a hollow victory. The Popperian may grant that experience can be reason-giving, but restrict this to the practical realm. That is, it is still open to the Popperian to deny that experience has epistemological import in the theoretical arena. In support of what may appear an arbitrary restriction the Popperian may point to an important disanalogy between the experience of pain and perceptual experience. The latter, it will be said, is representational, while the former is not.[3] Being representational, perceptual experience is essentially 'interpreted', and it is this interpretation that is epistemologically significant. On this view all experiences that purport to be representations function in reason only *qua* representation, not *qua* experience. Further, it will be said, the representative character of experience essentially involves concepts, so the Popperian stance is vindicated. To evaluate this claim we need to look at the second area in which Popper appears to assign to experience an essentially rational role.

3 Darwinian thoughts

In the development of his evolutionary epistemology Popper repeatedly remarks on the role of experience in enabling us to have theories die instead of us. The following is typical:

> My hypothesis is that the original task of consciousness was to anticipate success and failure in problem-solving and to signal to the organism in the form of pleasure and pain whether it was on the right or wrong path to the solution of the problem. . . . Through the experience of pleasure and pain consciousness assists the organism in its *voyages of discovery*, and in its *learning processes*.
>
> (Popper 1992, pp. 17–18, italics in original)

166

Here again it is clearly the nature of the experience itself that is crucial to the role it plays in enabling the organism to solve its problems. The task of consciousness, its function, cannot be replaced by anything less robust, less painful or pleasurable, than the 'raw feels' themselves. Imagine the situation in which experience is not given this pivotal role, it being replaced by something like a description of the experience, the equivalent of basic statements. For non-human animals, the equivalent of basic statements would be internal representations (non-conceptual representational content) of their external environment and, we are now presuming, of their internal environment, their experiences. By analogy with the account provided for scientific learning, we can imagine that the animal learns only by comparing these representations and remedying the situation when there is conflict. On this view the experiences (feelings of pleasure and pain) play no epistemic role in the learning process, where 'epistemic role' is cashed out in terms of whether the experience plays an essential role in explaining how the animal solves the problems it confronts. Not only would this be a totally implausible account of the way in which such experiences are crucial to the animal's ability to navigate its way around its environment, it would also deny the validity of Popper's insight about how the 'original task' of consciousness was accomplished. This task is not carried out by pumping further representations into the organism; it is a fundamental feature of Popper's account that it is pain itself, not a representation of pain, that does the work in signalling to the organism that trouble lies ahead.

Can one extend this feature of painful experience, its ability to act as a 'secondary' selector, to other modes of experience that enable us to gain knowledge? To see how the analogy with selection can be broadened it will be useful to look at the work of Donald Campbell, an evolutionary epistemologist influenced by Popper and who provided more substance to the idea of secondary selection. (In addition his thoughts on epistemology are highly relevant to our understanding of how Popper understood his own evolutionary epistemology, as Popper, commenting on Campbell's contribution to *The Philosophy of Karl Popper*, says that 'the most striking thing about Campbell's essay is the almost complete agreement, down even to the minute details, between Campbell's views and my own' (Popper 1974, p. 1059). Campbell claimed that all our inductive achievements were due to a 'blind-variation-and-selective-retention' (BVSR) model of learning.[4] There were three essential aspects to the BVSR model (see Campbell 1988, p. 402):

1   mechanism(s) for introducing variation;
2   consistent selection processes;
3   mechanism(s) for preserving and/or propagating the selected variants.

The analogy with natural selection is obvious. It is precisely this analogy that Popper exploited in his account of theory selection: 'We choose the theory which holds its own in competition with other theories, the one which, by natural selection, proves itself the fittest to survive' (Popper 1959, p. 108).

The differences from Darwinian natural selection are due to the different nature of the items selected and propagated, and the different way in which selection and propagation (inheritance) operate. For Popper the variation, the analogue of mutation, was introduced by the tentative 'trial' an animal would make, a trial aimed at solving a problem posed by the environment. If this attempted solution was a failure there would have to be 'error-elimination' (that is, selection) and further trials. There could be no further trials, though, if the selection process involved the death of the animal, so evolution provides ways of eliminating error that avoid this catastrophic consequence. Experiencing pain could be one such cause of error-elimination, costly but effective. Less costly is the use of sense organs that enable an animal to anticipate that it will experience pain, using what Popper calls the signal that pain, or worse, is in the offing.

It was Campbell who emphasised the significance of these signals and who made an important theoretical contribution to our understanding of them. At the most basic level he notes that an organism may avoid noxious substances when its chemoreceptors signal that the environment is becoming lethal. In this case it is the chemoreceptors that select the responses, these selectors having themselves been selected for precisely this task. What we find throughout nature, he claimed, is a Darwinian BVSR process spawning higher BVSR processes, which in turn spawn further such processes, all the way up the tree of knowledge. This begins with simple locomotion, whereby an animal learns, by the trial and error process of collision and further movement, which parts of its spatial environment are penetrable and which impenetrable. Echolocation is a further sophistication of essentially the same process, soundwaves substituting for locomotion, with vision providing yet a further means of economising on movement. The claim is that in general what BVSR processes construct are primarily means of producing economies in the creation of knowledge. On this view creative thought provides 'a *substitute* exploration of a *substitute* representation of the environment, the "solution" being selected from the multifarious exploratory thought trials according to a criterion which is in itself *substituting* for an external state of affairs' (Campbell 1987, p. 96).[5]

Yet a further step is taken with the ways we use language to impart knowledge, language itself functioning as a substitute for the individual organism's perceptual investigation of its environment. What language cannot do, though, is bypass this perceptual encounter entirely; the process of language acquisition relies on the transmitter and receiver being in the same perceived environment. As Campbell puts it, 'language cannot be learned by telephone, but requires visually or tactually present ostensive referents stimulating and editing the trial meanings' (Campbell 1988, p. 415).

Returning to our main theme, one can see that this conception of the role of perceptual experience in selecting out error does not permit the usurpation of that role by 'basic statements'. For Campbell, it is the world impinging on our senses that affords us the means to eliminate false trials. The best that language (and thought) can do is to function as a vicarious environment within which our errors are (fallibly) eliminated. It is only insofar as thought and language represent the environment accurately that they can succeed in their task, and the test of their success lies in our perceptual experience. Interestingly, Campbell connects this to the demarcation problem, implicitly criticising Popper's use of falsifiability relative to an agreed-on set of basic statements as the criterion assuring scientific status:

> The demarcation of science from other speculations is that the knowledge claims be testable, and that there be available mechanisms for testing or selecting which are more than social. In theology and the humanities there is certainly differential propagation among advocated beliefs, if only at the level of fads and fashions. What is characteristic of science is that the selective system which weeds out among the variety of conjectures involves deliberate contact with the environment through experiment and quantified prediction, designed so that outcomes quite independent of the preferences of the investigator are possible.
>
> (Campbell 1988, p. 416)

In as much as Popper talked of 'conjectures boldly put forward for trial, to be eliminated if they clashed with observations' (Popper 1963, p. 46), he would have to agree.

4 Non-conceptual 'thoughts'

It has been argued above that Popper did not consistently view experience as having no epistemological import; it is clear that in certain areas of his philosophy experience played an essential role. It is difficult to make sense of his negative utilitarianism without requiring that our experience of pain is such that we have reason to avoid it, and as Campbell's development of evolutionary epistemology shows, theoretical reason also requires perceptual experience to function an eliminator of false ideas. Nevertheless, in his 'official' philosophy of science Popper did consistently downgrade the importance of experience, and did so to such an extent that it was deemed critically impotent. Almost certainly one explanation of this neglect lies in Popper's hostility to the idea that what is provided by sensory experience is given to a passive subject, and consequently forms the basis for inductive generalisation. The notion that uninterpreted experience could form the basis upon which scientific justification rested, and from which scientific theorising began, was anathema to Popper, and in rejecting it he also rejected the idea that experience could have *any* epistemological significance. The Kantian lesson was that the mind was active, creative, and not merely a 'dumb' consumer of unvarnished experiences. Popper emphasises this in commenting on Campbell's claim that the BVSR method is similar to a blind man using a stick to move around obstacles. This is seen as showing that 'nothing is "given" to us by our senses; everything is interpreted, decoded: everything is the result of active experiments, under the control of an exploratory drive' (Popper 1974, p. 1062).

One need not, however, be committed to the passivity of the intellect, nor the notion that experience is absorbed 'uninterpreted', in order to accept its fundamental epistemological status. (After all, Campbell, who did see experience as crucial to the gaining of knowledge, was insistent that 'The blind-variation-and-selective-retention model of thought joins the Gestaltists in protest against the picture of the learning organisms as a passive induction machine accumulating contingencies' – Campbell 1960, p. 401.) The two crucial elements conjoined in this exegesis of Popper's position are *activity* and *interpretation*, so what will be critical in any attempt to combine the active intellect with a rational role for experience is the account one gives of the experience *as interpreted*. Presumably the reason why Popper thought the proposed combination to be impossible was the thought that interpretation itself was a product of the active intellect, it being the active intellect's imposition of concepts ('theory') on the uninterpreted deliverances of the senses. The further thought must be that if the deliverances of the senses are conceptually interpreted then it is the conceptual interpretation that does all the reason-giving work, that which is interpreted, the experience, thus dropping out as epistemologically irrelevant.

Given that there are these different aspects to the rejection of reason-giving experience a response can be formulated in two ways. One can make sense of the conceptual shaping of experience in such a way as to render the experiential component more visible, or one can attempt to characterise a notion of 'content', or interpretation, that is not conceptual content. The first tack is that taken by John McDowell, who in a number of influential papers has put forward a view in which some thoughts are individuated partly by the objects those thoughts are about (see McDowell 1986, 1994, 1999). The idea is that some thoughts we entertain, 'singular thoughts', would not be the thoughts they are, were the objects they purport to be about be non-existent; their content is said to be 'object-involving'. And we are liable to have such object-involving thoughts when we are in perceptual contact with the world about us. On this model, our perceptual experience provides a particularly good reason to commit to beliefs about the objects perceived, since those experiences would not have the conceptual content they do have were the objects perceived not there. This emphasises the role of experience while leaving in place the requirement that all reasons have conceptual content.

The significant difference from Popper's view is that this 'conceptualisation of experience' is not active; on this view, in experiencing the world our concepts are activated by the world acting on us. This passivity is distinctive of perceptual experience; the experience comes to us as interpreted. The agreement with Popper is with his insistence that only that which is conceptualised can function as a reason. So on this account, experience does not just motivate our beliefs, it also provides us with reason to believe.[6]

I mention this suggestion simply to flag it as a possibility. For present purposes I wish to briefly outline the second strategy, which is to try to make room for a notion of 'interpretation' that is non-conceptual. The advantage in this proposal is that it is consistent with that aspect of evolutionary epistemology, partly pioneered by Popper, which sees our cognitive capacities as continuous with those of other animals. The central thought is that, given there are animals with no apparent conceptual skills who know how to navigate their way around the world, there must be a *non-conceptual* content in their experience facilitating their movements. It is central to this approach that the content, even if non-conceptual, be representational. It is because the content is representational that it is appropriate to say that the content can be right or wrong, accurate or inaccurate. In this respect it accords with Popper's notion of an interpreted state.

It is not, however, sufficient for our purposes that the content can be assessed as right or wrong; this can be true of any informational state of an organism. Here we are concerned to outline a view in which the (non-conceptual) content can function as a reason for a commitment to a belief with an appropriate conceptual content. It is essential to the *rationality* of the transition from non-conceptual content to belief that the non-conceptual content be a component of the subject's experience. To constitute a person's reason for believing something, the person – the subject – must be sensitive to the non-conceptual content, such sensitivity resulting in the deployment of that content as a ground for having a belief. For the content to operate as a reason this sensitivity must be exercised within subjective space.

The details of such an account, one in which we can have reasons that are non-conceptually characterised, cannot be provided here, nor are they of immediate relevance.[7] The importance of this account for present purposes is that it allows Popper some of what he wants ('interpretation' or representation) without ceding to him the claim that basic statements (or, in terms Popper would dislike, basic beliefs) can function as theory-testers only courtesy of a non-justified agreement among scientists to treat those statements as basic. It opens up the possibility that perceptual experience can justify (or falsify) hypotheses, and does so in a way that accords with some of Popper's evolutionary thoughts about the similarity between our processes of knowledge-acquisition and those of other animals. It also allows for an appropriate insistence on the activity of the mind in its pursuit of knowledge. As Popper (and Campbell) emphasised, other animals are active in the investigation of their environments; they do not need to be conceptualisers to be explorers. Nor do we. Interpretation and activity are compatible with experiential justification. This is just as well, because without a rational (and critical) role for perceptual experience, Popper's account of scientific rationality would be fatally flawed.

Notes

1 The demarcation was sometimes said to be between science and metaphysics, at other times between science and pseudo-science, with the unfortunate consequence that pseudo-science and metaphysics looked to be equally indicted as something to be avoided. Popper later made it clear that he did not wish the two to be conflated.

2 I am putting aside the problem raised by A. J. Ayer in opposition to Carnap's and Neurath's protocol-sentences, as to how we decide whether scientists have accepted a certain set of statements as basic. Would it be by accepting a basic statement to the effect that scientists have accepted that set? Ayer suggested (1959, pp. 228–43) that it would have to be individual scientists' experiences that informed them of the agreement among the scientists to accept a set of basic statements.

3 The Popperian may be encouraged in this respect by Hume's insistence that reasons have to be representational. 'Reason is the discovery of truth and falsehood. Truth or falsehood consists in an agreement or disagreement either to the real relations of ideas, or to real existence and matter of fact' (Hume 1978 [1739], p. 458). Passions, volitions and actions, being original existences (not copies) 'are not susceptible of any such agreement or disagreement. . . . 'tis impossible, therefore, they can be pronounced either true or false, and be either contrary or conformable to reason' (ibid.).

4 Campbell claimed that his use of 'inductive' was broad enough to embrace learning by Popperian trial-and-error.

5 Campbell talks of a 'substitute representation'; it is charitable to take this as meaning 'a substitute that is a representation' rather than 'a substitute of a representation'.

6 'On my conception, to enjoy an experience in which all goes well is simply to have a fact available to one, so that it can be normatively behind a judgment one might make' (McDowell 1999, p. 16).

7 See Peacocke 2001 for a defence of this possibility.

References

Ayer, A. J. 1959 [1937]. 'Verification and Experience', in A. J. Ayer (ed.), *Logical Positivism*. New York: Free Press, pp. 228–43. (Originally published in *Proceedings of the Aristotelian Society*, vol. 37, pp. 137–56.)

Campbell, D. T. 1987 [1960]. 'Blind Variation and Selective Retention in Creative Thought as in Other Knowledge Processes', in G. Radnitzky and W. W. Bartley III (eds), *Evolutionary Epistemology, Rationality, and the Sociology of Knowledge*, La Salle, IL: Open Court, pp. 91–114. (Originally published in *The Psychological Review*, vol. 67, pp. 380–400.)

Campbell, D. T. 1988 [1974]. 'Evolutionary Epistemology', in *Methodology and Epistemology for Social Sciences: Selected Essays*. Chicago: University of Chicago Press, pp. 393–434. (Originally published in P. A. Schilpp (ed.), *The Philosophy of Karl Popper*. La Salle, IL: Open Court, pp. 413–63.)

Campbell, John. 2002. *Reference and Consciousness*, Oxford: Oxford University Press.

Heck, Richard. 2000. 'Nonconceptual Content and the "Space of Reasons"', in *The Philosophical Review*, vol. 109, pp. 483–523.

Hume, David. 1978 [1739]. *A Treatise of Human Nature*, ed. L. A. Selby-Bigge, Oxford: Clarendon Press.

McDowell, John. 1986. 'Singular Thought and the Extent of Inner Space', in J. McDowell and P. Pettit (eds), *Subject, Thought, and Context*, Oxford: Oxford University Press, pp. 137–68.

McDowell, John. 1994. *Mind and World*, Cambridge, MA: Harvard University Press.

McDowell, John. 1999. *Reason and Nature*, ed. Marcus Willaschek, Munster: Lit Verlag.

Peacocke, C. 2001. 'Does Perception Have a Nonconceptual Content?', in *Journal of Philosophy*, vol. 98, pp. 239–64.

Popper, Karl. 1959. *The Logic of Scientific Discovery*, London: Hutchinson.

Popper, Karl. 1963. *Conjectures and Refutations*, London: Routledge and Kegan Paul.

Popper, Karl. 1971. *The Open Society and Its Enemies*, vol. 1 *Plato*, vol. II *Hegel and Marx*, 5th edition, Princeton, NJ: Princeton University Press.

Popper, Karl. 1974. 'Replies to Critics', in P. A. Schilpp (ed.), *The Philosophy of Karl Popper*, La Salle, IL: Open Court, pp. 961–1200.

Popper, Karl. 1992. 'Knowledge and the Shaping of Reality', in his *In Search of a Better World: Lectures and Essays from Thirty Years*, London: Routledge, pp. 3–29.

9

POPPER'S POLITICS

Science and democracy

Alan Ryan

This chapter reflects on a familiar question: are science and democracy good for one another? The framing for the question is provided by the two books that constituted Karl Popper's 'war work' of The Open Society and Its Enemies *and* The Poverty of Historicism. *There, and in his autobiography,* Unended Quest, *Popper claims that there is an affinity between the critical rationalism that underpins well-conducted science and the procedures of a properly functioning democracy. Here, the familiar question is taken to mean three things: first, whether liberal democracies provide the best environment for scientific advance, second, whether there is a natural affinity between democractic procedures and scientific investigation, and third, whether science as at present practised assists the functioning of democratic politics. The chapter tentatively answers yes to the first question and no to the third. The philosophically more interesting question is the second. Hobbes's attempt to deduce an authoritarian monarchy from avowedly impregnable scientific considerations is contrasted with Popper's arguments in* The Open Society, *and Popper's difficulties in squaring his account of ideal scientific practice with its practice as described by T. S. Kuhn are briefly explored. The chapter's conclusion is that the affinity between all forms of the formation of an unforced consensus on what to do and what to think suggested by John Dewey and Jürgen Habermas usefully extends Popper's insights.*

* * *

This chapter aims at no novelties, and it preserves the informality of its origins as a lecture. The object of the chapter is to think again about a subject that is always fascinating, and perhaps inexhaustible – how far, and in what ways, the practice of science and the practice of democratic self-government are mutually supportive. Here this embraces three questions; the first and second I shall mostly ignore, much as Popper himself did, and the third I shall discuss at some length. The first question – and the last to be discussed – is: Is science good for democracy? (Meaning by 'science' the institutionalised inquiry into the natural world that we know in prosperous modern societies such as the United States, France, Britain or Japan and meaning by democracy the parliamentary or congressional system of representative democracy practised in such countries.) Second – and first to be discussed: Is democracy (so understood) good for science (so understood)? Third: Are the ways in which scientists come (or should come) to a consensus about the way the world works a model for the ways in which the citizenry comes (or should come) to a consensus on what government ought to do about those things that governments exist to do? Is the process of choosing governments and policies in democratic societies illuminated by the model of 'conjecture and refutation'? It is that third question that will preoccupy us.

The first two questions are factual and sociological, but they allow for much evasion and complication – science is really sciences; Popper was rather contemptuous of the technological applications of science, but it is not easy to draw the line between (pure) scientific and (applied) technological research; and which features of 'modern liberal democracies' are modern, liberal or democratic is debatable. Leaving the first question to the end, the answer to the second question is that democracy seems at first glance good for at least some sorts of science. Prosperous liberal democracies promote energetically the sciences that sustain the technology of high living standards and national prestige, but are bad at promoting other sorts of inquiry. (Think of the bias in the research effort behind genetically modified crops in favour of solving simple problems about resistance to pests and weedkillers relevant to industrialised first-world agriculture while ignoring the extraordinary gains that would come from a second green revolution in the less developed world; and think too of the disproportionate attention paid by medical researchers to the diseases of the rich, and perhaps even the disproportionate attention paid to medicine as distinct from a clearer understanding of why we make ourselves ill in the first place.)

Societies where the norms and practices of liberal democracy are solidly in place are favourable environments for scientific progress, although this may have more to do with the fact that the well-established liberal democracies are the richest countries in the world than with the fact that they are democracies. Claims for the impact of liberalism and democracy in themselves must be taken with a pinch of salt. That their antitheses provide a malign environment is a different matter. Stalin's Russia and Hitler's Germany both suffered intellectually from the way their politics were conducted, suggesting that totalitarianism is more obviously bad for creative science than liberal democracy is good. Theoretical innovation in Germany dried up under Hitler, even though the German war effort was technically very competent, and German industry was throughout more efficient than the British. There was a view in the 1950s, encapsulated in C. P. Snow's lecture on 'The Two Cultures' (1959) that the Soviet Union did better science than the West and applied it faster. With the exception of the first space flights, this was false; and the technology of those flights was the Second World War rocket technology of Germany, with the basic science for that much older again.

But German science was extraordinarily innovative at the level of pure theory throughout the late nineteenth century and the early twentieth century. During the Nazi disaster, German and other central European refugees created much of wartime and postwar natural science in the United States. The political system under which they had been trained and begun work was authoritarian, and even in 1914, it was moving only very slowly, if it was moving at all, in the direction of liberal democracy. In 1914, one might have thought that liberal democracies undervalued pure inquiry, and that autocratically and bureaucratically organised states had a clearer long-term view of society's need for scientific research and an easier time providing funding for it.

Even today, one might think that it was not the *democratic* aspects of modern liberal democracies that fostered scientific research after the Second World War so much as the demands of the Cold War and international economic competition; once prosperity was secure, the demands of national security were reinforced by the demands of medicine and the needs of the pharmaceutical industry. However, it goes too far to suggest that this is *all* that is needed to foster a climate that produces good science; Soviet science was not as good as Western science, and not only because Soviet scientists were short of money; more of the problem lay in the political interference to which scientists were subject. In that, the Soviet Union was unlike older autocracies. The natural sciences made more progress in the Wilhelmine Empire than anywhere else in Europe, but the German autocracy of the nineteenth and twentieth centuries preserved intellectual freedom to the degree that scientists needed it. That liberal – if not exactly democratic – ingredient seems essential.

Germany possessed an ideal of intellectual freedom – best thought of as German *Lehrfreiheit* – that took academic life out of oversight by the political system so long as academics returned the favour by being politically inactive. It was a narrow conception of academic freedom in the sense that it assured researchers that they were not imperilled by holding and teaching any view that fell within their professional competence. Scientists might research what they liked, discuss their results as they liked, and teach their students as they liked. That, however, was the extent of it; there was no licence for *political* free speech in the classroom or the laboratory. It was not the modern American thought that you do not lose your rights as a citizen when you enter the classroom as a teacher. So, any plausible claim about the impact of democracy on science must be cautious; the blanket suppression of freedom of speech and thought will wreck science, some institutionalised immunity of imagination and controversy from political control is essential to rapid progress in science. Liberal democracies are the best bet over a long run in providing those conditions, but may well need – as Popper more than once suggested – institutional means to counteract democracy's tendency towards short-termism.

Let us turn to the main question. Is scientific debate a model for democratic debate? Popper was one of the most famous defenders of the view that science, properly practised, was a model for democratic decision-making. It was a view that Russell put forward sometimes, but by no means always, and that Dewey put forward always but by no means with Popper's rhetorical verve. Popper's view that the defence of good science, the glories of European civilisation, and liberal democratic politics was all of a piece had considerable resonance at different points in his life. Popper was less influential in the United States than in Britain and Europe, but towards the end of his life he was greatly admired by politicians as well as philosophers throughout Europe – east as well as west. He had always been admired by intelligent politicians in Britain, particularly by Sir Edward Boyle.

George Soros's Open Society Foundations, which spread liberal-democratic ideas throughout the former Communist *bloc* in the 1970s and 1980s, took their title from Popper's great book on *The Open Society and Its Enemies*. Popper's impact on European politics was almost wholly to the good. There are, however, two large difficulties in Popper's case. One is whether political *decision-making* is really analogous to scientific *investigation*; the other is the divergence between Popper's *prescriptions* for scientific inquiry and some famous *descriptions* of how scientists behave in practice. If scientists do not and perhaps cannot behave in the way Popper thought they could and did, the case for thinking that science is intrinsically democratic is much weakened. This is why the chapter ends with some anxieties about the political and academic impact of 'science as practised'.

We should begin by recalling that the most striking of the twentieth-century literary representations of the impact of science on society have been *dystopian* rather than *utopian*. In New Zealand, it was a matter of some regret to leave to one side the orcs who feature so strikingly in the film of *The Lord of the Rings*; but they are the product of sorcery rather than science, and their creators were driven by pure malice. The more frightening, because more plausible, anxiety is not that science will be misused by the wicked but that it will be misused by the good-natured. Aldous Huxley's *Brave New World*, for instance, is a fantasy that is almost within our grasp to implement; at the time of his death thirty years ago Huxley thought we were well on the way to its realisation. In *Brave New World*, the Director ensures that a combination of genetic manipulation and psychological reinforcement creates a hierarchical society in which everyone gets what they want and everyone wants what they get. Alphas think, Betas manage and Gammas labour. It is not the savage depiction of an English Stalinism that Orwell set out in *1984* – which has no technological underpinning at all to speak of. Nor is it the terrified depiction of the world reduced to smoking rubble that fills any number of Bertrand Russell's post-1945 essays on the military impact of advanced science. *Brave New World* shows a world in which our desire for comfort and happiness has been satisfied. It is also a world from which every trace of political life has been expunged. Its intellectual ancestor was Russell's *Icarus*, the little pamphlet he wrote in 1924 as a *riposte* to the optimism of J. B. S. Haldane's *Daedalus*.

This is why the issue of the connection of science and democracy is interesting. The images of science that were most popular in the later twentieth century were those of the 'aviator' as he was usually called in 1930s novels, dropping bombs on civilians in perfect safety from 20,000 feet in the sky, and the psychologist conditioning babies in one of Huxley's eugenicist nurseries; a philosopher who wants to argue that science provides a model for democratic politics has (rhetorically) an uphill task.[1] There are some more narrowly conceptual difficulties; in particular, a philosopher who held, as Popper did when writing *The Open Society and Its Enemies*, that there is a logical divide between facts and decisions – Popper's version of Hume's 'is–ought' gap – has an uphill struggle.

On Popper's own account, the decision to support democratic institutions was just that, a decision. Whether scientific procedures were characteristically consensual, open, and deliberative, or more typically authoritarian and dogmatic would not on the face of it bear on that decision one way or another. A man might be a despot on the conductor's podium and a liberal in the voting booth, a tyrant to his students in the physics laboratory and an anarchist in his politics. The interest of Popper's work to the non-philosopher of science is that he knew this as well as anyone, but produced what one might in the idiom of a later age call an account of 'open discourse' as underpinning both democracy and science.

It was in New Zealand that he wrote the two books that endeared him to non-philosophers – and to philosophers who were not deeply interested in probability and formal logic. *The Open Society and Its Enemies* (1945) was one, and *The Poverty of Historicism* (1957) the other. New Zealand was a propitious environment. Although Popper was not well understood by his employers, he had enough friends and colleagues in subjects other than philosophy to provide him with the audience and critics he needed, while the country was an egalitarian, welfare state democracy far in advance of most of the countries of Europe. *The Open Society* is a heavily historical work. Volume One sets out to destroy Plato's reputation, and Volume Two that of Hegel and Marx. Part of the point of so doing is plain. Throughout history, and today as much as ever, science has been linked to authority. Plato thought philosophers should be kings and kings should be philosophers, because he thought that only those who *know* should govern. Hegel – on Popper's highly controversial reading of him – thought the same thing; he, Hegel, knew how Reason was destined to embody itself in the institutions of the Prussian state, and thought that the authority of the Prussian monarchy was the authority of Reason. In the same way, Marx believed that the new science of historical materialism answered all possible questions about the future course of social, economic and political life, and that the bearers of this knowledge were entitled to remake the future as they saw fit.

Here the historical skirmishing confronts Popper with Thomas Hobbes rather than the enemies he picked for himself, as a prelude to the suggestion that Dewey's version of Popper's case was even better than Popper's own. But, Popper was quite right to think that *most* thinkers have linked science to infallible knowledge, and have linked infallibility to a right to exercise unconstrained authority. That is, they have thought that science was intrinsically inimical to democracy; because the opinion of the many is no match for the knowledge of the wise. We ought also to keep in front of us the way in which today, the 'expert,' the person who really knows, is called in as a constraint on democratic decision-making. You don't, as the commonplace has it, want to take a vote on who is to perform brain surgery on you, you want the guy who knows how to do it.

By parity of reasoning, if there were scientifically trained leaders who *knew* what to do, they should be allowed to do it, and the rest of us should keep quiet. The idea that experts should be 'on tap, not on top' competes uneasily with the reverence for expertise as such.

Hobbes was born when his mother panicked at a rumour of the arrival of the Spanish Armada – on Good Friday, 1588, some six months before the Armada arrived off the Cornish coast in September. He said that fear and he were born twins into the world, and followed his own materialist psychology by suggesting that his birth in a climate of fear made him a good friend to peace. Intellectually, on the other hand, he was not a friend to peace but a violent controversialist. Much like Popper attacking Plato as the begetter of fascism, historicism, totalitarianism and much else, Hobbes attacked Aristotle as the begetter of scholasticism and superstition, and classical political authors more generally as the preachers of tyrannicide and rebellion; he wanted to replace the influence of philosophers and rhetoricians with the truths of the new science. But it was not for the *sake* of science that he took on the classical writers; he did it to re-establish political, ideological and religious authority. This authority was to be absolute and unchallengeable. And science was to be its basis.

Paradoxically, Hobbes was as much an individualist as Popper. But his picture of science could not have been more different. Where Popper thought that science was a matter of forming bold conjectures and seeking the evidence that would show up whatever weaknesses they had, Hobbes claimed that science was a matter of choosing correct definitions and following out their consequences. A concern with definitions was one of the things that Popper most loathed; and Hobbes really was obsessed with definitions. He had reasons for this that Popper would not have had much time for, but which are not foolish; a version of Hobbes's case was in fact explored by Popper, without reference to Hobbes, in a well known paper on the way the calculi of logic and mathematics apply to the world. Hobbes thought the model of science was geometry, and unlike us, who mostly side with Popper in thinking definitions are arbitrary, he thought well-chosen definitions were the path to true knowledge. If you get your definitions right and follow the train of inference exactly, you *cannot* be wrong. It is the thought that one *can* get definitions right that is the sticking point.

The nature of authority is now the issue. Although Hobbes's aim was to establish authority, he gave authority a limited role in the search for truth. Each individual is a cognitive enterprise entire and whole unto herself or himself. We are set, in the words of Burke, to trade on our own stock of reason, and the natural condition of humanity is that of having to make up their own minds as best they can in the light of the evidence and with the aid of their own reason. Unlike Burke, who thought each man's stock of reason was small, Hobbes thought it was quite large enough to reach important conclusions about life, death, peace and politics. It is very unBurkean, but a good foundation for a belief in social progress and a belief in the growth of knowledge – in the possibility of which Hobbes believed as strongly as Popper.

To rely uncritically on anyone else's beliefs, Hobbes thought, doubles the chance of being wrong; I may be wrong to trust the person on whom I rely, and he may be wrong about the matter in hand; I would be as wrong to trust his judgment without myself looking at the matter as the owner of a business would be to trust the accounts of his servants without going through them for himself. The wise man inspects the evidence and scrutinises the argument, and makes up his own mind. It is also an egalitarian view of reason. Against Plato, there is no class of persons whose judgments are infallible. As against Aristotle, we all have enough sense for the business of life, and there are no natural slaves, no natural rulers, no peoples incapable of political life. In what looks very like the same spirit as Popper's insistence that science is radically anti-authoritarian, Hobbes gives each of us the task of making up our own minds about how the world works, and our own place in it.

Hobbes, however, deduces absolute monarchy from these premises; Popper was always a liberal democrat – even if the socialist Popper of the 1930s was more than *merely* a liberal democrat, and the Popper of the 1970s and 1980s held conventional neo-conservative prejudices against the allegiances of his youth. Was Hobbes's invocation of science as the basis of absolute monarchy simply absurd? Not really. Is there a weaker connection between the methods of science and the methods of liberal democracy than Popper thought? Plainly yes, but not just like that.

Hobbes argued as follows. Individualism is not absolute; finding the best account of the nature of the world is a social matter. We must use our own reason; but we must take other people's views seriously. To prefer our own view just because it is *ours* is like insisting when we play cards that trumps should be whatever suit we have most of. We cannot just accept other people's claims, but we can share our opinions and improve our understanding. That Hobbes thought of science as a cooperative activity is not in doubt, even though he was appallingly prickly in his dealings with anyone who disagreed with him, and appears to have been refused membership of the Royal Society for just that reason: a man who observes that 'if he had read as much as other men he would have known as little as they' is not a natural cooperator. But Hobbes thought that one of the greatest benefits of civilisation was that it allows science to flourish; the state's fundamental task was to save us from sudden and violent death and to reduce fear and anxiety; but once it has done that basic work it shelters science and all the other arts of civilised society. And these are all cooperatively established.

Science tends towards consensus among careful investigators. This implies that in matters where there is a natural consensus, little authoritative direction is required. But there are many things about which no natural agreement can be had. These are things in which our desires and aversions are implicated. Science explains why we all want different things, and why each of us wants different things at different times, but science does not tell us *what to want*. This not only sounds very like Popper's sharp division between fact and decision; it has radical implications. What is '*good*' by nature depends on who uses the term and not on the object it is applied to; we apply it to the objects of our desire, just because they are the object of our desire. 'What each man desireth is that which he for his part calleth good.' Where description is concerned, we shape the names to the world, but where evaluation is concerned we shape the names to our desires. Whereas discussion and the sharing of views will lead us to impose the same names and come to agreement in the description and explanation of the world, no such convergence can be had in the realm of desire.

What, then, can science tell us? It can tell us two things. First, it can tell us that we need some conventional mechanism, some authority, that will *impose* standards of good and evil, and impose an agreement about what is just and unjust on the behaviour needed to make a society function peacefully. Hobbes weaves together the arbitrary and non-arbitrary in a way that needs a delicate touch to disentangle. The realm of *justice*, which Hobbes defines as the science of those things that follow from covenant is non-arbitrary; but there are many other matters that need some decision rather than none, but where the content of the decision is unimportant. Whether a man should pray with his head covered or bare provokes dissension and warfare between contending sects; reason suggests that an agreed convention about what constitutes the expression of an intention to honour the deity will keep the peace, so our need is for one convention and not several conflicting ones. Authority exists to impose it. The second thing science can tell us is what leads us into mutual conflict, and what we must do to get out of that state. Hobbes's famous account of the life of man in the state of nature – 'solitary, poor, nasty, brutish, and short' – is the culmination of his account of the horrors of life without a state to protect us from each other.

And, thinks Hobbes, what science tells us is that to leave that condition and enjoy the blessings of living in a pacified society, we must yield all our rights and powers into the hands of a sovereign. This may be one man, or a body of men, or even all of us collectively. However it is organised, it must have absolute authority to make laws that govern us hereafter, and those laws must be adequately enforced. All this, says Hobbes, is demonstrably true. What form of government works best is a matter of prudence and experience, which Hobbes believed argued in favour of monarchy. But all government must be absolute government.

In this light let us contemplate Popper's conviction in *The Open Society* and elsewhere that the methodology of science supports liberal democracy. Hobbes gives Popper more trouble than the targets Popper chose. He was neither a tribalist nor a historicist, so few of Popper's complaints about Plato, Hegel and Marx touch him. Now, in this light let us contemplate Popper's conviction in *The Open Society* and elsewhere that there is a natural consilience between science and liberal democracy. Hobbes's account of the political situation exemplifies Popperian virtue – not in terms of the philosophy of science broadly construed but in terms of Popper's own methodological prescriptions for social science. Popper came in middle age to think that the models of economic theory were a paradigm of good social science theorising; they are built around 'situational logic', and they explain behaviour as the reiteration of responses to situations that are themselves the unanticipated consequences of previous actions taken in response to situations with a certain logic. In just that fashion, Hobbes offered an analysis of the situational logic that would lead by one route into the state of war and by another out of that state and into political society.

A further reason for invoking Hobbes is that there is a deep affinity between Hobbes's insistence on the importance of peace and what became Popper's overwhelming concern during the last thirty years of his life – the avoidance of catastrophic nuclear war. Commentators on Popper tend to be obsessed by the philosophical puzzles attendant on the question, what if anything is democratic about science and what if anything is scientific about democracy? But a layman might be equally struck by the way in which the scientific community after 1945 was emotionally devastated by the invention of the atomic bomb and its successor weapons. Speculation is cheap, but one might see in the reaction of many nuclear scientists and scientifically trained philosophers such as Popper or Russell a metaphysical horror not only at the thought that humanity had become clever enough to kill itself off once and for all as a species, but at the thought that the most striking advances in our understanding of the world had been turned to such destructive purposes.

Popper's view was very much not a case of 'peace at any price', and he was ready in the best traditions of John Stuart Mill to envisage the need on appropriate occasions to go to war to preserve the peace. At that point, the comparison with Hobbes breaks down. Hobbes was not a natural liberal interventionist. None the less, Popper made the preservation of a stable peace the centrepiece of many of the political interviews he gave in the last decades of his life, and saw it as increasingly urgent when the collapse of the Soviet Union meant that a great deal of nuclear weaponry might fall into the hands of lunatics, fanatics and gangsters of every possible stripe. The advantage in the analysis lies with Hobbes, however. Hobbes thought that good men might kill one another as readily as bad men. It was the situation rather than their morality that we must repair. Popper on the contrary was always quick to make large moral judgments, and the fact that he is said never to have read the newspaper and never to have listened to the radio makes this moralising sometimes unpersuasive. Hobbes had a sharp eye for the way in which the absence of political authority may make persons who are neither mad nor fanatical nor sadistic into enemies of one another and under the wrong conditions may drag them into the mutual destruction which they wish at all costs to avoid.

What Hobbes and Popper share is an anxiety about undeterrable violence. In Hobbes's picture of interaction in the state of nature we have people who are frightened of each other, who may be in competition for the means of life, and who understand, crucially, that if the other manages to kill them, they have no recourse. But why should the other person try to kill them? The answer is because he is afraid they might strike first, and the only security against that is striking first himself. This is the seventeenth-century, two-person model of what became the nuclear nightmare in the early 1950s when both the United States and the

Soviet Union appeared to have enough first-strike nuclear capacity to destroy the other side's ability to respond. Paradoxically, MAD – the guarantee that each side could retaliate no matter what happened to it, known as Mutually Assured Destruction – meant that life became safer with more weapons around than it had been with fewer. Hobbes's sovereign is a universal second-strike capacity; because we all know that we will do badly if we behave badly, we are not tempted to behave badly, and because we know everyone else is in the same boat, we know we need not fear them, and our motive for attack vanishes. We get in and out of the state of nature by the same route. And one might say of this argument that not only does Hobbes provide a more persuasive analytical framework than Popper, he does it by using exactly the minimal apparatus that Popper recommended in his discussions of the methodology of the social sciences. For even though Hobbes writes at length of human nature, and Popper is deeply hostile to theories of human nature, they actually coincide at the crucial point – an austere theory of rationality and situational logic.

But, we must now recur to the great difference. For Hobbes we come out of the state of nature and put ourselves under the protection of an absolute government, absolute monarchy for preference. More crucially, it is a state whose rulers are legally and constitutionally unaccountable. This, of course, is exactly at the opposite pole from Popper's intentions. Popper was very much *not* a 'rule by the people' democrat. The need for accountability was the closest he ever came to a one-shot description of an acceptable political order. And, this is the moment to swing the argument around and tie the politics back to the philosophy of science. Popper was a mild sort of Marxist as a young man in Vienna at the end of the first war. Exactly what prompted him to abandon Marx is disputed; Popper's autobiographical account is more tidy in retrospect than life may have been at the time. He says, plausibly, that he thought the violence of the revolution proposed by Marxists was morally wrong – it was needlessly costly for the reforms expected – and practically foolish – the persons proposing to launch an insurrection were pacifists by temperament and no match for their right-wing military opponents, who were effective fighters and happy to shoot just about anyone on the left. But, Popper throws in for good measure the view that the Russian Revolution of 1917 was a falsification of Marxist theory. That it was a revolution was undeniable, but it was the wrong revolution and in the wrong place. If it was a socialist revolution, one half of Marx's theory was wrong, and if it was not, then much else was wrong.

In short, Marx's predictions had been falsified. If Marxists were scientifically minded, they would have abandoned Marx. Critics of Popper complain that because he had not yet arrived at the sophisticated understanding of the concept of falsification that his *Logik der Forschung* elaborates, he cannot have been disillusioned in quite the way he implies. It is also suggested that it was only when he came to write the most elaborate version of *The Poverty of Historicism* along with *The Open Society* that Marxist prophecy became as salient a target as assorted quasi-fascist views. This is true but not especially important. Innumerable quasi-Marxists at the time thought that the Russian Revolution was a blow *against* Marxism rather than a proof of Marx's correctness, and did so for essentially Popper's reasons, without ever elaborating a sophisticated theory of falsification. It is very easy to believe that a young man as clever as Popper and thinking with the intensity that he was at that stage of his life would have thought exactly what he later remembers thinking – even if the event later wore a significance it did not at the time.

So, let us try to nail down the connection between the falsificationist criterion for scientific respectability and democratic politics. Popper turned the conventional view of science on its head by arguing that scientists do not try to *prove* theories or hypotheses, but to *disprove* them. No amount of evidence can prove a theory is true, but one decisive experiment can show that it is false. One black swan disproves the hypothesis that swans have to be white. Newton's physics had received endless confirmations before the evidence from Eddington's eclipse expedition after the First World War (revealing the bending of starlight near the sun) showed that Einstein was more nearly right than he. Good science makes progress by what Popper calls conjecture and refutation; we should try to have lots of bright ideas and then look for ways of showing that the false ones are false. This has implications for the organisation of scientific inquiry; hypotheses must not be protected by the eminence or distinction of those who think them up or who learned them when young and don't want to abandon them. The ideal scientific community is one that allows anyone to propose an idea for experimental or other testing, and to the extent possible criticises it in a productive way – a difficult idea, since it combines the thought that we must give a new idea the chance to prove itself with the thought that we must also be hard on it to expose its defects.

Popper's politics are based on accountability. What is the great virtue of science? It is the notion that we are accountable for our beliefs. What this means is that Popper's philosophy of science does not so much support a liberal and democratic politics; it just is that politics in cognitive action. This is not to be taken as a biographical observation about how Popper himself thought of things. Most of the time, he seems not to have thought about politics in the everyday sense at all. He dealt in larger entities than those handled by day-to-day politics. It was at the level of large dichotomies – culture versus savagery, civilisation versus barbarism – that he thought when he thought about politics. The details of political institutions seem not to have interested him; it was tides of opinion that he noticed, not refinements of small-scale policy. Liberal democracy is the politics of responsible, non-tribalist, non-superstitious humanity; and science is the epistemology of those same persons. The connection between these large cultural values and the defence of liberal democratic politics is an empirical one. As a matter of fact – but it is an impressive and important matter of fact – liberal-democratic political regimes have been much better than their competitors at protecting the values that Popper minded about. Liberal democracies – mostly, and with many failings – are good at preventing racial cruelty, torture, judicial murder and much else of that sort. Still, this is an argument in favour of liberal democracy that is wholly free-standing; it is a good argument, but it does not illuminate the question we have been skirting: is the practice of science sufficiently like the practice of democratic politics for the first to illuminate the second?

The dissimilarities seem in the end too many for Popper to handle. One reason we have already mentioned. Popper, like Hobbes, distinguishes sharply between facts and decisions; *deciding* what to do is never determined by the facts. Science, ideally, rests on the fact that scientists are constrained in what they can say and think by the way the world actually is. Our wants are not thus constrained, though what we can do to satisfy them certainly is. Politics is much more about working out what we *want* in the light of the fact that we have to live together than it is about discovering how the world works; a process that works well for the second task cannot be assumed to have much to tell us about how best to reach a collective decision about what we should do next.

Moreover, the actual practices of both science and political democracy work against Popper's picture. The great historian of science, Thomas Kuhn, wrote a little book on *The Structure of Scientific Revolutions* that Popper regarded as a threat to civilisation and an encouragement to religious fanaticism. Since Kuhn had thought of himself as a disciple of Popper, he was more than slightly startled – and pained – by this. His offence was to claim two things. The first was that in everyday scientific practice, very little falsification is practised; bold hypotheses are not much wanted; young scientists are trained as apprentices before being allowed to think an original thought; and what Kuhn called 'normal' science is mostly 'gap-filling'. For long periods, scientists assume they know the broad out-lines of how particular bits of the natural world work, and devote themselves to filling in the details. The second claim was that the process by which large-scale transformations of a scientific world-view occur is very like the process of political revolution. The old regime loses credibility bit by bit, but only when a plausible rival appears is revolution possible. Then, for a long time it is unclear whether progress has actually occurred; eventually the dust settles and it becomes clear that *some* progress has occurred, though rarely as much as is claimed by enthusi-asts for the new model. The first sort of science is not democratically organised, not bold and exciting, and not very individualist in style. The second sort is not rational in the way Popper held it must be. The two things together threatened the idea that scientific inquiry was *the* model of rational conduct with important political implications. Conversely, much of contemporary democratic theory is also unPopperian. On at least one popular view, the central element of democra-tic politics is electing a team of leaders to run a government for a period of several years between elections. Although the effects of proposed policies are certainly debated, and although we should no doubt benefit from a more rational and evi-dence-based attitude to the formation of policy on all sorts of issues, the core of the matter is achieving a consensus not on the effects of policies but on the ques-tion of who is to govern us.

One writer who handled this better than Popper, while still maintaining that there is an affinity between the method of science and the method of democracy, was Dewey. The deep reasons for this are complicated, but the surface reasons are less so – and here we shall stay on the surface. Dewey rejected the split between facts and decisions that Popper insisted upon. For Dewey a 'fact' was less part of the structure of reality than a label we placed on beliefs that we did not need to reopen for the moment; by the same token, a 'decision' was a label we placed on the sense that what we were up to did not immediately need to be questioned. The distinction between facts and decisions was rarely important, and did not reflect some deep feature of reality; 'wanting' is a process of discovery, and seeing the facts is often a matter of deciding to accept one picture of the world rather than another.

So Dewey was not faced with the logical chasm between fact and decision into which Popper's account falls. By the same token, Dewey could provide a positive account of rationality in conduct that embraced individual choice, collective choice and 'science'. He did it by taking most of the weight off the idea of rationality. Human beings are like other animals. We are adapted to steering ourselves around the world in ways that promote the welfare both of the individual and of the species; good sense is a quality of the species. This is why he insisted that human beings could learn the art of rationally scrutinising *everything* about their activities (though not all at once), without receiving the gift of pure reason from Plato, Hegel, or God.

How far, though, will this take us? Further than Popper, but not far enough for anyone who wants to make the activities of scientists a model for democratic politics. Popper, faced with Kuhn, retreated to saying that *good* science was practised as he had described; that there was a lot of plodding and conservative work about was not news, but that was not science as he meant it. Yet such a response to Kuhn was a retreat to stipulative definitions of the sort Popper ordinarily disapproved of. Dewey had a more fruitful approach; in effect, he says that knowledge is increased by a continuous and open-ended process of reflection, not only on our beliefs but on our techniques, our philosophical prejudices, and whatever may get in the way of intellectual and reflective growth. Is this a model for democracy?

It tells you little about one-man, one-vote – about which Dewey was anyway pretty unkind, thinking that the major political parties had long ago sold themselves to economic interests. It may, however, tell you about the way a community can develop an unforced consensus about both belief and action. 'What do we think and what do we want?' invites an open-ended argument in which literally anything goes – though well-intentioned participants will introduce *fruitful* rather than merely idiosyncratic considerations. People who like formal logic dislike Dewey's allusive and loosely articulated approach, and prefer the Poppers, Carnaps and Reichenbachs of this world. But everyone other than Popper bought rigour so defined by splitting rationality defined in formal terms from political reasonableness and found themselves with nothing to say about the latter. Everyone who hopes for illumination has had to go down the Deweyan track – including Americans such as Richard Rorty and Europeans such as Jürgen Habermas.

If the question 'does scientific practice provide a model for democratic practice?'

gets a slightly blurred 'yes' for an answer – since even on the most Deweyan view, they can only supply a partial model for each other – we should turn to the question whether science as currently practised and funded is good for democratic politics, or for democracy in the wider social sense. We should now stare bleakly at the anxieties expressed in Huxley's *Brave New World* and in Russell's *Icarus*; they are the same anxieties – Russell complained that Huxley had stolen his central idea from his little book and had turned it into a best-selling novel. Since most of our anxieties seem to be about *technique* and *technology*, it might be thought that the pure inquiry into the world that Popper thought the only thing worthy of the name of science *could not* be alarming. Once we get down to practice, however, that distinction may begin to dissolve. The thought is this: most modern science is technological in aim, and therefore most of what passes for 'pure' science is dubiously anything of the sort. The modern version of Huxley's and, more particularly, Russell's fears thus boil down to the thought that our demand for *usefulness* in science will either result in our destroying ourselves in hi-tech war, or if we avoid that fate, in our agreeing to be entertained, fed and looked after by benign and well-intentioned experts, which will mean a safe and comfortable, but essentially infantilised existence. They would be different routes to the same destination: human extinction.

There are many reasons to be less fearful than that – at least about the second alternative. The paternalist task is too complicated to be described other than in a novel, and heaps an implausible degree of authority on one man's shoulders. Any actual Director, for instance, would have friends and rivals who disagree with him over both policy and technique. The illusion that we are heading towards brave new world by 'Amusing Ourselves to Death' as one recent book put it, has little to do with science and more to do with the extraordinary quantity of television and other forms of home entertainment available in an affluent society. Certainly modern science underpins the technology but the technology does not force itself on us. If there is any undermining of older ideals of citizen engagement going on, or any turning away from the ideal of the autonomous moral agent, it is we who are undermining ourselves, even if we are using more hi-tech instruments than our forebears might have done.

None the less, Popper and Dewey were interestingly wrong in ways that induce some unhappiness in anyone concerned for education. Popper, like Dewey, admired disciplines that need a clear head, a sharp pencil, and the back of an envelope. Both Popper's bold 'conjecture and refutation' and Dewey's more conversational accounts illuminate such disciplines, and both provide a model for democratic discourse. But, most observers think that science as practised is, if anything, inimical to democratic discourse. The sheer weight of information and accepted understanding that students must master before they can do research of their own is nowadays enormous. Undergraduate science teaching is more authoritarian than humanities teaching for a reason that is hard to resist or evade: in the humanities, learning the arts of reinterpreting a manageable number of events and artefacts is what education is about, and endless discussion is the natural tool of education. In the sciences, techniques and data multiply faster than anyone can keep up with them, and mastering the newest data and the newest techniques is more like intellectual boot camp than like a stroll in the Elysian Fields. And yet, Popper and Dewey were right to want a scientific education to provide the same exercise for the imagination as a traditional arts education.

Here as everywhere, money is the root of all evil, and the funding of science is bound to reflect the demands of the funders; the maintenance of the unity of the arts and sciences is not high on the priorities of governments or pharmaceutical companies, and exploring what it means cannot be very high on the priorities of students incurring a substantial indebtedness in the hope of a decent job after graduation. Popper could retort that this isn't what he's concerned with. Dewey would have thought it was a failure of democracy to allow anything to escape the net of discussion and intellectual accountability. The sheer difficulty of knowing how we could institutionalise that ideal is one reason why it is so easy to think of him as a utopian – and a reason to envy an optimism it is hard to share.

Note

1 Popper's early biography is worth bearing in mind when thinking about his politics. His autobiography, *Unended Quest* (1976), is a highly 'political' document. It is full of political lessons Popper meant us to draw from the world in which he grew up; and its selection of topics from his intellectual development is also slanted (perfectly properly) for political reasons. Karl Popper was born in Vienna in 1902. His father was a well-off liberal lawyer, his mother a highly cultivated woman and an excellent pianist; they were Jews who converted to Christianity out of a wish to get on with their Christian neighbours, and Popper later approved this gesture of politeness. The First World War broke out when he was twelve – on his birthday, in fact. He left school at the end of the war, joined the Communist Youth Movement for six weeks and left when they seemed bent on getting people killed for no good reason. He worked as an assistant in a psycho-analytic nursery school, and remained a committed socialist until the end of the Second World War; his education was patchy – his family were ruined by the post-war inflation, and he worked at odd jobs including taking an apprenticeship with a cabinet-maker and tutoring American students in German. But he got himself a PhD at the end of the 1920s, for the first part of what became his masterpiece: *The Logic of Scientific Discovery* (1935).

References

Hacohen, Malachi. 2000. *Karl Popper: The Formative Years*, Cambridge: Cambridge University Press.

Popper, Karl R. 1935. *Logik der Forschung*, Vienna: Springer.

Popper, Karl R. 1945. *The Open Society and Its Enemies*, two volumes, London: Routledge and Kegan Paul.

Popper, Karl R. 1957. *The Poverty of Historicism*, London: Routledge and Kegan Paul.

Popper, Karl R. 1976. *Unended Quest*, London: Fontana/Collins.

Snow, C. P. 1959. *The Two Cultures and the Scientific Revolution*, Cambridge: Cambridge University Press.

10

THE OPEN SOCIETY REVISITED

Anthony O'Hear

In this chapter, I will consider some of the themes of Karl Popper's Open Society and Its Enemies, *which was first published in 1945 in two volumes (referred to here as OS, and quoted from the fifth edition, 1966). In doing this, I will concentrate on the respects in which Popper's positive vision of the open society he is advocating strikes me as utopian. Many of the criticisms Popper makes of Marx in particular strike me as devastating, of vital importance in the time in which they were written, and also, eventually, a classic case of philosophy influencing world politics for the good. Nevertheless, while I am in no sense trying here to bury Popper, questioning of an admittedly somewhat under-described vision in what may in retrospect come to seem his most important book seems to me a more worthy response than simple praise, especially if it helps to initiate a discussion of just how Popper's positive vision might be fruitfully developed in the twenty-first century.*

* * *

Popper's open society is contrasted with closed societies, which are societies marked by what Popper would see as oppression and inhumanity. These closed societies may be tribal societies, dominated by tradition, irrational prejudice, xenophobia and rule by hereditary groups or oligarchies. Or they may be more modern types of dictatorship, run by rulers who claim superior (or even infallible) insights into history and society, and who claim on the basis of this knowledge to be able to produce a good (or better) life for everyone. 'Everyone', of course, simply has to submit to this superior knowledge, so there is considerable dictatorial potential in closed societies, which was very much in Popper's mind when he attacked closed societies in the 1940s.

Open societies, by contrast, are societies in which everything – policies, institutions, traditions, rulers – is open to criticism, and open to criticism from anyone. Anyone may criticise in an open society, especially those directly affected by a given policy or institution. In an open society policies and institutions are modified by continual monitoring of their effects, and in the light of their ability to solve the problems they are supposed to solve. Rulers do not attempt to impose blueprints for the good life on the whole of society. Instead they seek to rectify obvious problems and abuses through piecemeal social engineering, and the continual monitoring of effects.

The open spirit is one which listens, as Popper puts it, to the other fellow's point of view. Differences are resolved and decisions reached through this process of rational discussion, and the spirit of compromise and cooperation. Open societies will probably be democracies, as democracy is the form of social organisation most conducive to the sort of discussion and consultation characteristic of open societies; but democracy is not sufficient for openness. The majority can tyrannise (as Popper knew all too well from Germany and Austria in the 1930s). For Popper the most important feature of an open society is that in it rulers can be replaced regularly and peacefully – because in such a system the rulers are most likely to be sensitive to the feelings and needs of the ruled.

An initial comment on all this might well be that no actual society is completely open in Popper's sense. Even if the liberal democracies of the West are more open than other forms of society (as they surely are), they may not be wholly open, Popper's own admiration for Britain and the United States notwithstanding. Even in Britain and the United States, it would be said, some voices are systematically unheard, such as the unemployed, immigrants, the old and women. Perhaps, as some have argued, Popper himself should have been more aware than he was of the way that power structures, cognitive interest and control of the mass and other media can stifle discussion and marginalise potentially valuable inputs to discussion. Maybe more social equality than Popper was prepared to admit is necessary to achieve the sort of openness Popper desired.

But criticisms of this sort, even if valid, would not invalidate the idea of the open society. They would show only that Popper had not worked it out sufficiently. Nor would they have any tendency to reduce the significance of his repeated assertion that what is critical in an open society is not just the structural and institutional framework necessary to achieve openness, crucial as this is, but a spirit of openness in those who man those structures and institutions. More damaging for Popper's social philosophy is a doubt as to whether any society could actually operate, or even survive, given the degree of openness his proposals advocate. But before addressing this doubt head on, we need to say something about the ideological underpinning of Popper's open society.

Underlying the open society are five basic ideas, the first four of which are firmly within the tradition of Enlightenment rationalism and optimism. The first idea is that of the unity of mankind. That is to say, in the open society anyone may criticise and contribute, regardless of origin, race, religion, class or gender. In this context, it is noteworthy that Popper himself was resolutely anti-nationalistic, even to the extent of criticising the very existence of Israel. He also made himself unpopular in the 1960s by saying that Jews in the Germanic countries should have sought to suppress their differences from Germans and Austrians, so as not to have aroused antagonism (not that Popper had any truck with Pan-Germanism). In this dislike of national differences and distinctions, Popper parallels Kant's views on the topic, though whether, as some have suggested, he was yearning for the palmy days of the structurally multi-cultural post-1848 Austro-Hungarian Empire is perhaps more doubtful.

The second support to openness is the notion of individualism. Popper had an almost pathological hatred of any form of group rule or collectivism (even to the extent of refusing in his eighties to go round a Portuguese palace in a group). But his insistence on individualism, ontological, political and methodological, was not just pathological. It was based on a Kantian sense of the rational autonomy of each individual, *qua* individual.

Third, and connected to the first two notions, is that of impartiality. Any view may be worth hearing, whatever its provenance. This is not just an Enlightenment view. For Popper it is also an essential similarity between the open society and the ideal scientific community, in which valid criticism of a scientific theory can come from any quarter. The extent to which a human society, open or not, can actually resemble the community of science is something which will concern us later.

Then, fourth, there is humanitarianism. Popper was horrified from the time of his encounters with revolutionary socialists after the First World War by the readiness of idealists to sacrifice individual lives today in order to hasten the birth of some ideal society in the future. Even if there were a greater chance of the ideal society coming about through revolutionary terrorism than in fact is the case, it could never be justified to treat the lives of others as means to the end, again a striking parallel with Kant.

The fifth strand to Popper's thought is where, to a degree, he departs from the classical Enlightenment position. For Popper does not believe that the unfettered use of reason is bound to produce truth or absence from error. He is in no sense an epistemological optimist; he is, in fact, a fallibilist, one who believes that we can never rule out the possibility of error, even in the best regulated and conducted of enquiries. Neither truth nor desirable social outcomes are the inevitable fruit of the use of reason. It is partly because of this that Popper makes criticism and openness so central to the open society, because criticism and openness are the best ways we know of uncovering error and failure in the social sphere. And, as part of his fallibilism about social outcomes, Popper will stress the reality of human freedom, and the way the free decisions of individual human beings affect what happens in both big and small affairs. Not the least of his objections to Marxism is the arrogant assumption of the Marxists that they know how history is going, and that the rest of us simply have to submit both to history and to their superior knowledge of it. It is this idea, that history has a definite direction, which Popper characterises as historicism, and he thinks it is nonsense. We are free, and within limits we can act, individually and collectively, sometimes even to change what all the experts confidently assert to be the course of history (as, in their different ways President Reagan and Mrs Thatcher and their followers did both in their own countries and in the Evil Empire, and as the Ayatollah Khomeini and his followers did in Iran).

It is on fallibilism, freedom and unpredictability that Popper's social and polit-

191

ical views converge with those of Hayek (particularly in *The Fatal Conceit* (Hayek 1988)). For Hayek, like Popper, argues strongly for the undesirability of a centrally planned society, and against the optimism of the early Enlightenment thinkers, who believed in the possibility of designing an ideal society on rational first principles. Both Hayek and Popper will point to the limitations of human reason in this area.

It is, indeed, important to note at this point that not all the closed societies attacked by Popper are based on irrationalism, either of a primitive or a modern variety. In fact, quite to the contrary, the closed societies Popper spends most time attacking, those of Plato and Marx, both make big claims to be based on reason and science. They both claim that by rational or scientific means it is possible to plan a centrally directed society which will produce more happiness and human flourishing than any other, and this is still the dream of many intellectuals, who would claim no direct allegiance to either Plato or Marx.

But, say Popper and Hayek, it is just this knowledge which cannot be had. In Hayek's case, this is because of the complexity and instability of the information which would need to be centralised for planning purposes. There is an incalculable amount of it in any society of any size. It is also inherently unstable and unpredictable. People's choices and tastes are constantly altering, freely and unpredictably, right up to when they actually decide to do or buy something. And the decisions of the central authority itself interfere with and destabilise the very system it is supposed to be controlling and predicting. For Popper the argument is that, as in science, any policy or proposal is necessarily uncertain and fallible, because of our ignorance of the future. In the social case, any action or policy, however well meant and well planned, will have unintended and often unwelcome consequences. As in science we gain knowledge through attending to refutations, in this case the unintended consequences of our actions, rather than the falsifying observations of science, and by modifying our original theories and policies accordingly. Society as a whole thus becomes a microcosm of the scientific community: proposals are continually monitored and replaced by the efforts of individuals to discover new problems in old solutions, as a result of which new solutions are then proposed, which throw up further new problems in their turn, and so on and so on. The main difference between science and politics in this context is that in science the proposed solutions are theories aimed at discovering the truth in the physical world, whereas in politics they are policies aimed at removing manifest evils in society.

Before evaluating Popper's social and political thinking, it is worth briefly comparing Popper's and Hayek's deployment of their respective fallibilisms. For Hayek, ignorance in the social sphere leads to minimal government and a Smithian free market (in which the uncentralisable knowledge of the free decisions of a myriad individuals in a large economy is nevertheless spread around the system as a whole, to best advantage). For Popper, ignorance leads to a politics of negative utilitarianism. In politics, we should attempt to remedy manifest evils (which everyone can agree are evils, and on which there would be some consensus on what would count as a solution). We should not involve ourselves in applying blueprints for someone's vision of the good life (on whose value there may be considerable disagreement, and which may in any case have consequences quite different from those intended by its supporters). But Popperian negative utilitarianism is not incompatible with a degree of welfarism and even democratic socialism.

From Popper's perspective (as from Oakeshott's) the Hayekian directive against any form of central planning is itself dogmatic. A plan to avoid all planning might be better than state socialism, but it is still a plan, and it is one which may actually militate against measures needed to apply negative utilitarianism. So Popper is far less of a liberal than Hayek on economics and political planning.

On the other hand, on morality and social cohesion, the positions are reversed. Hayek, in his later thought anyway, is the conservative (despite his well known disclaimer in this regard), and Popper the liberal. Hayek thinks that a shared morality is needed to bind a society together, and to give it the values, such as those of honesty, work and the family, which the market needs to operate successfully. This morality may well have evolved non-rationally, in a quasi-evolutionary fashion, and in practice it may require some religion to back it up. For Popper, on the other hand, society needs no moral consensus of this sort, beyond what he thinks is the minimal consensus about manifest evils which is implicit in negative utilitarianism. In the case of an open society a shared disposition on the part of its members freely to criticise and to engage in rational discussion is enough to hold society together. It is this assumption which we now need to examine.

The open society is presented as an antidote to utopian dreams and nightmares. Certainly it is not based on any plan to be imposed centrally and forcibly on the whole of society, not on unattainable knowledge, supposedly vested in a few visionaries or some party committee furnished with insight into the course of history or the destiny of mankind. It is, by contrast, pluralist; and its underlying philosophy is negative utilitarianism, rather than some positive vision of heaven on earth.

Without denying these criticisms Popper makes of the closed societies he attacks, there are certain key respects in which the open society, as envisaged by Popper, is itself utopian; that is, it has at its heart an unrealised and unrealisable vision of human society, and one which will actually tend to loosen the bonds which in fact tie societies together.

In the first place, as already mentioned, the open society, like Popper's philosophy more generally, is built on a faith in reason, meaning by that a belief in the power of reasoned discussion to resolve disputes and create social harmony. This faith is combined with a form of cosmopolitan rationalism and Popper's own fallibilism. These are, as noted, characteristically enlightened beliefs, part of the world view bequeathed us by the Enlightenment. It is, as Popper himself observed, a question of two competing faiths (OS II, p. 246). We need now to compare these two faiths, as guides to social life.

From the point of view of irrationalists, such as nationalists and fundamentalist religious believers, Popper's fallibilism and cosmopolitanism will look as partial and tendentious as their beliefs do to the fallibilist Popper. What we and Popper will see as universal values inherent in Enlightenment rationalism and scepticism might, from the point of view of other cultures and faiths, appear as a manifestation of Western imperialism, to these other cultures and faiths, as objectionable and insidious as other more overt manifestations of imperialism. (On this point, see Huntington 1996, p. 184.)

In this context, Popper's insistence that it is all based on an irrational faith is, to put it mildly, disappointing. It leaves him open to the obvious rejoinder that the other faith could be just as true and useful as Popper's, and would determine a rather different attitude to those who disagree – rather more forceful, no doubt, than listening to the other fellow's point of view. So far, my point is that the liberalism espoused by Popper is not merely procedural, nor can it be justified in terms merely of negative utilitarianism. It is actually a substantive politico-ethical position, with its own substantive estimate of the value of rationalism, of autonomy and of individuality, just as much as, say, Catholicism or Serbian nationalism or Islam are, with their own rather different evaluations of these matters. What Popper needs at this point is some account of how his (or any other) form of rationalism contributes more to human flourishing and answers more to our needs than these other faiths. What he needs is some positive account of human nature, which will enable us to see the value of critical rationalism as an expression of that nature over its competitor faiths. But it is just this that he fails to offer.

This serious gap aside, have we any reason to think that critical rationalism is actually likely to promote a better form of politics than its competitors? One of its supposed advantages, and the one much emphasised by Popper himself, is that it enables disputes in society to be resolved peacefully, and that by discussions and continual monitoring of policies we may get nearer to the truth. All, of course, hangs on what is meant by 'resolved'.

The methods of science, on the whole, produce a consensus among scientific enquirers. But this is because there is a fairly general agreement within the scientific community about the aims and methods appropriate to science. As Popper himself acknowledged in the original edition of *Logik der Forschung*, though not subsequently, 'only those sharing the same goal can rationally argue over differences of opinion' (Popper 1935, p. 10). But Popper's open society will precisely not be a community in that sense. In his doctrine of negative utilitarianism he explicitly repudiates the requirement that in an open society there be any general consensus about the aims of human life, or about ethics more generally. He hopes to secure enough of a consensus on policies through insisting that any acceptable policy be guided by the principles of negative utilitarianism, that is that it should be aimed at the removal of manifest ills.

But this, too, is dubious. It is hard, if not impossible, to separate the notion of 'manifest ill' from some more general conception of what a good life is. What might be the serious oppression of women to one society might be according them their proper role and status in another. Is the mere existence of chains of abortion clinics a manifest ill? Or would their absence, and the prevalence of back-street abortions, be a manifest ill? Further, permissible means of removing ills are not always ethically neutral either. We can all agree that the existence of spina bifida is a manifest ill, and that getting rid of it is good. But by any means? By aborting babies with the condition? Many will think not, and others, perhaps against the majority in the West, will think that even if it could produce a cure for some terrible disease or affliction, research on embryos is not a permissible means either.

In such circumstances, decisions on policy will still have to be made. But given such entrenched disagreement at the level of principle as exists in the cases we have considered, and in other cases too in many areas, policy is not likely to be based on agreement. It is more likely to be based on pragmatism, not to put too fine a point on it, on what the majority will put up with. (On how policies on ethical matters in Western democracies are actually made, see the candid and revealing remarks of Mary Warnock – a legislator as well as a philosopher – in her 1998 An Intelligent Person's Guide to Ethics, pp. 49–50.)

Nor, in these circumstances, is the decision-making process necessarily going to lead to truth. It is certainly not aimed at truth. It is aimed rather at consensus and at a sort of tolerance. But just because a majority concurs or pragmatics dictates it, a decision is not thereby right. If abortion, or its criminalisation, or slavery, or tor-ture are wrong, then they are wrong, and wrong whatever a majority might think, and even if the majority view had arisen through as much openness and discussion as one could imagine or wish. Indeed, in some circumstances one could doubt that it would even be right to adopt the methods of critical rationalism. Should we say to someone who wants to torture the innocent or join the SS or sodomise children, 'I may be wrong and you may be right'? Even entertaining the thought that certain practices could, in certain circumstances, be permissible would be to concede too much, leading to weakening of moral commitment individually and collectively. A society which encourages such debates, particularly among the young, may end up in a state of moral uncertainty and decline, where no whiff of fallibilism should have been admitted in the first place (whatever Mill might have said about the value of putting even the firmest principles into question).

So Popper's faith in reason could lead us to a form of uncertainty where, in some matters, no uncertainty should be admitted, theoretically or practically, and which may actually take us away from the truth. It also evinces an approach to society and to institutions which is excessively instrumental. According to Popper, rationality in social life involves a continual willingness to test what Popper, like Mill, thinks of as experiments in living (that is, our actions, policies, traditions and institutions). According to Popper 'a social technology is needed whose results can be tested by piecemeal social engineering' (OS II, p. 222). In the words of Bryan Magee, 'the Popperian approach involves subjecting institutions to a permanently critical evaluation in order to monitor how well they are solving the problems they exist to solve – and involves moreover a permanent willingness to change them in the light of changing requirements'. (In Magee 1995, p. 266.) Magee makes this remark in an attempt to enlist Popper in the service of the political left, and he points out that Popper has a radical attitude to institutions and to society more generally, one that is quite at odds with conservatism.

Magee is right about the Popper of *The Open Society and Its Enemies*, but both are wrong about institutions. Not all institutions exist to solve problems, and many institutions will be undermined if they are subjected to the strictures of Popperian social engineering. An institution like a church or an ancient university or the Berlin Philharmonic Orchestra or even my son's rugby club does not exist to 'solve problems'. They may, once they exist, have plenty of problems to solve, such as keeping in existence or dealing with their staff or members, but it misunderstands their nature to think of them principally in terms of problem solving. In so far as they exist for anything at all, they exist to embody and pass on a certain form of life. They are the vessels through which particular traditions are transmitted and developed. They exist because the people who belong to them and support them find that they and the activities they promote are worthwhile in themselves.

To say, as Magee said in response to this point, that my son's rugby club exists to solve the problem of getting boys to play rugby is not simply a matter of a somewhat empty use of the term 'problem'; it actually mislocates what a rugby club's focus really is. The club's aim is rugby and its spirit – and companionship and hospitality, etc. – as ends in themselves. It no doubt needs to get members to do this, but to represent this truism by saying that it exists to solve the problem of getting boys to play rugby makes it sound as if it is involved in a kind of social work, a subtle transformation of its character, perhaps, but a transformation none the less. It is a transformation somewhat akin to the present British government's insistence that one of the things that what it calls 'cultural services' are about is 'social inclusion'. In this case the misunderstanding really matters, as literally thousands of museums and artistic companies dumb themselves down in the name of access. (Managerialism and instrumentalism regarding institutions are no preserve of the political right.)

And there are many other institutions which, though in a sense existing as means to some ulterior purpose (or for solving problems in Popper's terminology), cannot or should not, once they exist, be reduced to that purpose. They develop their own spirit and traditions and way of life which has a value, both for themselves and for the community of which they are a part, quite apart from their extrinsic aims. In this context, one can think of such institutions as regiments, parliaments, the law, schools, the monarchy, the stock exchange, and even some commercial institutions such as Harrods, say, or Nissan. What happens in such cases is that institutions originally formed to promote activities, such as fighting or selling or ruling, which clearly do have instrumental and problem-solving aspects, develop traditions and practices with their own intrinsic value, and which then endow the institutions with a value over and above the instrumental. But not only the institutions. The activities they are for are also thereby invested with a value beyond the instrumental, and, for those involved, have the potential to become forms of life worthwhile in and for themselves. It is for this reason, incomprehensible to bureaucrats or Popperian social engineers, that people feel aggrieved when a famous regiment is 'rationalised' by being amalgamated with another, or a school is forced by a bureaucracy unresponsive to its nature to change its character or status. A whole way of life may thereby be lost, and lamented by those to whom it was dear.

To subject institutions with their own spirit and life to the 'permanently critical evaluation' recommended by Popper is likely to destroy what is most valuable in them, because it will look not at what they are, in and for themselves, but at what they do, apart from themselves. As an example of the sort of managerialism I am criticising, consider the phrase 'no management without measurement'. One is tempted to say that if that is what management is, institutions with their own – unmeasurable – value and tradition would be better off with no management. But that would be unnecessarily perverse, if only because it was often the very unmeasurable and intrinsically valuable spirit of an institution which made it good at the measurable things too, something that often becomes clear only after an institution has been rationalised by social engineers, and its spirit and tradition stripped off in the name of efficient target setting and attaining. Similarly, an institution forced by Popperian social engineers to declare its aims and objectives and then held accountable against a diet of targets met and problems solved is more than likely to lose morale and to wither and decline, as happened to so many institutions in Britain in the 1980s when they were subjected to radical and 'permanently critical evaluation' under Margaret Thatcher's premiership, Margaret Thatcher being the only sort of conservative Magee sees as sitting happily with what he calls 'a Popperian approach to the requirements of institutional change' (Magee 1995, p. 267).

And this takes us to a basic difficulty with Popper's open society. Criticising the Enlightenment or Kantian view of man as a rational, autonomous, independent individual, de Maistre says this: 'In the course of my life, I have seen Frenchmen, Italians, Russians . . . I know, too, thanks to Montesquieu, that one can be a Persian. But as for man, I declare that I have never met him in my life; if he exists, he is unknown to me.'

The point is that, as Bradley pointed out, the man into whose essence his community with others does not enter, who does not include 'relation to other' in his very being, is a fiction. Popper's rational problem solver is just such a fiction. Like Kant's pure rational agent, abstracted from messy and partial human reality and commitment, it is too thin a conception on which to base an individual life, let alone a community.

Communities are not founded on rational decisions alone or on just the commitment to openness, as Popper himself acknowledges in 'Towards a Rational Theory of Tradition' (in Popper 1963, pp. 161–82, though originally written in 1949). For their very existence they require shared sentiment, shared allegiances, shared traditions and shared values. All this takes us far beyond the

197

considerations of 'appropriateness, efficiency and simplicity' which Popper thinks should concern the social engineer (cf. OS I, p. 24), and beyond the judgment of institutions, traditions, policies and the rest in terms of the externally and independently designatable problems they are supposed to be solving. It is of the essence of shared sentiment and shared life that much about it is partial, historical and contingent, and to that extent non-rational. Even though in his post *Open Society and its Enemies* work Popper admits the need for non-rational, historically contingent bonds, these are likely to wither if subjected to the sort of scrutiny in terms of 'reason' and 'problems' which Popper also advocated throughout his career, and which would seem to form the essence of the open society.

Perhaps sometimes they should be subjected to scrutiny, and sometimes be allowed to wither. We are here operating in the area of what counter-Enlightenment figures such as Burke and Herder referred to as 'prejudice'. Thus Herder (1774, quoted in Barnard 1969, pp. 186–7): 'Prejudice is good in its time and place, because it makes a people happy. It takes them back to their centre, attaches them firmly to their roots, lets them flourish in their own way.'

By contrast (ibid.), 'when people dream of emigrating to foreign lands to seek hope and salvation, they reveal the first symptoms of sickness and flatulence, of approaching death'.

One cannot fail to be struck by the fact that this, and kindred passages from Fichte, Herder's follower in this respect, sowed the seeds of German nationalism, a point of which Popper would not have needed reminding. I am not defending any and all traditions, nor am I denying that critical rationalism may not itself be part of a society's traditions. Indeed I think it is part of our tradition here, now, in contrast to, say, Islamic tradition which, these days at least, appears to be essentially theocratic and uncritical. But the fact that certain types of prejudice and certain types of nationalism are objectionable and should be rationally criticised does not show that a community can exist as such without a degree of Burkean prejudice. Or, as Wittgenstein would have put it, what we need is agreement not in judgment, but in form of life, in acceptance of certain values and institutions as settled, unspoken and uncriticised.

Burke himself insisted that, initially at least, we should cherish prejudices precisely because they are prejudices. Our first reaction should not be critical. We should always first 'employ (our) sagacity to discover the latent wisdom which prevails in them' (Burke 1968 [1790], p. 183). If we find what we seek, we should continue the prejudice, with the reason involved

> because prejudice, with its reason, has a motive to give action to that reason, and an affection which will give it permanence . . . (engaging) the mind in a steady course of wisdom and virtue . . . (and not leaving) the man hesitating in the moment of decision, sceptical, puzzled and unresolved.
>
> (Ibid.)

198

Much of this concerns a difference of attitude between the rationalist and the conservative, as to one's first reaction when confronted with a settled custom or a settled society. But there is also the Aristotelian point that we become virtuous not by reasoning, but by habit. Reason without virtue can as well argue in favour of vice as in favour of virtue, and is only too likely to do so if deployed by people without wisdom, experience of life and habits of virtue. Only if we have virtuous habits to start with can we reason well about morality, which in the individual at least suggests a certain priority of initially unreflective habit over reflection.

In this context the remarks Popper makes about moral education are relevant (cf. OS II, p. 276). Teachers may stimulate interest in values in their pupils, but they must not attempt to impose higher values on them. Nor should they pose as authorities, in science or morals, or anything else. These proposals are doubtless in the spirit of Popperian openness, but they fail to address the question of how children and young people are to acquire the relevant habits and virtues, including the intellectual virtues required for the practice of science, unless their teachers pose as authorities, etc. There is certainly a pedagogical case for arguing that, at a certain level, teachers can and should pose as authorities even where they might personally have doubts precisely in order that their pupils become capable of embarking on a journey which leads to informed fallibilism in a given area, as opposed to shallow scepticism.

These reflections on education point to just one aspect of the general problem raised by Popper's open society. The general problem is that a disposition to criticise and engage in rational discussion is not in itself enough to bind a community together, let alone to resolve a dispute between, say, a liberal democrat full of ideals of openness and an Islamic mullah insisting on Sharia law for his co-religionists even in a liberal democracy.

To think that a disposition to criticise might on its own be enough to hold a community together is itself utopian, and it could be as destructively utopian as some of the other utopias Popper correctly criticises. For encouragement of a relentlessly critical cast of mind concerning settled values and institutions may not be neutral regarding social bonds. It may, as we see in certain political projects today, actually loosen the bonds which tie a people together, by eroding the sentiment and prejudice on which a form of life depends. And once these ties are eroded, the impeccably liberal and critical community which emerges may not have within itself enough self-belief to defend itself effectively against an enemy which actually believes in something positive, and does not feel constrained by the niceties of rational discussion and openness.

In 1941, in an article entitled 'Wells, Hitler and the World State', George Orwell asked (at p. 84) what had kept England on its feet in the past year:

> In part, no doubt, some vague idea about a better future, but chiefly the atavistic emotion of patriotism, the ingrained feeling of the English-speaking peoples that they are superior to foreigners. For the last twenty

199

years the main object of English left-wing intellectuals has been to break this feeling down, and if they had succeeded, we might be watching SS men patrolling the London streets at the moment.

By contrast (ibid.), 'for the commonsense, essentially hedonistic world-view which Mr Wells puts forward, hardly a human creature is willing to shed a pint of blood'.

What about Sir Karl's open society? It is true that much blood was in the past, has been quite recently, and maybe will be, shed in defence of Britain and the United States, and Britain and the United States are, as far as any societies are, open societies. Our values are those Popper admired: tolerance, liberalism, democracy, free speech and the rule of law. No doubt part of what we fight for, when we fight, is the defence of these values. But in all probability values which are not part of their nature as open societies have also been crucial to the willingness of our fellow-countrymen to fight and shed their blood on many occasions in the past hundred years. With many of these non-liberal aspects, Popper was clearly uncomfortable, so he reconfigures his ideal society as Britain or the United States with the patriotic, atavistic bits airbrushed out.

To that extent, to the extent that it refers to no actual society and not even to the reality of those societies he most admired, Popper's open society is a utopian vision. And neither he, nor anyone else, so far knows whether a society which was completely open and relentlessly self-critical in his sense would be possible. Whether, even if it were possible, it would be desirable, or whether it would be a managerial nightmare is another question altogether.

Having made these criticisms of Popper's open society, it is perhaps fitting to end by putting them in the context of the development of Popper's own thought. The vision of society we have been considering is that to be found in *The Open Society and Its Enemies*. That book was written in New Zealand, in the early 1940s, but very much in response to events occurring in Europe, particularly in the lands dominated by Hitler and Stalin. As a counter-blast to those societies and ideologies, *The Open Society* is *sans pareil*. And, given its oft-repeated message – that any large-scale attempt to re-mould society centrally is bound to lead to tyranny – it is puzzling that in that book there are many statements which can be seen as, up to a point, friendly to Marxism. I would argue that from the perspective of *The Open Society*, communism cannot be a good idea which went wrong. Involving as it does radical and continual intervention by the state in all areas of life, it was always a terrible idea, and Popper shows us exactly why. Nevertheless, its great merits notwithstanding, *The Open Society* remains over-rationalistic and utopian about reason and about the sort of society it is advocating.

However, it is arguable that by the time he wrote 'Towards a Rational Theory of Tradition' (op. cit.) in 1949, Popper himself came to distance himself not only from the rationalists he explicitly criticises, but also from his own earlier rationalistic stance. In 1949 he castigated rationalists in rather Burkean terms: they think that they have the means to correct and disparage traditions on the basis of pure reason, through their own brains, rather than confining their criticisms to cases where actual problems were apparent. But doesn't this picture apply at least to some degree to the ideal, thoroughgoingly untraditional citizen of the earlier open society?

But by 1949, when he had appeared to qualify his rationalism in favour of tradition, Popper had experienced the traditional societies of New Zealand and Britain, and he liked them. He valued many of their traditions, such as their un-spoken and unargued for tolerance, their respect for the law, and their concern for the individual and the underdog, things which go to make up his own 'irrational faith in reason'. At around this time, in conversation at least, he also defended Hayek against critics from the political left. A liberal society, he said, requires a framework of conservative values.

So the implicit contrast of The Open Society is wrong. It is not that there are irrational communities, with no commitment to reason, and rational open soci-eties with no basis in tradition. The open society, where and in so far as it exists, exists as part of a given tradition. One may object to this being seen in terms of an 'irrational' faith in reason, and, to return to a point made earlier, one might have preferred Popper to have located his ideas about freedom, individualism and openness in a more fully worked-out notion of human flourishing and human nature, so as to give his – and our – views on society and our tradition a more sub-stantial basis than that of one faith confronting other faiths. Maybe he did not want to do this because he resisted talk of human good, rather than of human harm. But, this admittedly crucial point aside, one can also see some positive point of his talk of an irrational faith in reason if it leads us to see what is surely correct: that the open society itself is a substantive tradition, or a part of one. And openness in a society will be undermined if too many people in it do not share its values and traditions, including those other than openness itself. This is a problem which concerns many in the West today, and which has no prospect of a solution so long as we think only in terms of the procedures of critical rational-ism, and not in terms of the actual traditions and substantive beliefs which sustain those procedures.

References

Barnard, F. M. 1969. J. G. Herder on Social and Political Culture, Cambridge: Cambridge University Press.

Burke, Edmund. 1968 [1790]. Reflections on the Revolution in France. Conor Cruise O'Brien (ed.), Middlesex: Harmondsworth.

Hayek, F. A. 1988. The Fatal Conceit, London: Routledge.

Huntington, Samuel P. 1996. The Clash of Civilisations and the Remaking of World Order, New York: Simon and Schuster.

Magee, Bryan. 1995. 'What Use is Popper to a Politician?', in Anthony O'Hear (ed.), Karl Popper: Philosophy and Problems. Cambridge: Cambridge University Press, pp. 259–74.

Orwell, George. 1946 [1941]. 'Wells, Hitler and the World State', in his Critical Essays, London: Secker and Warburg.

Popper, Karl. 1935. *Logik der Forschung: Zur Erkenntnistheorie der modernen Natur-wissenschaft*, Vienna: Springer.

Popper, Karl. 1963. *Conjectures and Refutations*, London: Routledge and Kegan Paul.

Popper, Karl. 1966 [1945]. *The Open Society and Its Enemies*, vols I and II, London: Routledge and Kegan Paul.

Warnock, Mary. 1998. *An Intelligent Person's Guide to Ethics*, London: Duckworth.

11

TRIBALISM AND THE MYTH OF THE FRAMEWORK

Some Popperian thoughts on the politics of cultural recognition

Jeremy Waldron

Popper's critique of tribalism in The Open Society and Its Enemies *is something more than an attack on early forms of collectivism, and its relevance for modern political philosophy goes beyond the liberalism/communitarianism debate. Popper's critique focuses on nostalgic attempts to revive the sense of immanent normativity and ethical solidarity associated with tribal custom; he argues that these attitudes are futile and inauthentic in the modern world where peoples have complex dealings with one another and where their knowledge of the customs of other societies has enabled them to develop critical attitudes towards their own. This chapter applies that critique to the philosophy of modern cultural identity politics. It argues that partisans of cultural identity make many of the same mistakes as those whom Popper labelled tribalists make. It suggests that a better and more authentic stance for the members of minority cultures in modern societies is to engage their norms as political proposals for solving the problems of the wider society, rather than as fiercely defended aspects of individual identity. The chapter concludes by using Popper's arguments from 'The Myth of the Framework' to debunk the claim that customs and norms from different cultural settings are incommensurable and cannot engage one another in fruitful debate.*

I

A neglected theme in a neglected book is the critique of 'tribalism' in Karl Popper's *The Open Society and Its Enemies* (1966, two volumes – hereinafter 'OS 1' and 'OS 2').[1] It is tempting to read Popper's critique of tribalism as nothing more than an attack on primitive or prototypic forms of totalitarianism: the tribalist society is a closed collectivist society which dominates every aspect of the lives of its members. As such it is the ancient enemy of the open society, the antithesis of a liberal society and of societies organised around respect for the individual and the idea of human rights.

Popper develops his account of tribalism in the context of an attack on Plato. But on this reading – that is on a reading which sees tribalism as a prototype of totalitarian collectivism – his critique would be important also for modern political theory. It would be relevant, first and foremost, to the critique of collectivist forms of polity and economy – 'actually existing socialism and the like' – a critique which many believe has now entered its triumphalist phase. But it would be relevant also to the more philosophical issue between liberals and communitarians, that is, between those who are committed to exactly the values that Popper celebrated in his ideal of the open society and those who yearn nostalgically for forms of community and belonging that pull us back from the abyss of total choice and of a largely abstract concept of human relationships. In other words, the critique of tribalism could be read as a very early shot fired in the debate that took place in the 1980s between those political philosophers like John Rawls and Ronald Dworkin, who give pride of place to the rights of free and equal individuals, and those like Alasdair Macintyre, Charles Taylor, and Michael Sandel who are searching for a political philosophy answering to the needs of the embedded self, a self inseparable from a certain form of community. (On the liberal side, see Rawls 1971 and Dworkin 1977. On the communitarian side, see Macintyre 1981, Taylor 1985 and Sandel 1982.)

I do not want to dispute the importance of Popper's critique to this debate. But I would like to approach the relevance of his discussion of tribalism from a slightly different angle. The emphasis in this chapter will not be on the stand-off between individualist and communitarian conceptions; instead it will address a debate about the politics of cultural identity, in which some of the protagonists in the liberalism/communitarianism stand-off have also participated. The debate I want to consider is about the importance of a person's cultural background to the life that he makes for himself in the world. On one rather liberal version of cultural identity politics, an individual cannot constitute himself as an autonomous person without an available menu of cultural choices appropriate to his background, upbringing, and belonging, secured and sustained by a system of cultural rights. (See, e.g., Kymlicka 1989.) On another, somewhat less liberal version, the support and sustenance of cultural rights is needed by communities rather than individuals, especially in multicultural societies. Minority communities cannot be expected to flourish in the shadow of a dominant societal culture without some special support and solicitude from the state; and if they do not flourish, they will collapse into a communal vacuum of disorientation and alienation which, while they are certainly individual harms, are also tragedies from a strictly communal point of view. (See, e.g. Tully 1995.) Against these and other versions of what I shall label modern culturalism, liberal opponents have argued that people (and peoples) do not in fact need to have frameworks of cultural identity secured against change and domination in order to flourish. No doubt autonomy looks to an array of culturally defined options; but it does not need those options to be organised into a single culturally secure framework, corresponding to the social system of some historically existing group, in order for them to be made available for autonomous choice. The world is already a fluid mixture of cultures and, for that modern world, authentic choice has to respond to the fractured chaos of options that that mixture affords. (Cf. my 1992.) And liberal opponents are highly critical of the communal version of culturalism too; they do not see the survival of cultural forms (like particular languages) as an inherent value in itself; they are appalled at the abuses that might be licensed or protected (or subsidised or enforced) by an overly solicitous attitude towards ancient cultural forms; and they see the attempt to secure and sustain the cultural integrity of particular communities as simply the polite philosophical face of a social evil that is wreaking havoc in the modern world under the auspices of revanchist nationalism, with its attendant practices of inter-communal conflict and ethnic cleansing. (See Levy 2000.)

It would not take long to establish which side Karl Popper might have taken in this dispute. That is not the point of my chapter. Instead I want to use some aspects of Popper's critique of tribalism to reinforce some misgivings that many liberal opponents of culturalism have about the way in which culturalists regard cultural forms and the mores of the communities they are trying to protect. Many of us worry that this involves a form of artifice or fetishism, an inauthentic attitude towards cultural mores which is adopted by the philosophers I call culturalists largely because authentic forms of belonging and submission to such mores are simply not available, socially and psychologically, in the modern world.

The upshot of this critique need not be that groups and individuals should abandon the moral heritage they have grown up with. A multicultural society ought to be able to profit from the array of different and disparate insights that the customs and beliefs of various cultural groups make available in social and political debate. The presence of such various groups and ways of life ought surely to enrich the politics of the larger society that accommodates them. But many of the defenders of cultural identity politics deny that such enrichment is possible, at least at the level of dialogue or political debate. They say that many of the cultures concerned are not just disparate but incommensurable, oriented to such different values and embodying such a diversity of world-views, that it is impossible to bring them into relation with one another as (say) competing suggestions for policy choices faced by the larger society. (See the discussion in Lukes 2003.) And some liberal opponents of culturalism say this too: they say that public debate should be orchestrated around a very 'thin' set of common values and beliefs, and that we should shy away from a politics of thick cultural engagement, just as we should shy away from any attempt to bring competing religious and ethical views to bear on choices that are unavoidable for a society comprising a multitude of incompatible and incommensurable cultural, moral and religious communities. (See the discussion of 'public reason' in Rawls 1996. See also Nagel 1987.)

It seems to me that some of Karl Popper's scepticism about 'frameworks' and about the need for common definitions can be brought to bear to dispel some of these doubts. Popper has always stood for the proposition that we should not underestimate the ability of humans from disparate backgrounds to talk with one another and to deal with one another (to trade, fight, fuck and imitate), even when it appears to an outsider – e.g., to a defender of cultural identity politics or to a pusillanimous political liberal – that the *ex ante* prospects for the encounter are hopeless. So what I want to do in this chapter is relate that Popperian position – summed up most eloquently in his essay 'The Myth of the Framework' (Popper 1994) – to some aspects of his critique of tribalism in *The Open Society*, in order to expose the sly legerdemain associated with cultural identity politics and to refute the demand that minority communities must continue to offer safe havens for whose who pretend, inauthentically, to have closed minds in matters of culture and identity.

II

The Open Society and Its Enemies is about the 'transition from the tribal or "closed society"' . . . to the "open society," which sets free the critical powers of man' (OS 1, p. 1). What does Popper mean by tribalism?

When he introduced the idea in *The Open Society*, Popper associated tribalism with collectivism, with an 'emphasis on the supreme importance of the tribe without which the individual is nothing at all' (OS 1, p. 9). A tribalist form of society involves the subordination of the individual, his freedom and his powers of reason to collective necessities and collective enterprises like war. And much of what Popper carries forward, from his early critique of the tribal collectivism that Plato tried in vain to preserve to his critique of Hegel and Marx later in the book, is an attack on collectivism – the collectivism of the nation state and the collectivism of socialist economy. The critique of collectivism, as such, and of the collectivist elements present even in non-tribalist societies (OS 1, p. 9) is a familiar one, and it is bound up of course with Popper's defence of markets and the principle of individual rights and responsibilities. (For Popper's personal misgivings about socialist movements, see Notturno 1999, at pp. 51–4.)

Even so, the critique of tribalism in *The Open Society* is not just a critique of collectivist forms of social organisation. What Popper associates particularly with tribalism is not merely the subordination of individual interests to those of the group, but also the *attitude* taken by members of a society to the customs that constitute their tribal way of life. Of course the point is complicated by the fact that Popper refuses to offer a definition of 'tribalism': his own anti-essentialism counsels against that, particularly in the social sciences (OS 2, p. 14). Still the commonalities that he brings to light as between the Greek examples he concentrates on (in his attack on Plato) and other instances of tribalism are instructive:

> The early Greek tribal society resembles in many respects that of peoples like the Polynesians, the Maoris for instance. Small bands of warriors, usually living in fortified settlements, ruled by tribal chiefs or kings, or by aristocratic families, were waging war against one another on sea as

well as on land. There were, of course, many differences between the Greek and the Polynesian ways of life, for there is, admittedly, no uniformity in tribalism. . . . It seems to me, however, that there are some characteristics that can be found in most, if not all, of these tribal societies. I mean their magical or irrational attitude towards the customs of social life, and the corresponding rigidity of these customs.

(OS 1, pp. 171–2)

In a tribal society, life is determined almost in its entirety by social and religious taboos. Not only does everyone know his place, but 'everyone feels that his place is the proper, the "natural" place, assigned to him by the forces which rule the world' (OS 1, p. 12). There are, Popper says, very few problems engaging moral responsibility in such a society. Occasionally, an individual may be called upon to act heroically, but 'he will rarely find himself in the position of doubting how he ought to act' (OS 1, p. 172). Rules, roles and customs are not viewed as conventions which may be questioned or changed. In the magical attitudes that characterise a primitive tribal society, the laws of the society 'are felt to be as inevitable as the rising of the sun, or the cycle of the seasons, or similar obvious regularities of nature' (OS 1, p. 57).

Obviously, for Popper, it is the mark of an open society that social norms are viewed as conventions which, though they may not have been set up intentionally, can certainly be subject to intentional revision and change (OS 1, p. 61). (Popper counsels against the view that conventionality implies arbitrariness – 'that if we are free to choose any system of norms we like, then one system is as good as any other' (OS 1, p. 65). For discussion of Popper's meta-ethics, see my 1985.) He does not deny that 'the moral values of a society . . . are closely bound up with its institutions and traditions' (OS 2, p. 94). And he acknowledges that one must consider social context very carefully as one undertakes revision and reform; this is one source of his normative emphasis on the piecemeal character of social engineering (OS 1, p. 158). (So it is a mistake to see Popper's emphasis on piecemeal social engineering as simply an artifact of his methodology, as though the only reason for it were that it is easier to test hypotheses about the effects of small-scale reforms. Cf. Lessnoff 1980, p. 113.) Still, the 'open' attitude towards social norms is about as far as can be imagined from the attitudes definitive of a closed or tribal society, and the move from the one form of society to the other, Popper says, 'can be described as one of the deepest revolutions through which mankind has passed' (OS 1, p. 175). The open attitude – the breakdown of magic tribalism – springs from the knowledge that 'taboos are different in various tribes [and] that they are imposed and enforced by man' (OS 1, p. 60). Understanding of this kind is unavailable to all or most so long as the society remains exclusive and self-sufficient. But when war begins to require detailed and accurate knowledge of the enemy, when a society has to rely on trade for its subsistence and prosperity, when diplomacy and economy require some general knowledge of what is going on in a whole region of the world, then the magical attitude to

207

customary law necessarily starts to give way. (Cf. my 2003, pp. 30–6.) 'Close contact with other tribes is liable to undermine the feeling of necessity with which tribal institutions are viewed' (OS 1, p. 177). It may be going too far to say (as Popper says) that 'tribalist exclusiveness and self-sufficiency could be superseded only by some form of imperialism' (OS 1, p. 181), like the imperialism of Athens towards the end of the fifth century BC. But I think he is right to say that 'commerce and a new class involved in trade and seafaring' presents perhaps 'the worst danger to the closed society' (OS 1, p. 176), a danger only exacerbated by the concomitant increase of the tribal population (which trade makes possible) and by the differentiation of ways of life in the society and the growth of stratification beyond that required for elementary tribal leadership.

The growth of trade and interaction among those not necessarily bound together by tribal mores contributes to the decline of another feature of tribal society that Popper emphasises – the organic character of human relations.

> A closed society resembles a herd or a tribe in being a semi-organic unit whose members are held together by semi-biological ties – kinship, living together, sharing common efforts, common dangers, common joys and common distress. It is still a concrete group of concrete individuals, related to one another not merely by such abstract relationships as division of labour and exchange of commodities, but by concrete physical relationships such as touch, smell, and sight.
>
> (OS 1, p. 173)

This, too, cannot survive the growth of population, social complexity, and interaction with other societies. As Popper implies in the passage just quoted, an anthropologist may use abstract categories like function, exchange and division of labour to characterise even this concrete organic form. But the changes that come to a tribal society under the circumstances we are envisaging drive abstraction into the heart of social relations. One now deals with others *in their abstract capacities*, i.e. one deals with someone *as* a merchant or *as* a partner in exchange or *as* someone carrying out a necessary function in the social division of labour. Society becomes, by degrees, an 'abstract' society (OS 1, p. 174), functioning largely by interactions involving people who regard one another in an abstract way.

Though Popper associates this with the growth of individualism (and not just methodological individualism, but social or ethical individualism: for the distinction see Lukes 1973), there is actually an under-current of lament in what he says about it:

> There never will be or can be a completely abstract or even a predominantly abstract society. . . . Men still form real groups and enter into real social contacts of all kinds, and try to satisfy their emotional social needs as well as they can. But most of the social groups of a modern

open society (with the exception of some lucky family groups) are poor substitutes, since they do not provide for a common life.

(OS 1, p. 175)

This is one of the few places where one gets a sense of Popper's empathy for the motives of those he criticises, 'the desire of men to find and know their definite place in the world' (OS 2, p. 64), and the enterprise of those who seek, nostalgically, to lead us back to the lost dawn of tribal solidarity.

III

Thus far, we have talked about tribalism in terms of decline and fall. Once upon a time, there were primitive societies – tribal societies – whose members viewed their norms as natural or magical necessities; but that attitude could not survive the growth of interaction and interdependence. There is, however, another sense of tribalism that interests Popper – a sense of tribalism which represents a deliberate attempt to turn one's back on the worldly features that have undermined the naturalistic or magical attitude to social norms in order to recover the lost sense of tribal unity and stability.

Now, the attitude embodied in this nostalgic enterprise necessarily differs from the attitude embodied in the original form of tribal society. Much as the one tries to imitate the other, it is distinguished from it by the curse of self-consciousness, and by the fact that it seeks nostalgically *through human agency* to re-cultivate a shared sense that the forms of tribal life are beyond human agency and should be treated unreflectively as (though they were) natural or magical necessities.

This is how Popper views Plato's enterprise in *The Republic* and elsewhere. According to Popper, Plato 'made a serious attempt to reconstruct the ancient tribal forms of social life' (OS 1, p. 45): the political outlook expressed in his work is 'a symptom of nostalgia, of a longing for a unified and harmonious, an "organic" state: for a society of a more primitive kind' (OS 1, pp. 79–80). I have no wish to enter the lists for or against Popper's reading of the ancients, but it is worth noting that his points about the existence and importance of this sort of nostalgia are not confined to his reading of Plato. He applies them also to the crisis of ancient Judaism, suggesting that the rise of Christianity was in part

a protest against Jewish tribalism, against its rigid and empty tribal taboos, and against its tribal exclusiveness which expressed itself, for example, in the doctrine of the chosen people, i.e. in an interpretation of the deity as a tribal god. Such an emphasis upon tribal laws and tribal unity appears to be characteristic not so much of a primitive tribal society as of a desperate attempt to restore and arrest the old forms of tribal life; and in the case of Jewry, it seems to have originated as a reaction to the impact of the Babylonian conquest on Jewish tribal life.

(OS 2, p. 22)2

In this case, too, there is a sense that when the ancient taboos are made the subject of a campaign of restoration in this way, it is already too late to recapture the sense of implicit necessity associated with their original social existence.

Something similar is said in *The Open Society* about the attempts of modern nationalists to recapture the organic basis of national life. The ideology of nationalism looks to the sort of close ethnic affiliation characteristic of early tribal societies as a basis for political organisation. But there is no question of *literal* tribal nationalism in this sense, certainly not for the modern world, and probably not for the ancient world either:

> [W]ith Alexander's empire, genuine tribal nationalism disappears for ever from political practice, and for a long time from political theory. From Alexander onward, all the civilised states of Europe and Asia were empires, embracing populations of infinitely mixed origin. European civilisation and all the political units belonging to it have remained international or, more precisely, inter-tribal ever since.
>
> (OS 2, p. 50)

No-one but a fool (in which category Popper placed Woodrow Wilson) could think that nationality could possibly be the basis for a practicable principle of political self-determination:

> How anybody who had the slightest notion of European history, of the shifting and mixing of all kinds of tribes, of the countless waves of peoples who had come from their original Asian habitat and split up and mingled when reaching the maze of peninsulas called the European continent, how anybody who knew all this could ever have put forward such an inapplicable principle, is hard to understand.
>
> (OS 2, pp. 50–1)

Nevertheless the idea of national solidarity continues to entrance us. Though it is not based on tribal reality, the romantic myth of tribal collectivism answers 'to our tribal instincts, to passion and to prejudice, and to our nostalgic desire to be relieved from the strain of individual responsibility which it attempts to replace by a collective or group responsibility' (OS 2, p. 49). The dream is not entirely reprehensible. In the Napoleonic era, national feeling arose as a way of combating empire and oppression: it was 'a kind of cloak in which a humanitarian desire for freedom and equality was clad' (OS 2, p. 55). But it became dangerous when the 'mystical experience of community with the other members of the oppressed tribe' (OS 2, p. 55) took on a life of its own as a sort of 'yearning for the lost unity and shelter of tribalism' (OS 2, p. 228) – something which could be used to overwhelm the sentiments of liberty and equality which had earlier galvanised it.[3] This is particularly important for Popper's critique of Hegel: Hegel, he says, took it as his task 'to combat the liberal . . . leanings of nationalism' and to persuade the nationalists that the nostalgic side of their aspirations would be best realised in the modern world 'by an almighty state' (OS 2, p. 57).

Again, I don't want to plunge into the scholarly debate about Popper's reading of Hegel any more than I want to participate in the debate about his reading of Plato. My point in bringing all this up is not to highlight the 'reactionary and servile' aspects of 'the Hegelian farce' (OS 2, p. 51 and p. 79). Popper is certainly right to note Hegel's observation 'that nationalism answers a need – the desire of men to find and know their definite place in the world and to belong to a power-ful collective body' (OS 2, p. 64). What interests me, for the purposes of this chapter, is what the expression of that need does to people's attitude towards and engagement with the mores and customs which they take to define or to have defined the organic life of the nation or tribe they are nostalgic for.

In the original tribal milieu (if such a milieu ever existed), people are presum-ably in a situation where the mores and customs constitutive of their way of life simply govern their actions in a way that is beyond any question or reflection. Popper himself is inclined to associate this kind of normativity with what he calls 'naive naturalism' – a stage at which the distinction between natural and norma-tive law has not yet been made, i.e. '[n]o distinction is made between sanctions imposed by other men, if a normative taboo is broken, and unpleasant experi-ences suffered in the natural environment' (OS 1, pp. 59–60). But actually he pulls back a little from this, suggesting that this may be only 'an abstract possibil-ity which probably never was realised' (OS 1, p. 60). I think he is right to do so, for I am not sure that we can attribute the thought that there is no distinction between natural and normative law to the members of a genuine tribal society. If there is any assimilation, I suspect it is in the other direction – from natural to prescriptive law rather than the other way round. (Popper indicates that it might better be understood as 'a stage at which both natural and normative regularities are experienced as expressions of, and as dependent upon, the decisions of man-like gods or demons' – OS 1, p. 60.) Probably, though, we are dealing simply with immediate and unreflective prescriptivity. The mores are clearly normative – that is, they do occupy a *practical* role in the lives and choices of those they govern, only that practical role is not itself seen as appropriately subject to critical assess-ment. One just does as one ought; and the thought that one ought to do such and such is not itself a subject for searching reflection. Unreflective normativity rather than naive naturalism seems the best description here.

Now I am sure Popper is right to suggest that the primitive 'take' on social norms (however we describe it) cannot survive widespread understanding of their variability between societies. Certainly it cannot survive the emergence in a soci-ety of new sects with distinctive norms of their own, whether that is due to social fission or to the more or less permanent mingling of locals with outsiders. The mainstream mores of the group may remain prescriptive but their immunity from reflection cannot last. So, when, in the wake of these developments, attempts are made to return to the erstwhile solidarity of the tribe, those attempts are bound to orient themselves towards tribal norms in a way that sees them in a somewhat different light from the way in which they were originally and immemorially practised. At best, tribal solidarity is now something that has to be sought through the medium of the revival of tribalistic norms, rather than being something which is just characteristic of their being unquestioningly practised. *Nostalgic* tribalism is necessarily second-hand, making what was once immanent and unreflective the object of conscious reflection and resolve.

I don't mean that the nostalgic tribalist necessarily takes an *instrumentalist* attitude towards tribal mores, treating them just as a means to the end of the revival of tribal solidarity. That would be too cynical a reading. The mores are partly constitutive of the end that the nostalgic tribalist aims at, not a mere means to it. But even as a part of his end, the mores function and they are grasped and followed in a different spirit from that associated with their original immanence. The nostalgic campaign for their revival takes place against a different social background, where norms as such are now beginning to be regarded critically. Different sets of norms are now compared with one another, and the business of comparison may well give rise to the emergence of a critical standard by reference to which sets of norms may be assessed (OS 1, p. 61). (For discussion of the emergence of 'critical morality', see Hart 1994, pp. 169–84.) Of course, nostalgic tribalism is intended as a repudiation of that: the tribalist wishes to return to forms of normativity that are not reflective, or comparative or critical in this way. But that repudiation is already contaminated with reflection, comparison and criticism: the nostalgic tribalist has seen and considered the ways of life associated with the open or abstract society, and he does not like them. But what he looks for instead is not available.

Much the same can be said about phenomena like moral relativism and also what Popper calls 'ethical positivism':

> Positivism maintains that there are no other norms but the laws which have actually been set up (or 'posited') and therefore have a positive existence. Other standards are considered as unreal imaginations. The existing laws are the only possible standards of goodness: what is, is good.
>
> (OS 1, p. 71)

This may be a perfectly good outsider's description of the mentality of a tribal society. But this sort of positivism itself cannot be made into an ethical creed. I don't mean this as a refutation of relativism.[4] It may well be that sets of mores have immediate reality as existing ways of life, that defy the ethereal standards that a social critic or a practitioner of abstract moral philosophy might bring to bear on them. But if the key to that immediate reality is supposed to be the unreflective character of the normativity of such concrete mores and customs, it is simply too late to use as a reason or an argument in favour of the reactionary enterprise. Reflection has come into the world, and pointing out the insubstantiality of the critical standards that are conjured up out of the comparisons we make with other societies and the reflection we direct on our own does not open a way back to the world as it was before we began to compare and reflect. However insubstantial our critical standards are, we cannot go back to a time at which the idea of social and ethical criticism was unheard of.

IV

I said that I wanted to bring Popperian considerations to bear on the politics of cultural recognition. Today, in social philosophy, there is increasing support for the view that respect for persons, and proper recognition of their standing in society and of the claims that they have against others and against society as a whole, is impossible without a grasp of their cultural background and of the relation between their individual identity and a particular way of life. In a mono-cultural society, this background would be the same for all individuals, and respect for persons would be a matter of considering the particular identity – their values, allegiances and conception of the good life – that people carved out for themselves against that common background. But today almost all societies are *multi*-cultural: they comprise communities of many different ethnicities and cultures. In these circumstances, it is often thought more important from the point of view of respecting a given individual, x to find out (a) which culture x's identity was forged in, than to find out (b) what particular identity x forged as an individual within that culture. Indifference or misapprehension at level (a) is often thought to be a much worse affront to x's dignity than indifference or misapprehension at level (b). Or to put it the other way round, the most common basis for the most egregious affronts to people's identities is thought to be disrespect for or the slighting of a particular culture or ethnicity rather than disrespect for the particular identity an individual has crafted for himself within his culture or ethnicity. This is particularly so when the background or ethnicity in question is that of a minority community: an immigrant group, for example, or an indigenous people. Accordingly, the strongest demand that is made in modern identity politics is that we should respect the distinctive dignity of the cultural or ethnic background that each individual has or claims as his own (cf. Taylor 1992).

In our critical assessment of this movement in recent thought, I believe we need to think very carefully about what a culture is. It should not be thought of as something like a costume which a person might wear or as an individual lifestyle. In the first instance, a culture has social reality. As a shared way of life, it comprises mores and norms, laws and customs, that purport to govern the multitude of ways in which individuals live together and interact in society. It represents the heritage of the attempts that have been made in a particular context to address and to come to terms with the various problems of social life. So: a culture may comprise a particular way of dealing with relations between the sexes, the rearing of children, the organisation of an economy, the transmission of knowledge and the punishment of offences. Cultures represent an array of attempted social solutions to the vicissitudes that affect all the stages of human life in society from conception to the disposition of corpses, and from the deepest love to the most vengeful antipathies. So when a person talks about his identity as a Maori, or a Sunni Muslim, or a Jew, or a Scot, he is relating himself not just to a set of dances, costumes, recipes and incantations, but to a distinct set of practices in and through which his people (the people he identifies with when he claims this as his identity) have historically addressed and settled upon solutions to the serious problems of human life in society.

By emphasising the character of each culture as, in the first instance, an array of ways of dealing with the problems of social life, we can see some of the difficulties (and also some of the opportunities) that arise when diverse cultures coexist in a single (multi-cultural) society. For, obviously, the problems of social life, to which disparate cultures pose different solutions, are also problems that may have to be addressed at the level of the wider society, which comprises the various minority groups we are considering. The wider society has to address the question of the disposal of human remains, the upbringing of children, relations between the sexes, the organisation of the economy, the punishment of offences, issues of diet and hygiene, and so on. And so there are going to be hard questions about what the relation should be between the way the wider society addresses problems like these and any demands that are made in the name of minority cultural recognition.

One possibility is that the demands made in the name of minority cultural recognition will present themselves as constraints on possible solutions adopted at the level of the whole society. If the wider society, W, adopts a particular solution, s_w, to some problem, p, of social life which is at odds with the solution, s_c, embodied in the culture of a minority community, C, which is a sub-group of W, then the members of C may feel disrespected and oppressed. This, they will say, is because they have to bear not only their share of the burdens that s_w involves – assuming that s_w distributes benefits and burdens generally among the members of W including members of C – but also the additional burden of interference by s_w with the practicability of the solution posed by their own culture.

Here's an example (cf. the 24 Sept. 1997 *New York Times* news story 'Prison Terms for 2 Men In Marrying Young Girls', which I discuss at length in my 2002a). Suppose the wider society W faces the problem of how to regulate teenage sexuality. It imposes a particular complex solution (s_w), prohibiting all sexual contact below a certain age but requiring families to prepare their teenage children for responsible autonomous choice beyond that age. Since members of the sub-group C have children, they too have to bear the burden of this regime: they have to supervise their children but also to prepare them for and to bear the burden of their eventual autonomy. But culture C may also comprise its own distinctive perspective (s_c) on teenage sexuality: it may arrange marriages at an early age for teenage girls, in order to safeguard their chastity. Now s_w is incompatible with s_c: it prohibits teenage marriage and it frowns on arranged marriage. So, being regulated by s_w, the members of C not only bear the burdens that all families bear; they bear the additional burden of having to violate their deeply held beliefs about this matter. This, the members of C will say, is an extra burden that is unfairly placed on them. Moreover, if they really do associate their culture with their identity, they may regard the imposition of this extra burden as a form of profound disrespect. That is, they may argue against the imposition of s_w in a way that is similar to the way a liberal would argue against social solutions which violate individual rights. Though everyone must bear their fair share of the burdens of social life, no one should be required to sacrifice *themselves* for the social good; but in effect that is what the imposition of s_w does. It requires those who identify with a culture that dictates a different and incompatible solution, s_c, to give up or compromise part of their (cultural) identity, and that is just like having to give up or compromise their sense of who they are. Needless to say, once social and political claims begin to be put about in this spirit, it is going to be very difficult indeed for the members of W to come up with any viable common solution to p or to any of the other problems they face. At worst, they will face a deadly impasse.[5] At best, they will only be able to adopt solutions that are riddled with exceptions and accommodations for rival and disparate cultural practices – and that may well betray their sense of what counts as a solution to p.[6]

The dilemma seems a daunting one, until we begin to look more closely at the link between culture and identity that has brought us to this pass. The set of cultural practices at stake here – which includes the purported solution, s_c, to problem p – has a dual aspect. On the one hand, it represents a certain social reality – the traditions of a particular community (call it C^*) that once flourished with the culture in question, unaffected by the contagion of multi-culturalism. On the other hand, it represents a certain sort of individual identity, the identity of those members of W who happen to cherish the traditions that once were associated with C^*. Let me elaborate this distinction. Though we are imagining a minority culture, C, which is a sub-group of W, we know that the members of C look beyond their present sub-group status to a time or a place in which their culture was practised as a culture of a whole society. Once upon a time, the ancestors of the members of C lived as the members of an indigenous community, C^*, managing their own affairs, addressing and solving their own social problems. Or: elsewhere in the world the relatives or compatriots of the members of C live even now as a self-sufficient community, C^*, managing their own affairs and addressing and solving their social problems along the lines of their traditional way of life. So when some particular practice like s_c is in question, we may consider it as the artifact of a particular society – as a social solution to the problem of social living that developed in C^* – or we may think of it as a sort of badge of identity, by which certain people express their individual identification with a certain cultural heritage. They present themselves as pining nostalgically for the culture of C^*, that older homogenous society that their ancestors once belonged to, or they present themselves as pining in a homesick way for the culture of the homogenous society, C^*, from which they have emigrated. And their allegiance to this particular practice – and their sense that any derogation from it by the laws and customs of W is an unbearable individual affront – is a sort of token of this pining.

But treating what was once an aspect of social practice as now a constituent of individual identity may be a way of betraying rather than being true to the norms that constitute a culture. The key is the air of self-consciousness that tends to pervade the self-presentations associated with identity politics. The idea of identity connotes a struggle within each person to listen to his inner yearnings and to be, in some deep sense, true to himself. That involves a supreme effort of self-consciousness – as one strains to catch the urgings of one's inner voice or whatever. (See Taylor 1992, pp. 30–51.) But that very conscious straining is quite at odds with the normal or normative mode of existence of cultural norms. Indeed at the level of simple and straightforward participation in the culture of one's community, such obsessively self-conscious endeavour is likely to be quite distracting. Think for a moment about involvement in a given culture in a *non-multi-cultural* setting, i.e., involvement with a culture in the culture's natural habitat, so to speak. One is living in C* and the frame of culture C* is all any of us has been used to. In this setting, it is doubtful whether thoughts *about* one's culture – how marvellous it is; how colourful and distinctive; how important it is to the identity of each of us – will loom very large in people's involvement in the life of their community. In the homogenous social setting what one does is simply speak or marry or dance or worship. One participates in a form of life. *Proclaiming* or *advertising* that this is what one is doing would be viewed as rather strange. Certainly it would be to participate in a different form of life – a form of life only problematically related to the first. As I said, what one does in straightforward cultural engagement is simply speak or marry or dance or worship. In doing so, one does not say anything about the distinctive features of, say, the Irish heritage, or the peculiarities of the Maori wedding feast. One keeps faith with the mores of one's community just by following them, not by announcing slyly and self-consciously that it is the mores of one's community that one is following. (Cf. my 2000, pp. 168–9.)

I hope you see the connection between this and the Popperian critique of nostalgic tribalism, which I set out in section III. In both cases, the norms and mores of a homogenous community are made the object of longing, and perhaps even of political action, by people who no longer live in the circumstances in which those norms and mores once flourished. And in both cases, there is something inauthentic about the relation in which such people stand to the norms and mores in question. In the case of nostalgic tribalism, the unreflective aspect of those norms is cherished in a way that is already and irretrievably contaminated by reflection. That which was once unselfconscious – unreflective normativity – is now made the object of conscious nostalgic endeavour. And I want to argue that something similar is happening in the politics of cultural identity: individual identity claims of the sort we have been considering represent quite inauthentic ways of engaging with a culture.

<h1 style="text-align:center">V</h1>

I have been assuming a discipline of authenticity: one's cultural engagement must be true both to the reality of one's culture and to the limits on what is possible in the real circumstances in which one finds oneself. So: cursed with self-consciousness and living as they do in a modern multi-cultural society, what are the members of W who identify with a minority culture to do? Are they to abandon their cultural heritage altogether and the rules and practices, like s_c, worked out as ancient solutions to the problems of social living? Must they now submit meekly – as assimilated natives or as diffident newcomers – to the solutions to the problems of social life, like s_w, imposed imperiously by the dominant majority of W?

No; there is a third way. The members of C may present s_c as a contribution to the debate in the wider society as to how problem p should be solved. The majority may be inclined to favour s_w, but the presence of minority communities in their midst may offer them a chance to rethink their views (or their prejudices). At the crudest level, this involves putting s_c on the ballot, as it were, alongside s_w and whatever other candidates there are: it is now on the menu of available choices for the society as a whole. This may seem a lost cause, given s_c's status as the solution favoured only by a minority group. But the minority solution may enrich the debate in other and more subtle ways. It may add a perspective that deepens people's sense of what is at stake if they do not accept the precise solution that is sponsored from that perspective. Also, discussion need not always be oriented simply to the question 'Which solution to problem p is to be imposed – s_w supported by the majority, or s_c by the members of minority community C?' There is also a question about how the background problem, p, is to be conceived and in particular whether it is to be conceived as a problem that requires a single solution for all the members of the society, or whether instead it is the sort of problem on which there can be a diversity of coexisting solutions, or in respect of which some degree of exemption and accommodation is possible relative to whatever solution is agreed on. I cannot go into this in any detail here (but see my 2002b), except to say that whether a problem does admit of cultural exemptions and accommodations is something which the members of the wider society have no choice but to talk about and something to which their various cultural perspectives are undoubtedly relevant.

Now all this assumes that it is not unreasonable to require those who identify with s_c to step up to the bar of social and political debate in the wider society, W, and engage their favoured norms in the processes of reasoning that will determine an outcome for W. Is this an unreasonable requirement? Does it require members of C to break faith with their cultural heritage? I think not.

Consider again the original community, C*, from which they came, or in which their folkways were once followed as a homogenous way of life. Had C* encountered outsiders, but on something more like its own terms (i.e. not as a community of emigration or not as a community invaded by colonists), it would not necessarily have abandoned its mores. Instead the processes that Popper points to – the processes that we discussed in section II – would have taken place. The mores of C* would become objects of criticism, comparison and reflection. Practices like s_c would lose their immanent and unreflective normativity, but they might well survive as norms held now in something like a critical spirit, associated with reasons and capable of defending themselves or being defended against alternative solutions to the social problems they addressed. Adherence to them by members of C* would no longer just be an unreflective aspect of being a member of that social order; adherence to them would now involve accepting the reasons behind them. So if s_c were something like a norm prescribing arranged marriage, s_c would now be accepted by the members of C* because they believed (say) that arranged marriage is an appropriate way to deal with the ill-advised or unstable affections of teenagers. That would be part of what was said as people practised s_c, reflected on it, and defended it in relation to what they knew of contrary practices elsewhere.

I think it important to emphasise the integrity of this sort of reasoning and reason-giving. It is sometimes said by defenders of cultural or national identity that one accepts the norms of one's society just because they are the norms of one's society. Isaiah Berlin, for example, says (in his 1981, pp. 342–3) that for the nationalist

> one of the most compelling reasons . . . for holding a particular belief, pursuing a particular policy, serving a particular end, living a particular life, is that these ends, beliefs, policies, lives are ours. This is tantamount to saying that these rules or doctrines or principles should be followed not because they . . . are good and right in themselves . . . [but] because these values are those of my group – for the nationalist, of my nation.

But this is a very peculiar attitude to take – to insert the cultural provenance of a norm or value into what H. L. A. Hart called (in his 1994, pp. 88ff.) its 'internal aspect'. It seems very odd to regard the fact that this is 'our' norm – that this is what we Irishmen or we French or we Maori do – as part of the reason, if not the central reason, for having the norm and for sustaining and following it (cf. my 1989). From the perspective of an outsider that may be what we say about the place of norms in an unreflective order – that they are followed just because they are the norms of that society. But if the 'because' is supposed to pick up on the internal aspect of the norms, then it is misleading. In the early unreflective version of C*, the norms are simply prescribed and followed; they are not prescribed and followed *because* they are the norms of C*. And when C* later changes into a more critical, open society, the norms exist in a context of reasons and reasoning, where there is a story to be told, a story internal to each norm as to why this way of doing things is better or efficient or obligatory or appropriate. At either stage, it is a distortion of the internal aspect of the norms to say that they are followed because they are the norms of this particular community.

Perhaps the point needs slight qualification, in two ways, neither of them affecting the argument I am making. Some norms we have and follow as matters of indifference; they are pure conventions, solving straightforward problems of coordination. We drive on the left in New Zealand because that is what everyone does and one most wants to follow the same rule as others are following in this respect. No substantive reason justifying the left-hand side is required. So it seems not inappropriate to say, 'I follow this norm because it is the norm of my society.' But most cases of cultural norms are not like that. And even cases that are like this can still be characterised in terms of reasons – only, they will be reasons appropriate to problems of pure coordination. (See Ullman-Margalit 1977.) Second, some people follow the norms laid down in their society, not because of reasons relating to their content, but because of their authoritative imposition. And this too may make it seem as though being a member of the particular society – subject to its authority – is referenced in the internal aspect of such norm-following. But once again, the internal aspect can be unpacked in terms of reasons relating to the practice of authority – reasons for deferring to tradition, power or collective decision when one does not engage with the substantive merits. (For the best modern account of the reasoning associated with deference to authority, see Raz 1986, pp. 38 ff.) That is what the appeal to authority amounts to. It is not an invocation of cultural identity as such: it is a relation of cultural membership to a complex structure of reasons appropriate to those who are in a certain situation.

I don't want to suggest that the reasons that are associated with cultural norms and practices as a society emerges from its closed, unreflective phase are necessarily the familiar sorts of reasons that one would find in a work of analytic moral philosophy. If I ask an elder of the group to which I belong why we have a norm of arranged marriages, he may tell me a story about the need for teenagers to be guided by their parents and by their community in their most important decisions or he may tell me a story about the moon and the stars and about how the moon shepherds the stars into their familiar constellations. The reasoning in the later story may be opaque, difficult or deeply buried. Still – either way – *that* is the sort of thing that counts, in the group, as a reason for following the custom.

Some important points about modern cultural identity politics follow from this. Humans and human groups take their norms seriously, and to take them seriously is to think of them as embedded in something like a structure of reasons and reasoning. Whatever we think of them from the outside, from the inside they are not like the rules of games or the norms of fancy dress – things one can cast off as soon as it seems no longer important to display oneself as a member of a particular group. As a member of a modern multi-cultural society, I may not accept the reasoning associated with a given norm, s_c, in C^*, or I may find the story about the stars and the moon bewildering or unsatisfying. But if it *is* true, if I reject or cannot follow the reasoning associated with s_c, then that is all there is to say about the matter: I no longer respect the norm on the basis on which it claims my respect. I certainly do not show any respect for s_c by gutting it of *its* reasons, and replacing them as reasons with *my own* need to keep faith with my cultural roots. That is not the point of s_c at all, and to think of it as the point (or even as one reason among others) may be to give a quite misleading impression of the importance of s_c in its original cultural setting. In other words: if there are norms and practices that constitute 'our' way of life, and that matters to us, then the thing to do is wholeheartedly to embrace them and the reasoning that goes with them, not in a way that leaves it open for us to comment to others in the sort of stage-whisper that characterises modern identity politics: 'I am following the practices of my culture' or 'What I am doing here is revisiting my roots.'

All this opens the way to an affirmative account of what authentic cultural engagement might amount to in a modern multi-cultural society. If keeping faith with some normative element in one's cultural heritage is in part also a matter of keeping faith with the reasons embedded in the internal aspect of the norms in question, then one is in a position to participate as a member of C in a wider social debate about the appropriate way to solve the social problem, p, to which s_w and s_c might be seen as rival solutions. Each of the solutions on offer makes a deep claim about what sort of things are at stake in the areas of social life that they govern; and each of those claims is held to be *true*, which means that it offers to give a better account of what really matters in this regard than the reasoning associated with a different set of norms and practices. Now, that reasoning may bewilder and disconcert those who are unfamiliar with a given cultural background. But it is like all human reasoning at least in this: it holds out the promise of some extent of human wisdom and it offers that for assessment on the basis of, and in comparison with, whatever else there is in our society in the way of human wisdom and experience on questions such as those that the norm purports to address.

The culturalist position sometimes seems to imply that one must protect the norms of a minority culture from this sort of process, to avoid the peril of assimilation. The fear is that if one offers s_c up for consideration in the debate taking place in the wider society as one possible solution to a social problem, then one runs the risk that it will be rejected, outvoted, adapted or modified out of all recognition. But the fear is surely misplaced. In the modern world, s_c could only exist in a context of reasons and reasoning, where people compare norms critically with one another and consider a range of possibilities for solving the various problems of social living that they face. The time of unreflective normativity has vanished irretrievably. Now the context of reasoning is the natural habitat of cultural norms. Being predicated on reasons and making itself available for rational discussion and assessment – that now, is what a norm *is*. Protecting it from this process is therefore not a way of keeping faith with the norm; at best, it is the artificial preservation of a frozen simulacrum. And the fact that that simulacrum is paraded as a badge of cultural identity does not entitle the culturalists to object to the norm's immersion in the context of reasoning that now constitutes its life.

VI

Nothing I have said assumes that this reasoning will be easy, whether it is reasoning about which solution to p to accept, or about whether p actually requires a single exceptionless solution. I would like to consider also what Karl Popper has contributed to our understanding of the difficulties that are likely to arise in this regard.

What we are imagining involves reasoned debate among people associated with one culture and people associated with another. (We have imagined that at two levels: first (in section II) the debates that got the whole process of critical reasoning underway between seafarers and those whose ports they visited or between merchants and those they bought from; and secondly (in section V) between those members of W associated with its majority culture and those members of W associated with the minority culture C.) The difficulties of inter-cultural dialogue are often exaggerated, with glib talk about the incommensurability of cultural frameworks and the impossibility of conversation without a common conceptual scheme. (See the discussion in Lukes 2003, pp. 63–77.) In fact conversation between members of different cultural and religious communities is seldom a dialogue of the deaf, though there is inevitable tension and misunderstanding. Humans are enormously curious about each other's ideas and reasons, and, when they want to be, they are resourceful in listening to and trying to learn from one another across what appear to be barriers of cultural comprehensibility, often far beyond what philosophers and theorists of culture give them credit for. We theorists tend to think that deliberation requires a framework of common concepts and understandings; and we are less embarrassed than we ought to be when, time and again, various seafarers, and traders, and migrants prove us wrong.

Popper's position on this is well known from his 1965 essay, 'The Myth of the Framework'. Here is the way he summarises (in Popper 1994, at pp. 34–5) the 'myth' that he wants to criticise:

> A rational and fruitful discussion is impossible unless the participants share a common framework of basic assumptions or, at least, unless they have agreed on such a framework for the purpose of the discussion.

Popper goes on to say that the myth sounds like common sense, but is in fact 'a vicious statement which, if widely believed, must undermine the unity of mankind, and . . . greatly increase the likelihood of violence and war' (p. 35).[7] Now, whatever its effect on war and peace, the myth of the framework certainly tends to undermine the prospects of dialogue in a multi-cultural society. It convinces people that there is no alternative to simply clinging to one's culture as a badge of identity, for it discredits the alternative I have urged – good-faith participation in a wider debate about how to address social problems of the community as a whole, a debate which is enriched by the contributions from various cultures. It is therefore a matter of some importance for our enterprise to find out whether what Popper calls 'the myth of the framework' really can be refuted.

A 'framework,' in the sense that Popper criticises, may be thought of in the first instance as a language, and one of the things Popper talks about in 'The Myth of the Framework' (his 1994) is the problem of translation (see pp. 49–52).[8] It may happen, he says, that a particular statement in one language cannot be translated into another, and it is almost always the case that translations involve some loss of aesthetic value, but usually the difficulties can be surmounted, at least so far as scientific or political discourse is concerned (cf. his 1994, p. 49).[9]

A more troubling version of the myth, however, has to do not with translation conventions but with definitions: '[I]t is the view that, before discussion, we should agree on our vocabulary – perhaps by defining our terms' (Popper 1994, p. 59). Popper's argument against this position has been consistent since *The Open Society*. There he wrote that '[t]he problem of definitions and of the "meaning of terms"' . . . has been an inexhaustible source of confusion' and it is the source, he says, 'of all that verbal and empty scholasticism that haunts not only the Middle Ages, but our own contemporary philosophy' (OS 2, p. 9). In his attack on Aristotelian essentialism in *The Open Society*, he denounced the view that definitions were fruitful for science. Definitions do not contain any knowledge, he argued; they are simply shorthand labels introduced in order to cut a long story short.[10] '[T]he scientific view of the definition "A puppy is a young dog" would be that it is an answer to the question *"What shall we call a young dog?"* rather than an answer to the question *"What is a puppy?"*' (OS 2, p. 14).

So those who do not share definitions lack, at most, only a common set of abbreviations. That may be inconvenient, as when one party to the dialogue is using what it thinks of as abbreviations, which are not familiar to the party on the other side. It may make discussion laborious.[11] But it is hardly insuperable. And anyway, any attempt to resolve the problem of definitions in advance of discussion simply postpones or reduplicates whatever problems we are supposed to have by virtue of not agreeing on the meaning of the terms we use in our discussion.

> All definitions, so-called 'operational definitions' included, can only shift the problem of the meaning of the term in question to the defining term. Thus the demand for definitions leads to an infinite regress unless we admit so-called primitive terms, that is undefined terms. But these are as a rule no less problematic than most of the defined terms.
>
> (Popper 1994, p. 59)

The point applies as much in ethics and politics as in science. Even though political discourse contains troublesome terms like 'democracy' and 'liberty' which are (Popper says) much misused, he believes 'that any attempt to define them can . . . only make matters worse', since it would just push the issue of confusion and manipulation back to the terms of the definiens (OS 2, p. 17).

There is a view associated with the later Wittgenstein that fruitful discussion requires not only agreement in definitions but agreement in judgments.[12] I am not sure whether Popper would disagree with the position as Wittgenstein elaborated it in *Philosophical Investigations*, i.e. as a fairly straightforward point about measuring: '[W]hat we call "measuring" is partly determined by a certain constancy in the results of measurement' (idem). He certainly rejects what a number of people have drawn from the Wittgensteinian position, namely that fruitful discussion requires not only shared definitions but also certain common basic assumptions, values or fundamental intellectual positions.[13] On the contrary Popper argues that the whole point of dialogue is to bring contrast and disagreement into the open. Agreement or consensus is not as such the point of conversation:

> [A] discussion between people who share many views is unlikely to be fruitful, even though it may be pleasant; while a discussion between vastly different frameworks can be extremely fruitful, even though it may sometimes be extremely difficult, and perhaps not quite so pleasant (though we may learn to enjoy it).
>
> (Popper 1994, p. 35)

Think back to the traders and merchants we imagined in section II. The most important effect of their conversations with those foreigners whose goods they bought or in whose ports they sojourned was not consensus but a shaking of each party's unreflective attitude towards the norms they had grown up with. An Egyptian doesn't have to come to agreement with an Athenian about how to run a state in order to appreciate from an encounter with him that there are ways of organising a society other than theocratic monarchy. And that is Popper's criterion of fruitfulness – not consensus but

> the more interesting questions and difficult questions they were asked, the more new answers they were induced to think of, the more they were shaken in their opinions, and the more they could see things differently after the discussion.
>
> (Popper 1994, pp. 35–6)[14]

However, let me end this section on a conciliatory note, so far as common definitions and assumptions are concerned. Maybe it is the case that fruitful discussion cannot proceed in the absence of some sort of conceptual consonance and some sort of congruity about fundamental assumptions. Maybe it is the case that any fruitful dialogue will disclose such consonance and such congruity. But I think it is very important to see that this concession falls well short of the culturalist claim about incommensurability in two respects. First, it does not imply that conceptual consonance and congruity in fundamental assumptions must exist *in advance* of the conversation: it may be constructed – perhaps haphazardly – *in* the conversation and it may disclose itself – haltingly – *as the conversation goes along*. And second, the concession I have suggested does not in any way imply that the parties must share the sort of array of concepts and assumptions that is usually associated with *a cultural framework*. The assumptions and concepts that they show themselves to be using may be a jerry-built concoction of a little bit that each of their background cultures has to offer. It need not be an integrated whole, or if integrity is necessary, that integrity too may disclose itself in a new and unprecedented form in the very conversation that is taking place.

VII

Though Popper denies that the participants in an intercultural dialogue need to begin with some concepts, definitions and judgments in common, he accepts that the prospect of fruitful dialogue does depend on their sharing certain attitudes, such as 'a wish to get to, or nearer to, the truth, and willingness to share problems or to understand the aims and the problems of somebody else' (Popper 1994, p. 35). What they need to share, in other words, is an ethic of reasoning: the parties must both be prepared to say, 'I may be wrong and you may be right, and by an effort we may get nearer the truth' (OS 2, p. 238). In all his work, Popper has stressed the fundamental connection between this ethic and the methodology of what he calls critical rationalism, 'with its emphasis on argument and experience' (OS 2, p. 238), 'the tradition of critical discussion – of examining and testing propositions or theories by attempting to refute them' (Popper 1969, p. 352).

Now, in Popper's view, acceptance of this method and of the ethic that informs it 'establishes what might be called "the rational unity of mankind"' (OS 2, p. 225). Following his lead, I have argued that engagement in discussion with other traditions along the lines of Popper's critical rationalism is a way of keeping faith with one's own cultural traditions, as well as the most profitable mode of interaction between cultures, from a moral and social point of view. Indeed I have argued that, since there is no reasonable prospect of a return to tribalism, any attempt to insulate minority cultures from these processes represents an inauthentic mode of allegiance to their norms and practices, as though we should drain the life from these norms and practices, and treat them solicitously as museum pieces or as icons for individual self-adornment. In section VI we considered whether this sort of engagement in critical discussion is *possible*, given the wide disparity of the ideas and concepts implicated in these various cultures. Again, following Popper's attack on 'the myth of the framework', I argued that it was possible. It would be wrong to end, however, without considering one last culturalist line of attack. The culturalist may argue that requiring a minority culture to involve itself and its component practices and traditions in critical engagement with other cultures and in particular with mainstream culture of Western multi-cultural society is, in effect, a death sentence. For in any such engagement, the odds are rigged overwhelmingly against the minority culture – first, because the very terms of the engagement are modern Western ideas and thus systematically biased against minority cultures, and second, because even if the terms of engagement were neutral, the partisans of mainstream Western traditions have shown over and over again an unwillingness to practise the spirit of open engagement with alien ideas that they so piously preach.

Sadly, I suspect there is some merit in the second count in this indictment. Often the real resistance to genuine dialogue comes from the partisans of the mainstream or majority culture. (Cf. my 2000, pp. 171–2.) Either they rely on their numbers and their power to simply sideline and ignore alternative practices and perspectives, or they explicitly attempt to exclude them from discussion (often in the name of a 'thin theory' of public reason, that excludes anything that cannot be framed in the secular terminology of political liberalism).[15] Worse still, there is often an assumption that any challenge to the current cosy consensus associated with Western practices – for example, the consensus on the nature and contents of human rights – must be a relativist challenge to the universalist pretensions of our claim, rather than a universalist competitor. In the light of all this, there is no doubt that the critical edge of the Popperian case has to be directed as much to the mainstream culture as to the minority culturalists. It is we – mainstream partisans – who need to be taught to hold our social, moral and cultural positions in an open and critical spirit appropriate to their alleged status as rational universalistic claims. The only thing that can possibly entitle us to strut about enforcing our norms and practices to the exclusion of various cultural alternatives is that we have carefully considered everything that might be relevant to the moral and political assessment of our norms and practices. It is not enough that we have considered what Kant said to Fichte, or what Bruce Ackerman said to John Rawls. The price of legitimising our universalist moral posturing is that we make a good faith attempt to address whatever reservations, doubts and objections there are about our positions out there, in the world, no matter what society or culture or religious tradition they come from (cf. my 1999, p. 311). If we do not subject ourselves to that discipline and that responsibility, we will be 'turning our backs upon that tradition of critical thought (stemming from the Greeks and from culture clash) which has made us what we are' (Popper 1994, p. 61).

What, finally, of the first claim in the indictment I mentioned at the beginning of this section – the claim that the tradition of critical thought (stemming from the Greeks etc.) is itself just an aspect of one culture, rather than a neutral arbiter between cultures, or a neutral framework within which cultures can interact fairly and reasonably with one another?

There are two things to say about this. The first is that the premise of the indictment is almost certainly true: surely any methodology, any ethos or tradition of dialogue and interaction, will have been first arrived at and articulated in a particular cultural setting. (If Popper is right, critical rationalism emerged in the clash of cultures that took place among particular peoples in a particular region of the world.) It did not disclose itself from the skies in abstract form. But that does not establish the charge of cultural bias, for Popper could reply that establishing the provenance of a methodology (or of any theory or idea) is not a way of refuting its universal applicability. There is nothing about the time or place or region where a set of propositions have been formed, generated or nurtured which restricts the range of their appropriate application. Just as penicillin kills bacteria in Cambodia even though it was discovered and first tested by a Scotsman, and the categorical imperative may explain why it is wrong for one Nigerian to tell lies to another even though the categorical imperative was first formulated and theorised in East Prussia, so critical rationalism may be an appropriate methodology and ethic for everyone to use even though it grew up among the Greeks and was articulated in a book by an Austrian philosopher living in New Zealand.

But the second thing to say about the charge of cultural bias is that it might be true. That is, it might be the case that the ethic and methodology of critical rationalism is mistaken and that only our imperious cultural prejudices prevent us from seeing this. Certainly there has been enough critical discussion of Popper's methodological views, even by Western philosophers of science, to dispel any illusion of its self-evidence!

With this in mind, it seems there is nothing to do but to adopt a fallibilist stance to our critical rationalism and consider – openly and fairly – each challenge to critical rationalism as it comes up. Other methodologies have been proposed – including other methodologies for evaluating the social practices of various cultures or for engaging in intercultural dialogue. Now such methodologies are not true or acceptable simply because they exist; nor are they true or acceptable simply because of their association with a given cultural tradition (not even for the people who belong to that tradition). *Any* view may be mistaken, for or in the hands of *any* person inclined (for whatever reason) to hold it. So we need to consider the alternatives to critical rationalism on their merits, in exactly the same spirit of critical openness as we consider the first-order cultural practices themselves.

But here's the rub. That last sentence seems to suggest that we should use the methods of critical rationalism to evaluate the method of critical rationalism. But it is one of the canons of Popper's rationalism that no one – and no method, presumably – should be judge in its own cause (OS 2, p. 238). (See also Popper 1969, p. 356.) Can we find a perspective from which critical rationalism can itself be judged? There are places where Popper seems to suggest that this problem is as easy to solve as moving from an object language to a meta-language. (Cf. Popper 1994, pp. 51–2.) But that establishes at most the possibility of talking critically about critical rationalism; it does not rebut the charge that such meta-talk is itself infected with the mistakes or biases of critical rationalism.

It is tempting to conclude lamely that we have no alternative to using the methodology of critical rationalism if we are to evaluate methodological proposals (such as the proposal that critical rationalism should be given up or replaced by an alternative rooted in another culture). And in a way that has to be the conclusion. We can only proceed from where we are. Still we can proceed on that basis in a tentative spirit or we could proceed in a complacent and a self-assured spirit. The Popperian position must surely be that we proceed in a tentative spirit. The mere fact that we have to start from where we are is no sort of *warrant* or *justification* for our methodological approach, once that approach has been called in question. And the situation is exactly analogous for our interlocutor in this cultural dialogue. If we imagine that members of minority culture C are accustomed to defending and evaluating proposals (such as s_c) with a methodology quite different from our own, then if we want to convince them that the methodology of critical rationalism (such as it is) is a better way to evaluate proposals than theirs, we must expect that they, too, will begin from where *they* are, and evaluate not just the case we make (say for s_w) using their methodology, but also evaluate the case we make for critical rationalism using *their* methodology. Once again, we should not expect that dialogue at this level will be anything other than difficult. But we are not entitled to assume that it is impossible, or that at this second level of methodology there is no choice but for each side to retreat into the incommensurable framework of its tribal heritage.

Notes

1 *The Open Society* is not given much attention in modern political philosophy. The most prominent journals for publishing essays in political theory or political philosophy are *Ethics*, *Philosophy and Public Affairs* and *Political Theory*. A quick search on the 'JSTOR' data-base – searching for 'Popper' within ten words of 'Open' in the full text of articles published in these journals between 1960 and 1999 – indicates that Popper's book has been cited in just 23 articles in that period. Of those 23 citations, almost all are perfunctory: they cite Popper either as a source for a particular phrase (like 'radical social engineering') or in order to mention, without elaboration, his attacks on Plato, Hegel and Marx. Six of them devote a sentence or two to his views on topics like utopianism, psychologism, the fact/value gap and negative utilitarianism. Only three offer anything more than a paragraph, and of the articles published in these journals over the last forty years, only one – Lefevre 1974 – is devoted in its entirety to a discussion of Popper's thought. I should add that there are one or two articles on Popper's political philosophy published in other journals: for examples, see Lessnoff 1980, p. 113, Popper 1994, p. 49, and note 9 below. (I am grateful to Julia Maskivker for research assistance on this and other matters for this chapter.)

2 One worries a little bit about the tenor of this attack on Jewish tribalism and also about passages like the following: '[T]he survival in the Ghettos of eastern Europe, down to 1914 and even longer, of arrested and petrified forms of Jewish tribalism is very interesting (cp. the way in which the Scottish tribes attempted to cling to their tribal life)' (OS 2, p. 301n). We should remember, though, that Popper wrote as a refugee from Austria in the late 1930s and as a person of Jewish background (albeit from a family that had converted to Lutheranism). For some discussion, see Edmonds and Eidinow 2001, ch. 10.

3 For a suggestion that Popper might have been brought to a more favourable view of 'liberal nationalism', see Agassi 1999.

4 Certainly it is not a refutation of the historicism that Popper thinks Hegel associates with his ethical positivism (OS 2, p. 49). The move from one form of society to another – whether or not that involves members of the society in transition taking a critical attitude towards their mores – may well be susceptible to historical explanation, may well even be inevitable under certain conditions; and it may well be the case, too, that we cannot formulate these laws of historical change without 'positivising' the mores of the societies we are studying.

5 I have elaborated this argument at greater length in my 2000, at pp. 156–65.

6 Many members of W may believe that p does not admit of any solution which allows for cultural exceptions. This may or may not be true of the practice of arranged teenage marriages. (I suspect it is.) It is certain to be true of some problems that have this character. Think of the problem of domestic violence, for example: the rationale for the solution favoured by the majority of members of the wider society – a strict ban on spousal abuse – may rule out any accommodation for members of minority cultures whose norms approve of (or even require) wife-beating in certain circumstances.

7 I must acknowledge, however, that there are a couple of passages in *The Open Society*,

where Popper seems to accept some version of the myth of the framework: he says that 'scientists try to avoid talking at cross-purposes' and that they must use a common language of experience for corroboration and refutation (OS 2, p. 218); he also writes that 'the adoption of rationalism implies . . . that there is a common medium of communication, a common language of reason', and that people have 'something like a moral obligation towards that language, the obligation to keep up its standards of clarity and to use it in such a way that it can retain its function as the vehicle of argument' (OS 2, p. 239).

8 Popper also offers this comment in *The Open Society*: '[M]ankind is united by the fact that our different mother tongues, in so far as they are rational, can be translated into one another' (OS 2, p. 239).

9 Popper adds the following observation from his experience of dealing with Third World students at the London School of Economics: 'I have found that the difficulties could usually be conquered with a little patience, on both sides. Whenever there was a major obstacle to overcome, it was, as a rule, the result of indoctrination with Western ideas. Dogmatic, uncritical teaching in bad Westernised schools and universities, and especially training in Western verbosity and in some Western ideology were, in my experience, much graver obstacles to rational discussion than any cultural or linguistic gap' (Popper 1994, p. 51).

10 However, for a critique of the proliferation of labels, often without definitions, used in *The Open Society*, see Robinson 1951, p. 502.

11 No doubt these nominalist definitions are 'extremely useful' (OS 2, p. 14); consider, Popper says, 'the extreme difficulties that would arise if a bacteriologist, whenever he spoke of a certain strain of bacteria, had to repeat its whole description (including the methods of dyeing, etc., by which it is distinguished from a number of similar species)' (OS 2, p. 15). But they add nothing substantial to the storehouse of knowledge or opinion; they add only to its manageability. In Popper's view, questions like 'What is energy?' or 'What is an atom?' are never important for physics. The scientist 'will attach importance to a question like: "How can the energy of the sun be made useful?" or . . . "Under what conditions does an atom radiate light?" And to those philosophers who tell him that before having answered the "what is" question he cannot hope to give exact answers to any of the "how" questions, he will reply, if at all, by pointing out how much he prefers the modest degree of exactness which he can achieve by his methods to the pretentious muddle which they have achieved by theirs' (OS 1, p. 32).

12 See Wittgenstein's *Philosophical Investigations*, 2002, p. 75e (para 242): 'If language is to be a means of communication there must be agreement not only in definitions but also (queer as this may sound) in judgments.'

13 Popper's hostility to Wittgenstein and to the influence he has had in philosophy is well documented. He attacks Wittgenstein's philosophy of language in *The Open Society* (OS 2, p. 297 ff.), he labels his approach 'verbal and empty scholasticism' (OS 2, p. 9), and he attacks the philosophic ethos of Wittgenstein's circle on the ground that it 'addresses its subtle analyses exclusively to the small esoteric circle of the initiated' (OS 2, p. 20). (There is no doubt that Popper felt himself an outsider in relation to the influence that Wittgenstein had: see Edmonds and Eidinow 2001, pp. 206 ff.).

14 See Popper 1969, p. 352: 'Thus the value of a discussion depends largely upon the variety of the competing views. Had there been no Tower of Babel, we should invent it.'

15 As I mentioned at the beginning of the chapter – see the second-to-last paragraph of Section I, p. 205 – this is often motivated by exactly the apprehensions about incommensurability that I discussed in section VI.

References

Agassi, Joseph. 1999. 'The Notion of the Modern Nation-State: Popper and Nationalism', in I. Jarvie and S. Pralong (eds), *Popper's Open Society after 50 Years*. London and New York: Routledge, pp. 182–96.

Berlin, Isaiah. 1981. *Against the Current: Essays in the History of Ideas*, Oxford: Oxford University Press.

Dworkin, Ronald. 1977. *Taking Rights Seriously*, revised edition, London: Duckworth.

Edmonds, David, and John Eidinow. 2001. *Wittgenstein's Poker: The Story of a Ten-Minute Argument Between Two Great Philosophers*, New York: HarperCollins.

Hart, H. L. A. 1994. *The Concept of Law*, second edition, Oxford: Clarendon Press.

Kymlicka, Will. 1989. *Liberalism, Community, and Culture*, Oxford: Clarendon Press.

Lefevre, Stephen R. 1974. 'Science and the Liberal Mind: the Methodological Recommendations of Karl Popper', in *Political Theory*, vol. 2, pp. 94–107.

Levy, Jacob. 2000. *The Multiculturalism of Fear*, Oxford: Oxford University Press.

Lessnoff, Michael. 1980. 'Review Article: The Political Philosophy of Karl Popper', in *British Journal of Political Science*, vol. 10, pp. 99–120.

Lukes, Steven. 1973. *Individualism*, Oxford: Basil Blackwell.

Lukes, Steven. 2003. *Liberals and Cannibals*, London: Verso.

Macintyre, Alasdair. 1981. *After Virtue*, London: Duckworth.

Nagel, Thomas. 1987. 'Moral Conflict and Political Legitimacy', in *Philosophy and Public Affairs*, vol. 16, pp. 215–40.

Notturno, Mark A. 1999. 'The Open Society and Its Enemies: Authority, Community, and Bureaucracy', in Ian Jarvie and Sandra Pralong (eds), *Popper's Open Society After Fifty Years: The Continuing Relevance of Karl Popper*, London: Routledge, pp. 41–55.

Popper, Karl. 1969. *Conjectures and Refutations: The Growth of Scientific Knowledge*, third edition. London: Routledge and Kegan Paul.

Popper, Karl. 1994. *The Myth of the Framework: In Defense of Science and Rationality*, ed. M. A. Notturno, London: Routledge.

Popper, Karl. 1996. *The Open Society and Its Enemies*, two volumes, Princeton, NJ: Princeton University Press.

Rawls, John. 1971. *A Theory of Justice*, Cambridge, MA: Harvard University Press.

Rawls, John. 1996. *Political Liberalism*, new edition, New York: Columbia University Press.

Raz, Joseph. 1986. *The Morality of Freedom*, Oxford: Clarendon Press.

Robinson, Richard. 1951. 'Dr. Popper's Defense of Democracy', in *Philosophical Review*, vol. 60, pp. 487–507.

Sandel, Michael. 1982. *Liberalism and the Limits of Justice*, Cambridge: Cambridge University Press.

Taylor, Charles. 1985. 'Atomism', in his collection *Philosophy and the Human Sciences: Philosophical Papers 2*, Cambridge: Cambridge University Press, pp. 187–210.

Taylor, Charles. 1992. *Multiculturalism and 'The Politics of Recognition'*, Princeton, NJ: Princeton University Press.

Tully, James. 1995. *Strange Multiplicity: Constitutionalism in an Age of Diversity*, Cambridge: Cambridge University Press.

Ullman-Margalit, Edna. 1977. *The Emergence of Norms*, Oxford: Clarendon Press.

Waldron, Jeremy. 1985. 'Making Sense of Critical Dualism', in Gregory Currie and Alan Musgrave (eds), *Popper and the Human Sciences*, Dordrecht: Martinus Nijhoff, pp. 105–20.

Waldron, Jeremy. 1989. 'Particular Values and Critical Morality', in *California Law Review*, vol. 77, pp. 561–89. Reprinted in my collection, *Liberal Rights: Collected Papers 1981–91*. Cambridge: Cambridge University Press, 1993, pp. 168–202.

Waldron, Jeremy. 1992. 'Minority Cultures and the Cosmopolitan Alternative', in *University of Michigan Journal of Law Reform*, vol. 25, pp. 751–92, reprinted in Will Kymlicka (ed.), *The Rights of Minority Cultures*, Oxford: Oxford University Press, 1995, pp. 93–119.

Waldron, Jeremy. 1999. 'How to Argue for a Universal Claim', in *Columbia Human Rights Review*, vol. 30, pp. 305–14.

Waldron, Jeremy. 2000. 'Cultural Identity and Civic Responsibility', in Will Kymlicka and Wayne Norman (eds), *Citizenship in Diverse Societies*, Oxford: Oxford University Press, pp. 155–74.

Waldron, Jeremy. 2002a. 'Taking Group Rights Carefully', in Grant Huscroft and Paul Rishworth (eds), *Litigating Rights: Perspectives from Domestic and International Law*, Oxford: Hart Publishing, pp. 203–20.

Waldron, Jeremy. 2002b. 'One Law for All: The Logic of Cultural Accommodation', in *Washington and Lee Law Review*, vol. 59, pp. 3–34.

Waldron, Jeremy. 2003. 'Teaching Cosmopolitan Right', in Kevin McDonough and Walter Feinberg (eds), *Education and Citizenship in Liberal-Democratic Societies: Cosmopolitan Values and Cultural Identities*, New York: Oxford University Press, pp. 23–55.

Wittgenstein, Ludwig. 2002. *Philosophical Investigations*, Oxford: Basil Blackwell.

INDEX